SOCIAL ISSUES, JUSTICE AND STATUS

COMMUNICATING PREJUDICE

AN APPRECIATIVE INQUIRY APPROACH

SOCIAL ISSUES, JUSTICE AND STATUS

Additional books in this series can be found on Nova's website under the Series tab.

Additional e-books in this series can be found on Nova's website under the eBooks tab.

SOCIAL ISSUES, JUSTICE AND STATUS

COMMUNICATING PREJUDICE

AN APPRECIATIVE INQUIRY APPROACH

SAKILE KAI CAMARA
AND
DARLENE K. DRUMMOND
EDITORS

nova publishers

New York

NOTICE TO THE READER

Library of Congress Cataloging-in-Publication Data

ISBN: 978-1-53610-167-6

Published by Nova Science Publishers, Inc. † New York

CONTENTS

FOREWORD

Tina M. Harris
University of Georgia

The two-term election of Senator Barack Obama in 2008 and 2012 to the highest political office in North American (U. S.) was a celebrated moment in our nation's history. As the first-ever elected African American president, Mr. Obama's ascendance to the position of the 44th President was a momentous occasion. Many professed this a public declaration of a post-racial America, an era whereby racial prejudices and tensions between ingroup and outgroup members, namely Whites and communities of color, had been overcome. We had theoretically, and some believed literally, realized Dr. Martin Luther King's vision of and dream that the human race had ideologically evolved to a point where the content of one's character outweighed the color of one's skin. Unfortunately, this public fervor for a post-racial America eventually revealed deep-seated prejudices espoused by many segments of the population related to differences across race, ethnicity, culture, and sexual orientation.

This ideological shift is essentially a revelation of biases and prejudices that pre-date Obama's presidency. Much like other countries, the U.S. is a nation with a sordid past where colonialism, slavery, and institutionalized racism were woven into its moral fabric, serving as a compass of sorts in determining how, if at all, human interactions should evolve. Interactions between individuals with seemingly marked differences are often times fraught with pre-existing notions about what the "other" is perceived to be. In an idyllic world, these differences would only enrich our relationships with each other; however, the reality is that we have all been socialized to view each other as possessing vast differences that are deemed either worthless or valuable, depending on one's placement on a given spectrum. These frameworks are the result of the socialization processes to which we have been exposed through our interpersonal networks, society at large, and various social media platforms. More specifically, it is the communicative exchanges that occur within these different interpersonal relationships and contexts that facilitate the acceptance and/or rejection of ideologies that create barriers between ingroup and outgroup members.

In order to better understand the relationship between prejudice and communication, noted communication scholar Michael Hecht published the book *Communicating Prejudice* (1998). His edited book was comprised of a collection of studies from scholars both within and outside of the communication discipline exploring the different ways in which prejudicial thoughts and behaviors manifest themselves in the lives of people from diverse backgrounds while also offering interventions for preventing such problematic ideologies from thriving in an increasingly diverse world. This book was important in articulating stressors that are unnecessarily problematizing myriad interpersonal relationships, and as recent tensions in the U. S. have demonstrated, prejudices against historically marginalized groups – African Americans, Hispanics, Latinos, the LGBTQ, Middle Easterners, and women – have increased, which has resulted in physical violence, racial profiling, sexual assaults, and cyber bullying. Thus, it is safe to argue that prejudices remain a salient factor in our interactions with others on an interpersonal, societal, and global level. This static observation is troubling, as it offers evidence that interventions are still needed if prejudices are to be reduced and/or eliminated.

Building on the work of Hecht, Camara and Drummond have assumed the ambitious yet important task of publishing this book, *Communicating Prejudice: An Appreciative Inquiry Approach,* with the goal of identifying the ways in which prejudice continues to problematizes our relationships. They enrich the pre-existing work by introducing methodologies, theories, and relational contexts that demonstrate the pervasive role that communication plays in the continued salience of stereotyping and bias, which are foundational to prejudice. Moreover, each chapter offers insight into the complex nature of prejudice as an ideological framework to which people are either knowingly or unknowingly wedded. Using communication as the lens, the authors provide inductive and deductive data that prejudice is perpetuated and preserved through the very act of communicating. A more important theme or observation across all chapters is that the authors provide strategies for identifying and responding to prejudices that ultimately function as barriers to positive communication interactions and, in some cases, self-perceptions.

The various methodologies that the authors introduce as a means for understanding prejudice include, for example, grounded theory and sense-making methodology (Chapter 1 and), duoethnography, appreciative inquiry (Chapter 5), autoethnography (Chapter 6), self-reflexivity (Chapter 8), and textual analysis (Chapter 11), among others. Each theoretical framework is used to identify communication behaviors that convey to others the prejudicial thought patterns that result from people being socialized to view others from a very negative perspective. The various authors advance the argument that intercultural contact and dialogue are at the core of dismantling prejudices. By using these frameworks, the authors are able to provide evidence that social science research has value in real world contexts. This is made apparent in Chapter 1 where the authors examine how individuals revise previously held stereotypes about their communication partner. Using Brenda Dervin's Sense-Making Methodology, the authors identify a variety of methods or strategies that individuals employ to unlearn years of socializing that has informed their current ideals about others from a different race, ethnicity or culture.

These diverse methodologies are pivotal to understandings of communicating prejudice in that they function as templates for other social scientists to translate theory to practice by translating their research into a form of social justice, as envisioned by Hecht's earlier work. To that end, Camara and Drummond uphold the principles of transformative research by identifying scholarship that advances an appreciative inquiry approach to understandings of prejudice in various contexts. This is exemplified in Chapter 11, where the author offers a critique of artifacts (e.g., t-shirts) through her narrative inquiry of women's traumatic experiences with assault and domestic violence vis-a-vis the Clothesline Project. The use of this qualitative methodology with such a vulnerable population speaks to the saliency and social significance of scholarship on the very real problem of abuse within romantic relationships. Moreover, the author identifies specific ways in while female victims of violence are subjected to prejudice from society, family, and others. The preconceived notions people hold of them ultimately affect how they choose to cope (or not) with varying degrees of abuse. The narratives that are inscribed on the t-shirts in concert with the interviews offer a richly nuanced understanding of the extent to which biases against women function to oppress them, essentially silencing many and rendering them voiceless. Such scholarship as this functions to not only offer an account of prejudice in its most violent form, but to empower other similarly oppressed persons to defy and survive their unhealthy circumstances.

In addition to diverse methodologies, this book utilizes multiple theoretical frameworks that can be used to articulate how prejudice manifests itself in different interpersonal and social contexts. Such theories as intergroup dialogue pedagogy (Chapter 2), co-cultural theory (Chapter 6), semiotics theory (Chapter 8), and social identity theory (Chapter 10) are used by different scholars to understand how prejudice is dealt with by either the perpetrator or the victim, per se. The methodologies give voice to these oppressive and traumatic experiences; however, this would not be possible were it not for the theories used to explain these phenomena in very compelling and enlightening ways. Although both quantitative and qualitative methodologies have been employed, Camara and Drummond are to be lauded for recognizing both the worth and value of both approaches to social science research. Inclusion of these approaches functions to inspire scholars across all disciplines to fulfill the original mission of Hecht, which is to facilitate social justice where injustices resultant of prejudice abound.

A main theme relative to these theories is self-reflexivity, which is an important quality of this collection of essays. For example, Chapter 8 is an excellent example of the richness that comes from a qualitative approach to communicating prejudice. It is from the perspective of a Latino immigrant graduate student that readers are able to understand the systemic nature of racism, which is a profound form of prejudice. The author recalls multiple interpersonal encounters where he is subjected overtly to a culture of rejection because of his otherness as a raced/cultured outsider in a predominately White community both on and off campus. With incredible detail, he describes the verbal assaults to which he was subjected throughout his tenure at a university in Colorado. His accounts offer both breadth and depth to the role of communication in perpetuating prejudice. It is disheartening to read this narrative (along with the others), as the disclosures are jarring and poignant, reminding readers of the reality of prejudice even in the most innocuous of social situations (e.g., party). The use of a self-reflexive approach to telling the story of discrimination is critical. Scholars and laypeople alike are made privy to forms of systemic oppression that sadly remain an integral part of the daily lives of many.

Another unique quality of this book is that it explores prejudice within a variety of contexts. One key element is that the various scholars used interpersonal relationships between friends, family members, and organization members (e.g., graduate school) to understand how prejudice is communicated between interactants (e.g., the oppressor and the oppressed). By including research that spans these contexts, the editors are offering further evidence of the pervasive nature of this social ill. Readers are afforded the opportunity to not only gain insight into how the relational dynamics typically occur, but they are made privy to the ways in which prejudiced ideologies ultimately function to marginalize the victims of such mistreatment, thereby creating an "alternate reality" that many either cannot or refuse to understand. Towards that end, these essays articulate for audiences the realness of a phenomenon that has become an all too common occurrence.

Chapter 12 is an excellent and powerful example of the potential richness that may be garnered from qualitative methodology in social science research. In this essay, the author describes for audiences how she navigated the difficult terrain of graduate school as part of a cadre of graduate students who overtly experienced prejudice because of their race/ethnicity. Verbal confrontations in very egregious degrees are recounted that speak to the deep-rooted prejudices that directly inform how some people choose to interact and communicate with people of color. The great detail provided offers a heartbreaking yet profound account of the impact that such harmful communication can have on the mental, emotional, and relational well-being on an individual. Unfortunately, the accounts are plenteous in her retelling of many encounters with prejudiced individuals at her graduate institution. They are important, however, because they demonstrate to readers that prejudiced behaviors are repetitive and cumulative. It is not necessarily isolated incidents that scar the victims of prejudice; rather, it is the accumulation of these encounters over time that ultimately function to create a reality stemmed in oppression because of one's membership in a marginalized group.

In keeping with the mission and vision of Hecht's *Communicating Prejudice*, Camara and Drummond's extension of that work in this book is to be lauded for its commitment to illuminating the many ways in which prejudice manifests itself in a variety of communicative exchanges. Whether it is through artifacts, familial relationships, or an organization, experiences with prejudice are plenteous, and this collection of studies demonstrate that although 28 years have passed, prejudice remains a critical and pervasive part of the moral fabric of the U. S. The assumption that we are living in an era where racial, ethnic, and cultural differences no longer matter is being dispelled by current events, such as #BlackLivesMatter and laws regarding the LGBTQ community, that collectively attest to the willingness of many to remain committed to ideologies that perpetuate systemic oppression. Thus, it is imperative that social scientists use their research to educate audiences about the reality of this very troubling phenomenon. More importantly, audiences should be challenged and empowered to facilitate social change in the fight against prejudice.

ACKNOWLEDGMENTS

Perhaps you find it odd that a book would have guest writers to craft the introduction, but this was not odd to us. It was an honor to have Michael Hecht, the author of *Communicating Prejudice*, and his co-author Emily Reichert write the introduction. Michael Hecht's scholarship in the area of identity formation, maintenance and transformation has been inspirational in the direction of several of our own works. We also thank Tina Harris for writing the foreword. We view her as a major scholar at the forefront of research on interracial romantic relationships and intercultural communication generally.

Thank you to the wonderfully gifted individuals who helped us see this project through to completion. First, to the author(s) of the chapters. You provided the foundation for this book and we applaud each of you. Many of you shared personal experiences that will help others understand the daily impact of prejudice and give them hope for addressing this problem proactively and positively in their own lives. We know that such sharing was not easy. Too often words can be misinterpreted, so we appreciate the risks taken. Second, we thank Danny Hoey, who initially started this project with us, but for personal reasons could not finish. Third, thank you to Nova Science Publishers for giving us this opportunity and believing in our vision.

In addition, there are individuals who may not have contributed a chapter to this work, but have nonetheless been instrumental in its completion. Key individuals have been there when we needed direction, advice or emotional support. Marsha Houston, Brenda J. Allen, Ronald J. Jackson, II and Mark Orbe generously mentored us through our PhD program and as professors at various institutions. In addition, we found a "home" within the African-

American Communication and Culture Division of the National Communication Association that has been invaluable.

We thank our families and friends for supporting us through the good times, tears and some very difficult experiences. Finally, we thank each other for over 20 years of friendship, support, and encouragement.

The Editors,

Sakile K. Camara
Darlene K. Drummond

INTRODUCTION TO PREJUDICE AND COMMUNICATION

Michael L. Hecht and Emily Reichert

Prejudice is a pervasive process in social relations. Some would say that only religious figures such as the Buddha could exist in the social world without valuing some things and some people over others. The world is filled with so much information and diversity and some short cuts are needed for all but the most talented minds. For the rest of us, categories are developed for processing information and forming social bonds. At its most innocent, this is prejudice – valuing some things or people over others. Gilder discusses Bloom's TED talk about the rational and moral elements of these processes that allow us to make often effective educated guesses about new encounters. This introductory chapter will lay the groundwork for the contributions of this book to build upon. To start, the theoretical underpinnings of prejudice will be presented, which will be followed by key terms used in this book along with their respective definitions and relevant contexts. This will lead into a discussion about how this book, *Communicating Prejudice: An Appreciative Inquiry Approach,* continues the study of prejudice communication that debuted in 1998 with *Communicating Prejudice*. The discussion will cover not only continuation, but how the chapters in this book expand the field by contributing new and innovative approaches. Following an overview of the contributions this book makes, opportunities and challenges in studying prejudice communication are presented. Finally, summaries of the chapters preclude the closing of this introduction.

THEORIZING PREJUDICE

Prejudice is rarely innocent; instead its insidious bias tends to take on properties of social structure that privilege entire groups not based on merit but merely on membership. And with privilege comes disadvantage, systematic disadvantage based on categorization rather than personal characteristics. Even worse, Gilder (Chapter 10) points to the horrific historical events that manifest from prejudice, like slave trade and genocide.

There are a number of theories that attempt to explain this phenomenon. On the one hand, there are evolutionary perspectives that suggest intolerance has a biological basis. The argument is that groups tend to defend their territory and seek to perpetuate themselves, putting them in competition with other groups and thus intolerance has an evolutionary value (Ross, 1991). A step away are sociological approaches that see the competition for resources as group-based but not necessarily evolutionary (Omi & Winant, 1986). Moving from there to more individualistic approaches, social psychologists starting with Allport (1954) and Stephan (1985) see prejudice as a learned belief system or cognitive processes. Between the individual and social is the analysis is offered by social identity theorists (e.g., Tajfel & Turner, 19826) who see these processes as emerging from competing identities or perceptual distinctions between in- and out-groups.

Incorporating multiple perspectives is often encouraged in the study of prejudice because a criticism common to most approaches are that they only focus on one single aspect of a phenomenon and do not view things holistically. Critical theory, for example, is based on a multidisciplinary approach of pulling from various fields such as political and social sciences while emphasizing the central role that power and values hold in any given observation (Kellner, 1989). Cultural studies theorists view prejudice as borne out of ideology, or in other words, values derived from a society or a culture (Hall, 1985; 1986). Rhetorical studies can examine phenomena such as prejudice through any of the given assumptions provided in these perspectives, but the level of analysis is based in the message (Zur, 1991).

While multidisciplinary perspectives bear many strengths, they are still subject to similar risks as singular perspectives. Cultural studies and critical theory approaches can often be too fixated on the influence of power in prejudice, and as a result, alternative ways of viewing prejudice, such as what happens through intolerance of the powerless towards the powerful, can be ignored (Baldwin, 1998). One proposal to overcoming these limitations has been through adopting the layered perspective on prejudice (Hecht & Baldwin, 1998).

The layered perspective on prejudice is based on the assumption that prejudice exists and occurs in multiple levels and expressions, often simultaneously (Hecht & Baldwin, 1998). The metaphor of a layer is used, specifically a holographic layering, to visualize how alternative epistemologies can exist together. In this existence these ways of knowing are not just piled on top of each other like a stack of cards, but like a hologram, perspectives act as the laser mechanism in a camera where they bounce off the object being photographed, then bounce again off of a second laser which measures the reflected light. This interchange is what occurs when a camera captures a photograph on film, and it can be used as a metaphor to understand prejudice. This is because "although there may be an underlying, global, or unifying construction of prejudice, there also are various intolerances," meaning that prejudice can exist in patterns, but can also be expressed uniquely (Hecht & Baldwin, 1998, p. 58). Through the holographic layering metaphor, five assumptions about prejudice can be drawn:

1) A given intolerance, even though culturally and historically defined, will have a commonality with other intolerances
2) A given intolerance, at a given time and place, can be seen at various levels of the society in which it is found
3) Intolerances can share common components across different spheres (such as race and gender)
4) Each angle of prejudice reveals a different (although interconnected) picture
5) An understanding of prejudice is maximized by examining the interference patterns—intersections, interpenetrations, connections, interactions—between and among the various approaches to prejudice, types of prejudice, and terrains of prejudice.

The layered perspective of prejudice is unique to studying intolerance because it facilitates not only methodological collaboration, but epistemological as well. It also makes room for sociological and individual approaches without keeping them at odds with each other. Foucault (1977) offers an explanation of how the two can be acknowledged in scholarship while studying the same phenomenon. He describes the power of subjugation as something of a symphony. It is not so simple as to say that structures determine all imbalances of power within the human world, but that these structures are maintained and perpetuated through the small menial rituals that occur in everyday life—a teacher taking roll in a classroom, a doctor compiling a checklist of symptoms for a patient—and through these performances power is evidenced, reinforced, perpetuated, spurred to continue in future rituals. It is in these small patterned moments—otherwise called instances of communication—that lie opportunities for disruption to the structures of domination. These instances for domination—ways of communicating prejudice-- are the central focus of this book.

DEFINITIONS USED IN THIS BOOK

This book and these chapters personalize and individualize the processes involved in prejudice and its siblings: stigma, stereotyping, and discrimination. Stereotypes can be thought of as beliefs or cognitions that are rigidly applied based on group membership while discrimination is the behavioral manifestation of prejudice in overt action to exclude, avoid or distance (Hecht, 1998). Moreover, discussions of prejudice are based on four metaphors (Hecht, 1998):

- Prejudice as fear of difference or the unknown (i.e., difference as threat)
- Prejudice as dislike of difference or the unknown (i.e., differences as aversive) – CH 10, fear response P. 10).
- Prejudice as competition with difference for scarce resources (i.e., difference as competition)
- Prejudice as hierarchy and structure (i.e., difference as power)

Stereotypes, discussed in further detail by Chapters 1 and 10, are conceptualized differently based on the field they draw upon. Cognitive-based ideas about stereotypes define them through belief systems that people hold about categories of people. These belief systems are used to justify behavior enacted for reasons related to the relevant categories (Lippmann, 1922; Allport, 1979). Relational definitions of stereotypes emphasize the creation of impressions that people form through the sending and receiving of communicative information—the phenomena of stereotyping initiates social distancing in social relationships (Semin, 2008). Either way, stereotypes are acquired through cultural learning, or more specifically the learning that occurs during the early period of life.

When viewed comprehensively, these processes contribute and gain from one another. Stereotyping is a tool of categorization used in prejudice. According to Bobbi Van Gilder (Chapter 10), stereotyping is a process that "is at the root of prejudice." Prejudice has been defined as "antipathy based on faulty or inflexible generalizations" (Allport, 1979, p. 9). It is a system comprised of belief systems that are rooted in the common theme of difference (stereotyping), whether that difference originates from the fear of the unknown, dislike of the unknown, competition for resources, or in hierarchy and structure (Hecht, 1998).

The "other" is another term that commonly appears throughout this book. Other can be a noun if it refers to a person or persons or may reference a process of "othering" or the act of casting someone as another. In either case, the word calls attention to the potentially pernicious process of marking someone as an outsider. References to "others" as foreign, strange, different, alien, etc. resound in recent natavistic rhetoric emerging around the world in response to massive immigration upheavals due to the unsafe conditions around the world as well as income inequalities. Sometimes, this othering is subtle, as in John McCain's reference to President Obama as "that one" portraying him as an object rather than a person. Other times, as in the rhetoric of presidential candidate Donald Trump, this othering is not so subtle. In either case, the sense of separation, what social psychologists perhaps more neutrally or objectively refer to as ingroup versus outgroup, is key.

While prejudice and stereotyping can sometimes be passive, their behavioral expression, discrimination, is not. Discrimination refers to an outcome that is behavioral, resulting from stereotyping and prejudice. It inherently disadvantages as observable deficits in housing, education, nutrition and health care. For example, the U.S. history of slavery manifests itself in inequalities to this day (Gaskin et al., 2005). Discrimination, disenfranchisement, and loss of status are all outcomes that can result from stereotyping, prejudice, and stigma. These are the outcomes that are usually of interest when topics such as stigma and prejudice are being studied because they cause harm.

CONTRIBUTIONS OF THIS BOOK

Almost twenty years after *Communicating Prejudice* in 1998, this book, *Communicating Prejudice: An Appreciative Inquiry Approach* enriches and reinvigorates the field of prejudice communication for the future.

The most notable contribution is the introduction of appreciative inquiry as a methodology to study prejudice communication. Hecht (1998) closed the first book with an observation that much of what is known about prejudice has to do with understanding its origins and the effects it bears on others. At that time there was a gap in the literature. As Hecht pointed out, "we have paid little attention to appreciation—what it is, how it is expressed, what appreciative relationships are like, what an appreciative structure would be like, and so on" (p. 337). The current volume addresses this missing piece in understanding prejudice—it takes the next step.

Appreciative Inquiry (AI), originally theorized by David Cooperrider and Whitney (2001), include five principles and four processes to enact change in living social systems. The five principles are as follows:

i.   The Constructionist Principle states that reality is co-constructed and re-constructed through the negotiation of beliefs in communication.

ii. The Principle of Simultaneity describes how actions as simple as just beginning to inquire about reality is enough to begin to change it.

iii. The Poetic Principle is a recommendation that when planning for a better future, we should rewrite stories from the past as how we would want it to have been.

iv. The Anticipatory Principle, similar to the Principle of Simultaneity, states that our imagination is what can inspire change in the future.

v.   The Positive Principle claims that change needs to be sustained, and this is done through developing strong relationships with those who are around you.

These principles are enacted into four phases that describe how change is evidenced in practice (Srivastava et al., 1999). Discovery is the first phase, where exploration is needed in order to identify cultural artifacts that are positive in a specific community (Conklin, 2014). The dream phase follows discovery, activating imagination and encouraging the visualization of what can be possible. The design phase is the third process and requires investigation as to the specific actions needed in order for positive change to actually occur. The final phase, destiny, encourages investing energy into questioning reality in order to facilitate learning.

While appreciation is present in every chapter of this book, AI is specifically used in unique ways throughout. In Chapter 3, Herakova and Correa utilize a critical version of AI that emphasizes a social justice perspective in appreciation. Wynter in Chapter 5 utilizes Srivastva, Fry, and Cooperrider's (1999) 4-D Model of Appreciative Inquiry in order to evaluate children's television shows featuring Black characters. In Chapter 12, Camara advances understandings of prejudice through the application of the five principles of AI (constructionist, simultaneity, poetic, anticipatory, and positive). Other chapters employ various theories in order to capture elements of appreciation as described in AI. In Chapter 6, Orbe and colleagues investigate possible paths to communication that transcends through and beyond prejudice into appreciation using autoethnographic data in co-cultural contexts. In Chapter 8, Alvarez uses semiotics theory and the communication theory of identity in order to explore possibilities for communal appreciation.

In addition to providing a space to explore appreciation in prejudice, this book supplements narratives about experiences involving prejudice. As quoted by Hecht (1998), "These narratives are intended as an alternative way of knowing—a mode invested in narrativity as a way of knowing, understanding, studying, and expressing" (p. 17). In Chapter 9, Womack illustrates the experiences of being a majority member and a minority member within different spheres. Lastly, Lang shares various stories in Chapter 11 about domestic violence and sexual assault among Clothesline Project participants.

Young (1998) writes about educational interventions, about what agents it will take to enact change of prejudice in both secondary and primary education. The focus of prejudice within education and imagining possibilities for change is a central focus of many chapters in this book. Scott discusses intergroup dialogue in college classrooms in the second chapter. The transformative potential of facilitating shared contact in order to move from "other" to simply "different." In Chapter 4, Drummond discusses strategies to promote intercultural communication competence in community colleges— especially given that the majority of faculty in these institutions are often white, disproportionate to the student body. And in Chapter 7, Jones shares examples of how fear and prejudice in a classroom can be confronted and reformed through fostering an environment of truth telling. These chapters contribute to the growing body of work focusing specifically on the problem of prejudice in classroom settings.

Possibly most importantly, this book provides a much needed outlet to explore the communication of prejudice, and all of its subsequent pathways. In the spirit of Appreciative Inquiry, the principle of simultaneity seems most appropriate to call upon: That the act of simply inquiring is enough to spark action and change. This book is realized through these five principles, by questioning current standards, imagining possible futures, rewriting possible pasts, and by fostering positive relationships between others—both interpersonally and empirically.

OPPORTUNITIES AND CHALLENGES

Communication holds such value for this subject because of its potential to illuminate not just the mechanisms behind prejudice, but also the potential to make theoretical and practical discoveries towards transformation away from and beyond prejudice. Gilder, for example, in Chapter 10, describes how mindfulness practices can be used to help people develop skills for respectfully engaging "others" or outgroups while appreciating difference. Rather than glossing over difference, the chapter calls for transformational learning based on intergroup communication, mindfulness, and empathy.

A challenge to studying prejudice communication is in locating our place in the realm of facts and hard science. While exploring new and unseen terrain, it can be difficult to distinguish what is to be categorized as a 'fact' or a 'scientific,' or 'true' observation. How can scholars know the difference between a fact and a false? At what point do scientific expeditions stop being considered scholarly, and turn into pseudoscience? In other words, how can we 'make room' for underrepresented identities in scholarship without tainting what others consider the facts and knowledge in the process?

Researchers have shown that membership in privileged groups and/or occupy powerful positions within societies can define which theories get distributed or prioritized (Porter, 1996; Haraway, 2003; Collins, 2004). This happens even while the sciences pledge to operate under complete objectivity. To make matters worse, the nature of objectivity in the sciences has been shown to be contradictory at best and at its worst only consistent with spheres of privilege (or said differently, those who have privilege are considered 'objective'). Some would claim that the very "science of race" was political rather than scientific. Claeys (2000) argues that race was constructed to validate the superiority of "whites" (read Europeans) and that the original "research" itself was deliberately misleading. It also may be argued that Charles Darwin's theory of evolution was used to justify ideas about "survival of the fittest" and rationalize inequality. Coined in 1864 by Herbert Spencer, the phrase describes an adaption of the theory of evolution to human socialization, where the "fittest" humans will outlive the weaker humans. It has been contended that theories of social Darwinism were justification for eugenics, or oppressing people in the name of evolution. This habit of the sciences has been shown to be harmful because it erases the experiences of others and creates opportunities for injustice to occur and continue without any awareness of the problem to begin with.

Possible solutions or at least a counter-weight to this predicament are many—one that is particularly popular is to gather or give voice to narratives from groups of people who do not hold powerful positions in society. As a harbor of narrative theory and methods, communication studies broadly defined are an obvious channel for exploring prejudice in this way. This solution, however, is not absolute and with it comes epistemological questions about how narrative accounts fit into the "hard sciences" of facts and truths. Are we to completely do away with the previous system of "facts" objective or otherwise? The implications of living in a "fact free world" are, for example, ignoring climate change or the effects of tax cuts in redistributing wealth. Ironically, the claim of both cultural studies and right wing rhetoric calls for all information/facts to be contested, the implications of which have been a slow reaction to serious problems such as climate change.

This issue manifests itself in educational practices as well as policy. In Chapter 7, Jones describes his experience in trying to disentangle his positions of power in the classroom in order to allow students to learn about their own positions of power. As Jones explains, this is easier said than done, and he describes the struggle of abandoning fact-based teaching in order to make room for the omitted stories of the oppressed. Doing so does, indeed, allows for previously silenced voices to be heard, but it also may have the unintended effect of allowing harmful and misinformed voices to carry the same validity. Jones raises important questions as to how communication can wrangle the fraught tension between interpretation and objectivism in prejudice. However, how do we respond to claims that do not comport themselves with known information? What about the statement that women and minorities are not disadvantaged in the U.S. (they are) or that welfare only goes to lazy people who do not want to work (it does not)? Are these to be allowed to float uncontested in an educational environment in the name of free speech and empowering the disadvantaged or silenced?

A second challenge to be faced in prejudice communication will be determining the stance to be taken in referencing forms of prejudice, stereotyping, stigma, and discrimination. It is habitual for studies dealing with prejudice to assume an inherent binary between the ingroup and outgroup— that even with intersectionally, when multiple in- and out-groups are accounted for, these boundaries are fixed and clear cut. Without problematizing memberships to consider the full array. For example, what is the membership of someone who is white, women, upper SES, educated, teacher, and Lesbian? Does it matter if only some of these are known or public? While in the process of creating a metaphorical map of prejudice, the nature of the map seems to have been prematurely decided on: a fixed print map on canvas that only changes when the viewer rotates the angle from the original perspective. Moreover, as Womack illustrates in Chapter 9, the status can be contextually fluid, especially as people travel.

But this is not only a sojourner experience from which people quickly return to their majority status but, instead reflects our increasingly diverse world where heterosexual privilege can be challenged in LGBT contexts; white privilege can be challenged in ethnic minority contexts. The 2016 U.S. election, for example, seems to highlight the threat felt by some whites that they were losing "their country". However, some political polling demonstrates that "white males" are not monolithic in this view, even those how are lower SES. One almost wishes to more fully problematize this process through engaging a narrative from the perspective of whites who fear this loss, or at least from those who do not experience "white privilege" based on socio-economic or disability status, at least as fully as others. It seems that the predetermined layout for mapping prejudice lends itself to studies putting undo weight upon the subjects of prejudice as opposed to the prejudice itself or even prejudice as process.

The problem with this assumption is that prejudice is not inherently white, male, Western or straight. These categories are not inherently privileged, the same way that disadvantaged categories are not designated based on inherent inferiority. When this is forgotten, when the map is a permanent sheet of parchment, problems arise. For example, stigma reduction programs focus often exclusively on a specific subject, such as mental illness. And regardless of the effectiveness of these programs, these programs do little to prevent stigma from popping up in other subject areas—namely in smoking reduction and anti-obesity issues to name a couple (Evans-Polce et al., 2015; MacLean et al., 2009). A call for a more overarching understanding of stigma has been proposed in order to allow to allow for stigma prevention efforts to be distributed (Reichert, 2016).

Theories derived from communication provide tools for attempting these challenges that are privy to the risks involved. The issue of opening up the dialogue to include silenced voices runs an obvious risk of also opening opportunities for equally harmful voices to bolster themselves.

CHAPTER SUMMARIES

We close with brief summaries of the various selections. These are not intended to provide a shorthand to each but rather to peak the readers interested in exploring the varying points of view.

In chapter one, Pariyadath and Kline explore how stereotypes are overcome through communicative strategies such as opening a dialogue with others, seeking similarities, displaying empathy, holding appreciation for difference, and adopting the perspectives of others. Pariyadath and Kline explore how people become aware of stereotypes that they personally hold in interpersonal encounters. This is done using Dervin's Sense-Making Methodology (SMM) which emphasizes the role of cognitive processes, such as the ways they define situations, and the past experiences that they call upon to compare with current situations, as opposed to an emphasis on identity. Pariyadath and Kline add new insights into stereotype change by expressly targeting the variances that exist in social encounters, and studying them in relation to stereotype change.

Scott shares insights in Chapter 2 as to how university settings are ideal locations, particularly for communication professors, to facilitate intergroup dialogue along boundaries of race, gender, and class, to name a few. According to Scott, universities at this point in history in America are becoming globalized in such a way that they offer instances of contact with the "other," whether that be through race or otherwise, and this is an opportunity that is becoming increasingly absent in virtually all other aspects of American life. Communication among students of different races is difficult to do, but is an important obligation as universities offer opportunities for groups to intersect in ways they may not have been able to before. Communication between races is often halted by white guilt and white privilege—the emergence of these feelings means an end to listening. Scott describes the goal of this communication as finding ways for white students to experience the pain expressed by students of color while still acknowledging that they are complicit in it.

In the third chapter, Herakova and Correa present a duoethnographic narrative project that delves into how prejudice is coped with and repaired through interactions with family. In the chapter, Herakova and Correa demonstrate ways that communication with family can connect disjointed experiences in ways that other interactions may not be able to. Appreciative Inquiry within family communication can integrate stories from the private and the social lives of a person. It can also bring together past and present experiences in order to create links with new possibilities for the future. Through this ethnography, Appreciative Inquiry in familial interactions serves as an additional resource for transforming the harmful reality of prejudice into something different.

Drummond documents in Chapter 4, how, despite the fact that community college students are primarily of color, over eighty percent of community college faculty fall within the categories of white and over 50 years of age. This imbalance, according to Drummond, puts undo pressure onto faculty who are outside of those spheres of white and older to educate students on diversity. A solution that Drummond proposes and records is to provide faculty with a course specifically designed to provide training in cultural competency. Similar to Pariyadath and Klines (Chapter 1) findings, Drummond reported success with a course that encouraged taking the perspectives of others, sitting with uncomfortable truths, and engaging in dialogue with others outside of their own categories.

Representation in the media, in the form of stereotypical portrayals or the lack of representation altogether, is examined by Wynter in the fifth chapter: "Identifying Stereotypes: The Stories TV Tells Black Children and How to 'Appreciate' Them." Three Nickelodeon children's programs are discussed in terms of how the stereotypes that are portrayed can be useful in coming up with solutions to the harm caused by such portrayals. The three programs chosen include *True Jackson VP*, *NFL Guardians of the Core*, and *The Haunted Hathaways*. Wynter uses the Appreciative Inquiry 4-D Model to guide these solutions by informing parents of black children to assess the quality of programming that their children consume.

Razzante and Orbe use self-generated autoethnographic narratives to explore how communication can be used to work through prejudice and lead to understanding within interpersonal relationships in Chapter 6. Co-cultural theory is used to understand how instances of difference can not just harm relationships, but also how they can be enhanced by them. They explain how prejudgements can prevent any form of genuine communication from happening between people and how adding accommodations into communicative encounters inoculate for issues that arise from prejudgements. This chapter is an example of how something underlying prejudice—difference—can be used in a way that promotes positive communication between people.

In Chapter 7, Jones presents a critical pedagogical framework for changing a classroom community of prejudice and fear into a community of truth telling and tolerance. He starts by recounting his own mistakes in dealing with this issue and then recounts how turning to a new pedagogy helped him remove prejudice, in his words, "without creating a power struggle". Jones invokes a metaphor of being on the same bus to explore gendered identities as a means for leveling the power in the classroom and argues for a dialogical approach to teaching rather than conveying information.

Alvarez unpacks experiences in Boulder, Colorado as well as in graduate school to reveal deeply ingrained prejudice in chapter 8. He describes what he sees as a form of liberalism that is "inclusive of the white lived experienced in the United States." The complement modified by "for a Hispanic" becomes a central metaphor describing how others views of him invalidated his accomplishments and the exhaustion he and many other minorities feel in that everyday world. Alvarez then applies a semiotics analysis and then moves on to integrate the Communication Theory of Identity with appreciation as a central element of identity and a means to ameliorate the prejudicial world.

Womack shares intimate stories and lessons learned about teaching intercultural communication in Chapter 9, "From Majority to Minority: How My Experiences as a Member of, first, a Majority Culture, then a Minority Culture, and finally, a Mixed Race Family." In this chapter, Womack discusses her experiences as alternatively a majority and minority group member and how this informs her teaching. These experiences translate into an experiential pedagogy, illustrated through teaching devices such as films. The chapter highlights the fluid nature of ingroup-outgroup status.

Gilder compiles a comprehensive literature review as to the historical origin and consequences of prejudice in Chapter 10. develop their communication skills to more effectively engage in intergroup communication. As such, this essay highlights the importance of practicing mindfulness in intergroup encounters. By practicing mindfulness, and by communicating respect and appreciation for difference, negative prejudicial behaviors and the harmful consequences of such actions may be reduced.

Chapter 11, written by Sorensen-Lang, presents a narrative inquiry approach to inform options toward empowerment for women facing violence from the Clothesline Project. Two central questions that guide this chapter deal with how advocacy workers use written communication to help women address domestic violence and trauma, and with identifying the feminist orientations that guide these staff workers. Findings implicate the state of violence against women in the US and those that aim to help them.

In the final chapter, Camara explores personal experiences of prejudice while matriculating through a PhD program in a Midwestern majority white institution. Using these experiences as a starting point, Camara applies the five principles of Appreciative Inquiry in order to imagine and transform the future and all of its possibilities. The chapter is an example of how AI can be used on autoethnographic accounts in order to generate new opportunities for transformation away from prejudice.

CONCLUSION

We "conclude" this introduction by suggesting that these contributions open more doors than they shut because they challenge traditional ways of seeing social life. While primarily applied to educational settings, one is left wondering of Jones' suggestions about what we might call the liminal classroom with the open flow of ideas would work equally well in a business environment? Technology-based companies often create spaces with few walls to emphasize the free flow of ideas. Open-source software like the Linux Operating System are examples of how this can operate more broadly. Perhaps in the online world such barriers are even more easily broached. On the other hand, in the emerging "fact-free" political discourse such structures may be problematic to the social well-being.

Within the arena of studying disadvantage and social phenomena generally there is a gut reaction to study the subject from a post-hoc point of view—observe things how they are currently and investigate the factors that led to their emergence. These points of view are certainly crucial and invaluable towards the study of prejudice, but they are also not nearly enough to bring about desired change. In their discussion of agency Emirbayer and Mische (1998) explain that an exclusivity to iterative elements of agency limit understandings of societal schemas and how they "can be challenged, reconsidered, and reformulated" (p. 983). A harmful phenomenon, like prejudice, can be understood entirely through contributing factors and influences, but this knowledge will invariably lead to the resulting question of, 'we know this about prejudice, so what do we do now?' The literature needs to make room for points of view that anchor themselves in the future—however 'unscientific' these points of view may feel at first. It is traditional to look upon the future through inferences of data gathered from the past and present. It is revolutionary to travel (so to speak) to the future, and look back onto the past. To observe possible futures before they are realized. To discuss alternate pasts that may have resulted in different presents. These are ways of viewing the world that sound more like science fiction than social science. *Communicating Prejudice: An Appreciative Inquiry Approach* challenges such an assumption and turns it onto its head. This book demonstrates through multiple methods, such as Appreciative Inquiry and narratives, how an orientation towards the future holds value matched with traditional scientific approaches and illuminates just how understudied the area is.

Terms like appreciation and empowerment are two that are used to describe ideal futures to prejudice and stigma. Questions that need to be asked are to wonder whether there are only two desirable futures for disadvantage? Is prejudice a binary of sorts, where on the one end there is disadvantage and on the other appreciation? Or is it more complex than that—so complex that thinking of it as a holographic layering may prove useful? These are questions that need to be asked, and are questions that this book continues to pose. *Communicating Prejudice: An Appreciative Inquiry Approach* begins the interrogation of prejudice with the future in mind. With that said, we can hope that this book will encourage and inspire each other to integrate creativity into our scholarly pursuits of the communication of prejudice. Let this book be the beginning of much more to come.

REFERENCES

Allport, G.W. (1979). The nature of prejudice. Reading, MA: Addison-Wesley (originally published in 1954).

Brewer, M.B. (1996). When contact is not enough: Social identity and intergroup cooperation. *International Journal of Intercultural Relations,* 20, 291-304.

Claeys, G. (2000). The "Survival of the Fittest" and the Origins of Social Darwinism. *Journal of the History of Ideas*, 61(2), 223-240.

Collins, P. H. (2004). Feminist Thought. The feminist standpoint theory reader: *Intellectual and political controversies*, 103.

Cooperrider, D. L., & Whitney, D. (2001). A positive revolution in change: Appreciative inquiry. *Public administration and public policy*, 87, 611-630.

Emirbayer, M., & Mische, A. (1998). What is agency? 1. *American journal of sociology*, 103(4), 962-1023.

Foucault, M. (1977). *Discipline and punish: The birth of the prison*. Vintage.

Gaskin, D. J., Headen, A. E., & White-Means, S. I. (2005). Racial disparities in health and wealth: The effects of slavery and past discrimination. *The Review of Black Political Economy*, 32(3), 95-110.

Hall, S. (1985). Signification, representation, ideology: Althusser and the post-structuralist debates. *Critical Studies in Mass Communication*, 2, 91-114.

Hall, S. (1986). Gramsci's relevance for the study of race and ethnicity. *Journal of Communication Inquiry*, 10(2), 5-27.

Haraway, D. (2003). Situated knowledges: The science question in feminism and the privilege of partial perspective. Turning points in qualitative research: *Tying knots in a handkerchief*, 2003, 21-46.

Hecht, M. L. & Baldin, J. R. (1998). Tolerance/Intolerance; A Multidisciplinary View of Prejudice. In M. L. Hecht (Ed) *Communicating Prejudice,* Newbury Park, CA: Sage.

Hecht, M.L. (Ed.) (1998). *Communicating prejudice*. Newbury Park, CA: Sage.

Kellner, D. (1989). Critical Theory, Marxism and modernity. Balimore, MD: Johns Hopkins University Press.

Lippmann, W. (1922). *The world outside and the pictures in our heads*.

Omi, M. & Winant, H. (1986). *Racial formation in the United States: From the 1960s to the 1980s* (rev. ed.). NY: Routledge.

Porter, T. M. (1996). Trust in numbers: The pursuit of objectivity in science and public life. Princeton University Press.

Ross, R.H. (1991). The role of evolution in ethnocentric conflict and its management. *Journal of Social Issues*, 47, 167-185.

Semin, G. R. (2008). Stereotypes in the wild. Y., Kashima, K. Fiedler, & P. Freytag (Eds.), Stereotype dynamics: Language-based approaches to the formation, maintenance and transformation of stereotypes, 11-28.

Srivastva, S., Fry, R., & Cooperrider, D. (1999). The call for executive appreciation. In *Appreciative management and leadership* (pp. 1-35). Williams Custom Publishing, Euclid, OH.

Stephan, W. (1985). Intergroup relations. In G. Lindsey & E. Aronson (Eds.), *Handbook of social psychology* (3rd ed., Vol. 2, pp. 599-658). NY: Random House.

Tajfel, H. & Turner, J.C. (1982). The social identity of intergroup behavior. In S. Worchel & W.G. Austin (Eds.), *Psychology of intergroup relations* (pp. 7-24). Chicago: Nelson-Hall.

Young, G. (1998). Educational Interventions. In M. L. Hecht (Ed) Communicating Prejudice, Newbury Park, CA: Sage.

Zur, O. (1991). The love of hating: The psychology of enmity. *History of European Ideas,* 13, 345-369.

In: Communicating Prejudice   ISBN: 978-1-53610-167-6
Editors: S. Camara and D. Drummond   © 2016 Nova Science Publishers, Inc.

Chapter 1

BRIDGING DIFFERENCE: A SENSE-MAKING STUDY OF THE ROLE OF COMMUNICATION IN STEREOTYPE CHANGE[1]

Renu Pariyadath and Susan L. Kline

Department of Fine Arts and Communication Studies
University of South Carolina Upstate
Spartanburg, SC, US
School of Communication, Ohio State University
Columbus, OH, US

ABSTRACT

Responding to calls for studies privileging participants' own accounts of intercultural contact, we employed Dervin's Sense-Making Methodology (SMM) to study the types of intercultural contact that led to stereotype revision. A grounded theory analysis of interviews with participants who had revised stereotypes about cultural others showed that participants overcame stereotypes by refocusing attention on the other and opening dialogue with them, through perspective-taking, showing empathy, seeing similarities, seeing the other as equal, and appreciating difference. The study suggests that both the content of in situ communicative acts and the dialogic form of communication between cultural others influence stereotype review.

---

[1] Address correspondence to: renup@uscupstate.edu.

INTRODUCTION

A recent example of prejudice resulting from holding a stereotype was the media controversy that erupted in the fall of 2014. Controversial television host Bill Maher pronounced on his show that the vast majority of the Muslim world was violent (Maher, September 26, 2014) and cited female genital mutilation and honor killing as evidence, ignoring the well-documented prevalence of these practices in non-Islamic regions and communities. No amount of counter evidence presented on the show would help Maher and his supporters shed or reconsider their stereotypes about Muslims leading to a polarizing debate involving news analysts, philosophers, religious studies experts, and celebrities.

Stereotypes about cultural and ethnic groups and their link to prejudice present continuing challenges to egalitarianism in multicultural societies. Maintaining stereotypes about others may lead to prejudice; stereotypes may also be used to justify prejudice against groups (Allport, 1954; Stangor, 2000). Given that dialogue is a key enabler of an engaged civil society, we were interested in studying the role of stereotyping in enabling and constraining dialogue. Generally, an openness to and respect for the other's views are defining characteristics of dialogue (Pearce & Pearce, 2004). Yet, relating to another person in communication as "Thou" rather than "it" (Buber, 1958) is impossible when one holds a stereotype about the other person. Situations such as the Maher case where an entire group is assigned negatively valenced characteristics work to affirm qualities ascribed to the dominant cultural group, creating rifts within the polity.

Fortunately, stereotypes are mutable. Obtaining positive information about and/or regular contact with stereotyped groups have been shown to lead to stereotype review and revision. Still, contact theory, a productive avenue for research on reducing prejudice, has not been able to offer an explanation for "how" prejudice is overcome (Pettigrew, 2008) and studies have been largely confined to laboratory settings (Connolly, 2000). Hence, there is a need to study how real life intercultural interactions may result in the maintenance or revision of stereotypes about others.

Rather than adopting a problem-solving approach to stereotype change, we embarked on a project that embodied the spirit of appreciative inquiry (Cooperrider & Whitney, 2005). We focused on individuals who had reframed their contact with stereotyped others as an experience that led to a positive change. To learn about the critical/interpretive processes of internal dialogue and the role of interpersonal communication involved in stereotype review, we studied intercultural contact and stereotyping using Brenda Dervin's Sense-Making Methodology or SMM (Dervin, 2003; Dervin 2008). Specifically, we examined when and how people interpreted communicative acts in an intercultural contact situation positively, leading them to revise a held stereotype about the communication partner. In the next section, we review relevant scholarship on dialogue and stereotypes, on contact theory as a way of overcoming prejudice, and introduce SMM and its utility in studying stereotype change.

LITERATURE REVIEW

In the last few decades, a range of philosophers and social theorists have theorized dialogue, as a way of conversing and thinking with each other. Scholars have produced various insights about communication practices that facilitate dialogue, such as having conversations about different biographical experiences and making explicit shared understandings (Bohman, 2000), listening and suspending certainty (Issacs, 1999), and recognizing that dialogue is responsive (Stewart, 1995). However, while dialogue scholarship has focused on theorizing productive practices for engaging in dialogue, deliberation scholarship has discovered its obstacles. Citizens are more likely to express their views if they think their opinions are more popular, while those who have less popular opinions are more likely to remain silent (Noelle-Neumann, 1974), resulting in more polarizing viewpoints being expressed by the perceived dominant group. Discussions that involve more polarizing viewpoints may also involve the expression of stereotypes, which may further impede the possibility for productive dialogue.

Conceptions of Stereotypes

Walter Lippmann (1922) first used the word, stereotype, to describe the way people deal with others separated by physical distance, when they lacked the time to get to know them intimately. Later, Allport referred to a stereotype as "an exaggerated belief associated with a category" that functions to justify conduct related to that category (1954, p. 191). Subsequent conceptions have viewed stereotypes as resulting from the psychological and cognitive need to categorize and simplify a complex social world (Augoustinos & Walker, 1998).

Much of the literature on stereotypes assumes that information about group members is obtained through direct observation or social interaction (Kashima, Fiedler & Freytag, 2008). Social cognitive researchers (e.g., Semin, 2008) contend that stereotype formation, maintenance and change involve the interplay of interpersonal as well as intrapersonal processes. These researchers argue that stereotypes are more than cognitive schemas; rather, they occur as people interact, form impressions and create relationships with one another (Yzerbyt & Carnaghi, 2008). The cultural or structural discourses that circulate in a society through mass media further support the stereotypes formed about others in social interaction. The social attributes of stereotypes led Semin (2008) to define stereotypes as "specific social phenomena that are manifested in communicative contexts and have the characteristic of inducing social distance between a speaker and a receiver" (p. 12). So, unlike Lippman's stereotype that formed as a result of physical distance, stereotyping, in this conception produced social distance between individuals and groups of people. Like social cognitive researchers, we conceptualize a stereotype as a pre-packaged way of thinking about another that is constituted, maintained, reinforced, and transformed through the discourses one engages in. We are especially interested in the potential for stereotype change through communication between people.

Two main strategies for effecting a change in stereotype have been addressed in previous research. The first is to make highly prejudiced people aware of consensus information or positive information about the stereotyped group shared by in-group members (Sechrist and Stangor, 2000). A second way of bringing about stereotype change has been through inter-group contact. Contact theory (Allport, 1954) proposes that stereotypes can be changed among members of different groups through increased contact between these groups. Pettigrew and Tropp's (2008) meta-analysis has substantiated a relationship between contact and prejudice reduction, and identified several factors that mediate this relationship, such as learning and reducing anxiety about the out-group, empathy, and perspective-taking. Since hostility between groups is presumably due to unfamiliarity and separation, increasing contact between these groups may reduce prejudice. Inter-group contact is expected to produce enough positive experiences to lead to disconfirming evidence that results in a revision of held stereotypes (Brewer & Gaertner, 2004).

Contact Theory and Prejudice Reduction

Allport's (1954) original hypothesis had four essential conditions or prerequisites for a positive contact outcome, including (1) equal status between majority and minority groups, (2) the pursuit of common goals, (3) legal sanction for the contact and (4) contact that which allows for members to perceive common interests and humanity between groups. Contact theory has been shown to be useful in laboratory settings and through researcher-derived categories. However, participants' own views of contact and their perspectives as to how they overcame prejudice or revised their stereotypes about another person are less studied. Dixon et al. (2005) noted that studying the optimal conditions of contact under the supposition that these conditions determine the success or failure of contact without paying heed to actual contact experiences across time and space neglected the contextual rootedness and specificity of social relations. Over the years researchers (e.g., Dixon, 2005; Connolly, 2000) have argued for developing a methodology that attends more closely to the socioeconomic and political context in which prejudice occurs and we believe employing SMM attends to both calls.

Studying Stereotype Change with Sense-Making Methodology

SMM, in development by Brenda Dervin since 1972, is an approach to comparative theory (Dervin, 2003) that focuses on processes rather than identity-related differences between individuals. It is a methodology that compares communicative behavior by examining individuals' definition of situations, use of past experiences, and connections they make (Foreman-Wernet, 2003). SMM has been used to understand how individuals make sense of communication and information in a variety of domains, such as libraries, the medical system, and art museums.

An assumption is that that reality can sometimes be orderly and sometimes chaotic, underscoring the fundamental human need for sense making. Human beings are seen as agents, moving from one situation to the other, sometimes using repetitive past responses to find responses to these situations, and at other times creating a new response to the situation (Dervin, 2003). As an individual moves through time and space they may be facilitated or hindered by power or societal forces. A core premise is the need for human beings to make sense as they move through a reality that is inherently filled with gaps, or ambiguities in understandings and SMM focuses on how people respond when faced with such gaps (Naumer, Fisher & Dervin, 2008). The individual is conceived as a "constructing, creating, sometimes repeating carrier of communicatings" (Dervin, 2003, p. 67) and *gaps* are where *communicatings* or the process of communication takes place. Communicatings are situated in structures at specific moments in time and space, and constructed in a "time line linked to the past." Therefore, to examine the essence of the communicating moment, SMM advocates studying how actors interpret the moment as a gap and deal with *gappiness*, in the moment of communicating.

We believe the concept of the gap in SMM is useful for describing an intercultural communication situation where an individual is faced with a stereotype about the person they are interacting with. As an individual moves through time-space a person can choose to see people of another culture in stereotypical ways or as dynamic individuals, and they may find these ways of viewing others beneficial or harmful. SMM's concept of the sense-making moment as the point in time-space when a person experiences a gap may thus be a productive way of conceptualizing the process that unfolds when one encounters a stereotype about another person (Naumer, Fisher & Dervin, 2008).

Study Aims and Research Questions

As detailed above, research on stereotype change has identified cognitive processes that people use to revise or change their stereotypes and work on contact theory has identified various conditions and mediating processes that facilitates the reduction of prejudice. While profitable, these lines of work generally neglect the social situatedness of stereotyping and do not provide a full understanding of the interpersonal and interpretive processes involved in revising or changing stereotypes. To address this gap in the literature, the aim of our study was to employ SMM to learn how persons who encounter stereotypes in an interpersonal contact situation make sense of these stereotypes. We focused on situations in which persons had become aware of having stereotypes about cultural others in the course of interacting with them. Some of the questions that guided us initially were: How does the person characterize the interpretive process and practices used in revising his/her stereotype? How does the person make sense of the other person's communicative acts and how does the meaning the person attaches to communicative acts lead to revised thinking about the other person? Also, what are the in situ communication processes that lead to revised insights about the other person? These foci led to two research questions, namely: RQ1) How do people make sense of an intercultural contact situation that leads them to review and revise a held stereotype? RQ2) What role does communication play in helping people revise a stereotype?

METHOD

Participants

We utilized a specific purposeful sampling strategy called intensity sampling to recruit individuals for our study in which individuals are recruited if they can relate rich examples of a phenomenon of interest, provided they are not unusual cases (Patton, 2004). We recruited individuals if they identified themselves as seeking intercultural contact situations, evidenced by engagement in at least one of these activities: attending intercultural events hosted by the university's multicultural center, voluntarily rooming with a person from a different culture, or having studied or worked abroad. There were no restrictions placed on nationality, race or gender.

Ten individuals (5 females, 5 males) were recruited for the study, whose ages ranged from 22 years to 45 years ($M = 27$). Five participants self-identified as Caucasian or European American, four as Indian (from India) and one as Latina. All participants were students who were graduates from or currently enrolled in a large, multicultural university. Occupations held by participants included research assistant, teaching assistant, medical interpreter, software professional and academic adviser. Participation in the study was voluntary and participants were not compensated for their time.

Procedures and Interview Instrument

Participants were interviewed one-on-one in a private room for about an hour. After the interview they were asked to complete a questionnaire to capture information that may have been missed during the interview. The interview instrument used was SMM's Micro-Moment Time-Line interview (Dervin, 2008) in which participants are led through a series of questions about how they made sense of a specific situation they experienced. The method has participants identify their experience as a series of time-line steps

(Dervin, 2008). Typically the interview begins with the interviewer reading the informant the critical entry or the research specific trigger question on which the interview is based. After the participant identifies the specific situation they would discuss, the interviewer asks a series of questions, called Level 1 Triangulation questions to learn how the participant makes sense of each moment of the situation in terms of their questions and thoughts, sense of self, and views of society. An interviewer may probe further using a set of questions called Level 2 Triangulation, in order to obtain a more complete picture of a participant's subjective understanding of the situation and their responses to the situation.

To implement the SMM, we emailed participants ahead of time with the critical entry for the interview, so they could begin reflecting on the situation they would later discuss. (For our critical entry see Appendix). When participants arrived for their interview, they were shown the SMM Metaphor (Dervin, 2008), a pictorial representation of a person trying to cross a bridge which conceptualizes a moment in time-space as a step one takes across gaps between one situation and the next. Participants were asked to imagine they were the person in the picture facing a gap or gaps related to the critical entry and asked how they bridged the gaps in the specific situation they were thinking about. Participants were also shown the questions they would be asked during the interview and were given ample time to reflect on the situation again. Once participants indicated they were ready to be interviewed, they were read the critical entry again.

Participants were first asked to describe their experience as a series of steps as if they were scenes in a movie that they could talk about. These time-line steps were put on note-cards so that participants could look at their time-line steps during the interview. For each step listed by the participant, the interviewer asked a series of questions from SMM that collectively formed the Level 1 Triangulation (for questions, see Appendix). Once participants answered the above questions, the interviewer picked from the responses anything she heard that needed further explanation or in-depth discussion. For instance, one of the participants in the study said: "I guess I have a negative association with arranged marriage." The interviewer chose this response for a Level 2 Triangulation, which involved re-anchoring interview questions to the participant's response about arranged marriage. This procedure invited more in-depth discussion from the participant (for an example, see Appendix).

The interviews were tape- and/or digitally recorded. One researcher interviewed all the participants and took detailed notes in addition to the recordings. At the end of each interview participants were thanked and given a questionnaire to complete. The questionnaire contained six open-ended questions that asked participants for how they had come across their stereotype, their definition of culture, what cultures they considered similar to and different from their own, and how contact with similar cultures and different cultures have helped and/or hurt them. Participants took about 20 minutes to complete the questionnaire, which was used to further understand the interview responses.

Data Analysis

All interviews were transcribed, which yielded about 95 single-spaced pages of transcription. The transcribed data were then analyzed inductively using constant comparative procedures to form categories and their properties, following grounded theory procedures (Charmaz, 2006; Corbin & Strauss, 2008). The interviews were first open coded (Strauss & Corbin, 1990) for concepts keeping in mind the research questions. Interview transcripts were closely read and re-read and memos were made about the codes that were identified. We especially focused on what the participants seemed to be "doing" in the situation, as we were interested in describing interpretive activities and processes. After initial categories about phenomena were developed, we looked for relationships between categories and how they linked to one another.

We adopted several of Lather's (1986) guidelines for validity as well as Lincoln and Guba's (1985) criteria for establishing trustworthiness. Credibility (Lincoln & Guba, 1985) was attended to by having participants construct their own realities through the time-line steps. The repetition and clarification of participant responses built into the sense-making interviewing process ensured that triangulation of sources was addressed. Methodological triangulation was attended to by analyzing participants' oral and written responses and by using in vivo terms in category formation. Both of us developed codes for the initial interview transcripts and then compared them. We found that categories derived from both our codes were almost identical. Throughout the coding process we then looked for disconfirming evidence and revised categories when necessary. We conducted a member check with one participant to ensure we were representing our participants' ideas accurately. We also attended to what Lather (1986) identifies as catalytic validity and took note of participants' remarks about how the interview had made them think about the situation differently.

RESULTS

The accounts of intercultural contact that we elicited from the ten participants spanned a variety of interactional situations and stereotypes. Hence, we present our analysis by first categorizing and summarizing the situations and stereotypes participants encounter. Then, we present an analysis of the interpretive activities participants engaged in to overcome the stereotype they held (addressing Research Question #1). Finally we present the communicative practices that the informants participated in, which facilitated revisions in their stereotypes (addressing Research Question #2). Descriptions of the themes that emerged from both research questions are illustrated with examples drawn from the interviews.

Interpretive Activities in Stereotype Change

In Table 1, we present a description of the stereotypes that participants discussed, along with their interactive contexts. Participants' stereotypes clustered into five categories: race (3), gender (3), nationality (5), and social class or cultural practices (2). Half of the participants focused on nationality stereotypes, or preconceived notions about a particular nationality, language, or interaction type. A single participant's stereotype could encompass more than one type of stereotype (such as #10; See Table 1).

Sequence of Interpretive Activities

Our first research question asked what interpretive activities lead to overcoming stereotypes. Our analysis showed that participants pursued a sequence of distinct interpretive activities as they overcame their held stereotypes. When the participant interpreted a move of the other person as confounding their prior notions, a sequence was set into motion, the steps of which are depicted in Figure 1.

Table 1. Stereotypes and situations

Stereotype	Stereotype attributes	Interaction leading to stereotype change and time taken
# 1 Lower-class persons cannot be good professors	Less civilized, deficient in English, shy, lack confidence, no presentation skills	A male Indian student's (age 27) interpretation of the opening lines of a Quantum Physics lecture by a professor hired through reservations, i.e., affirmative action in India. Stereotype changed over an hour-long class lecture
# 2 Hispanics have low education and low income	Frugal, lack knowledge and need to have technical vocabulary explained	A one-time interaction between a White male (age 25) working at an insurance firm and a Hispanic client. Stereotype changed over a brief interaction in less than an hour
# 3 Arranged marriages are an overly conservative and traditional practice	Practice indicates a lack of independence and control over life, non-critical and traditional thinking	A specific interaction between a White male (age 31) and an Indian friend he regularly talks to on his daily commute to work. Stereotype changed in less than an hour
# 4 White, blonde people are usually not culturally sensitive	Selfish, condescending to other ethnicities, objectify other cultures	A Latina medical interpreter (age 22) interacts with a White female volunteer at a free health clinic over a period of time. Stereotype changed over a few weeks
# 5 Rwandans are likely not able to communicate well	Heavy accent, cannot understand questions or respond to them in English	A White female returning student's (age 45) interacts with a female returning student from Rwanda for group activities on orientation day. Stereotype changed in a day's time
# 6 African-Americans are violent	Unsafe, high-crime and tough neighborhoods. Takes advantage of others, deceive people	An Indian female student's (age 23) interactions with an African-American man and woman over a bus journey. Stereotype changed over the course of the 20-hour journey
# 7 Americans do not participate in the customs of other cultures.	Objectify Eastern cultures, restrained and inhibited in cultural situations	An Indian male student's (age 25) interactions with different American guests at an Indian wedding. Stereotype changed over a day
# 8 Spaniards do not value time	Rude and disrespectful, do not adhere to normal US time patterns	A White female's (age 27) interactions with different Spaniards over a time spent studying in Spain. Stereotype changed over a four-month period
# 9 The Chinese have cliques that exclude other cultures	Cling together as a group, exclude others, deficient in English	An Indian female's (age 27) interactions with a Chinese female study partner over two academic years. Stereotype changed along the course of these interactions
# 10 Ecuadorean males are untrustworthy and conniving	Deceptive, interested in American women only for their money or bragging rights	A White female's (age 26) interactions with a male Ecuadorean host brother/friend over an academic term spent in Ecuador. Stereotype changed over 10 weeks

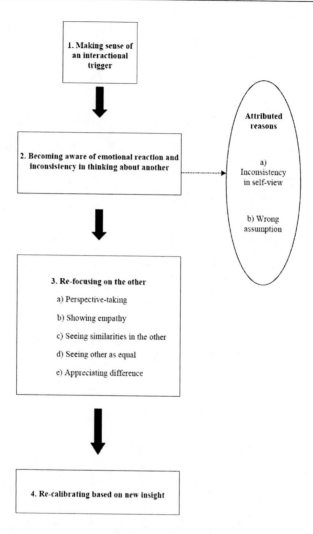

Figure 1. Interpretive processes in overcoming stereotypes.

Making sense of an interactional trigger. In symbolic interactionist terms, a trigger event is an object that participants indicate to themselves and to which they assign meaning (Blumer, 1969). In this context, trigger situations were identified by all participants as the moment they encountered evidence that disconfirmed a held stereotype about the other person; typically the other person had just interacted in way that violated something the participant had believed to be true up until that moment. For instance, participant #3 discussed his shock when his friend from India disclosed to him that he had had an arranged marriage:

> He described, 'I got to meet her for ten minutes before I made a choice'... and I was like 'how can you make a decision in ten minutes?' 'Oh you just know'... that really shocked. That was a situation where everything else I knew about him, I didn't associate.... [In My] past experiences with him ... he would have been somebody making jokes about arranged marriages as opposed to him having an arranged marriage.

There was a perceived lack of fit between what the participant had previously believed about his friend and what he had just found out about him; the conflict in the meaning the participant ascribed to the practice of arranged marriage and the meaning he associated with his friend triggered an interpretive process within the participant.

Becoming aware of one's emotional reaction and inconsistency in thinking. The next step comprised of two parts. The first involved becoming aware of an inconsistency in one's stereotype when compared with the person they were interacting with. The second involved becoming aware of a strong emotion. Over half the participants discussed noticing a change in their emotional state. For instance, participant #3 talked about his reaction to his friend's description of how he got married:

> Surprise. This feeling of everything I know about this person previously would have made me think different from that... I was prejudiced or I don't know if 'prejudiced' was the right word but I thought because he acts this other way, he seems to not be very traditional in many other ways and I didn't expect him to be traditional...

The intense emotion about the other's actions surprised the participant and led him to examine the reason for his strong feelings, such as if he was prejudiced. Similarly, participant #1 described his shock on discovering that he was prejudiced about a professor in India from a 'backward caste'. The professor had opened his lecture in an unexpectedly refreshing manner:

> I think I'm being receptive ... until he opens his mouth. And the first thing he says is, the Copenhagen Interpretation of Quantum Mechanics is that we don't really know what's happening. Clear, direct and it's as though someone else was speaking and that's the first thought that came in my head and I realized that I expected this person not to say this... and

that is just shocking, ... here I am thinking that... everyone deserves a chance, they're as bright as we are and I shouldn't even be thinking of they, them and us.

Participant #1 was not only shocked to hear the professor's words but was also shocked at his emotional reaction.

Reasons attributed to one's emotional reaction and inconsistency in thinking. Participants mentioned two reasons for the intense emotional reaction to the lack of fit between the other person in the interaction and their own stereotypes about the other person. One reason had to do with *not having their predictions right* or having *wrongly predicted:*

> Well, the predominant feeling was that of, ... pure and simple shock.... First of all, I was shocked, and I was a little pissed with myself that I had got it wrong. I had made a prediction and I had got it so wrong.

A second reason participants gave was that *they thought of themselves as open-minded and tolerant* people and did not like that they were stereotyping others. Participants compared their view of themselves in the situation with what they had previously thought about themselves, and realized that they had caught themselves stereotyping the other person:

> Usually in my experience I try not to stereotype people or group them into categories and make assumptions about them before I know anything about the individual. I realized that I had been doing that and I didn't want to do that. I would like to think that I wouldn't use these stereotypes... I'd like to think I'm the kind of person who wouldn't do that.

Participants compared their thought process in this interaction with what they supposed was their "true self" and they found it disturbing because they had not reacted as they thought they should have reacted.

Re-Focusing on the Other Person

Once participants realized they had been stereotyping the other person and that this act was not in line with how they viewed themselves, they shifted their focus to the other. *All* of the participants made one of five different communication or relationship moves, including taking the other's perspective, showing empathy, seeing similarities, appreciating differences and seeing the other an equal. These moves allowed participants to repair the inconsistencies in their views about themselves and their emotional reactions.

Taking the other's perspective. One of the other-focused moves that participants engaged in was to take the other's perspective. Here participants said they put themselves in the other's place and imagined the situation from the other's point of view. For instance, in talking about how his friend gave him a different perspective on arranged marriage, participant #3 said: "[my friend] didn't see it as conformity, maybe he saw it as celebrating something... embracing something he liked about that culture, that tradition." In a similar vein, informant #6, in the course of her interaction with an African-American lady on the bus, began to see similarities and also began to appreciate how she handled her troubles:

We were just talking all along the way about the books we like, the college she goes to, troubles she had as a single mom, balancing her education and the child and bringing her up and the situation in Harlem and everything that goes on there, ... I didn't know what to talk to her. I was feeling small in a way... that people ... are struggling through so much.

Experiencing empathy. Some participants were able to emotionally relate to the other person. This involved not just taking their perspective, but also being able to imagine what they must have felt like. For instance, participant #5 expressed her anger, on finding out that her group partner already had a nursing degree from her country Rwanda, but had to go to school all over again because her degree wasn't recognized in the U.S: "Her situation angered me... I felt anger and related it to my own situation."

Expressing shared experiences, interests, values. Participants also began to see similarities in the other person in terms of shared experiences, interests and values. This new knowledge about the other person helped them bridge prior differences and brought them closer to the other person. For instance, participant #5 said she felt empathy for her Rwandan group partner and related it to her own inability to go to college when she was younger: "I felt like we, that shared experience ... I don't want to say a bond, but we had a shared moment and a shared experience, we found something in common. So that made me feel closer to her."

Appreciating the other person. When similarities were not apparent, participants tried to appreciate or celebrate differences. For instance, participant #3 began to appreciate his friend's point of view on arranged marriage: "The amount of confidence, the level of commitment he has, maybe there's things to be appreciated, maybe it's not as negative a practice as I thought before. ...[I] found myself changing my position not completely but shifting it, more accepting of it."

Seeing the other as an equal. A final way participants shifted their focus to the other person was by seeing them as an equal. Any inequalities or differences that participants had assumed at the beginning of the interaction were bridged, based on some aspect of the interaction that was meaningful to the participant. For instance, participant #2 saw his Hispanic client differently after he displayed knowledge of insurance terms: "I suppose that I saw him as more like me at that time. To some degree you realize that they're in a position of power as much as you are because they have the same knowledge and abilities."

Re-Calibrating Based on New Insight

Once participants began to question their stereotypes they re-calibrated prior meanings they had attached to cultures, its members and practices with the insight they had gained from the situation. For instance, informant #3 initially viewed arranged marriage as a practice where "it felt like other people were controlling." He then gained a new perspective on this practice: "...the way he described it... someone that he was going to love, care for consistently, day after day, and I really had a lot of respect for that type of love and commitment to standing by somebody." The apparent alignment in interactants' beliefs about love and marriage led the participant to soften his views on arranged marriage: "And seeing his apparent happiness, that gave me a different perspective and I thought to myself that if it ends up in happy marriages, who am I to look down upon them?... I was reassessing my... values and my earlier assessment of that particular tradition." The participant now began to view the practice differently: "I had this more refined view of arranged marriages where I think that they could be good or OK in certain situations."

Reflections on the Situation

Despite the topic, our participants were extremely open and self-reflexive throughout the course of the interview. Participants talked about the valuable lessons they had gleaned from the incident, such as about what they learned about themselves, about culture, and about stereotypes. Participants saw themselves as having been prejudiced individuals. For instance, participant #1 confessed, "I was a little upset with myself that this had happened but I was... really satisfied with myself that this had occurred. I had a chance to let... this prejudice in me get exposed. I was also happy that it was very easy for me to deal with it. It happened very easily." The initial negativity and strong responses participants had during the situation were now seen as positive and as an experience that helped them learn about themselves.

Participants also talked about how they *saw themselves evolve* over the course of the situation, or how it helped them stay true to who they were. Participant #10 said:

> It definitely took me full circle back to being a pretty trusting person and maybe a little smarter. Going through the discernment of Ecuadorean guys... and meeting my host brother and realizing that he was a really good guy. I think it took me back to being that trusting person, definitely a big part of who I am. I generally trust people unless I have a reason not to whereas when I went to Ecuador, it was backward so I think this process allowed me to come back to my roots, I guess.

Participants generally indicated that they had gained more clarity about the situation and were able to appreciate what it had taught them about themselves.

Communicative Activities that Influenced Stereotype Change

Although interpretive processes played an important part in helping participants change their views of the other person, some participants mentioned specific communicative activities that they saw as important in facilitating this change. *Open communication* with the other was a recurring theme in five interviews, and involved participants being able to express themselves freely and without fearing judgment from their interactants. For instance, participant #9 commented about her "very successful study partnership over two years" with her Chinese study group partner, in spite of her partner not being fluent in English:

> When two people have different propensity to speak a language, typically the person with less propensity will speak less, right? That's the

hypothesis we always make. I never found that with her and I found that despite her difficulty with the language, she never stopped short of expressing herself. Expressing her ideas, disagreeing with stuff I was saying, which was so important.

Six participants, mostly those with nationality-related stereotypes, noted that the other's use of language was not as hindering as they had believed it would be. Three participants talked about the value of *asking questions* to clarify their misconceptions about the other person, which become an important factor in overcoming stereotypes about them. For participant #6, talking to her other and asking "taboo" questions about the African-American community helped to rid her of the misconceptions she said she had acquired from the media and her friends:

> I was mostly interviewing her – How do you do it? How do you feel? …Whatever confusion I had, I was talking to her and asking her. I was very comfortable with her... asking her, is it all right to call you Black? Why do you have a white child? How do you feel about Harlem when everyone says that it's a bad place... Basically I asked her all the taboo questions.

For participant #5, her interaction partner contributed by simply *having a conversation, listening without judgment* and allowing the participant to relate to her. Participant #5 saw this gesture as going beyond what was required; by focusing away from the task at hand and engaging in a conversation, participant #5 felt that her interaction partner "participated in the moment."

DISCUSSION

We set out to do a socially situated study of stereotype review to address gaps in current research on stereotype change and respond to contact theory researchers' calls for more studies privileging the experiences of those who had overcome prejudice. We were specifically interested in knowing more about how communication with another in an intercultural contact situation influenced stereotype review. We were also curious about the process of meaning making that would lead to a stereotype not being applied in a contact situation. To study this we employed Dervin's Sense-Making Methodology and conceptualized a gap situation where the person holding a stereotype was stopped in their thinking about a cultural other and interviewed persons on how they bridged this gap.

Our participants described what we have called the trigger event, something in the content or manner of the other's communication that stood out as disconfirming evidence and signaled to the participant that they had been stereotyping. Encountering the trigger event was often accompanied with an affective component that drew attention to the participant's held stereotype. Once participants realized that they had stereotyped the other, they were quick to move into damage control mode by refocusing their attention on the other and opening dialogue with the other in five primary ways: by taking their perspective, experiencing empathy, appreciating difference, expressing similarities, and/or seeing the other as an equal.

We first discuss the theoretical implications of the interpretive moves made by the participants (research question 1). Our findings are consistent with research on the cognitive processes undergirding stereotype change. For instance, similar to Richards and Hewstone (2001), participants engaged in subgrouping or the removal of the targeted individual from the stereotyped group as they considered discrepant information about the individual. Research on stereotype control has found that individuals committed to the goal of egalitarianism are able to prevent activation of their stereotypes (Moskowitz, Gollwitzer, Wasel, & Schaal, 1999).

The final interpretive activity of re-calibrating based on new insight can be likened to Kelly's (1955) findings about construct revisions. According to Kelly (1955), revisions begin with the invalidation of one's construct repertory and involve circumspection and choosing simpler constructs to understand what one is dealing with. Participants' reflections about their interactions were also an important factor in helping them overcome their stereotype, much like what Denzin has called "relived epiphanies," where "effects are immediate but their meanings are given only later in retrospection and in the reliving of the event" (1989, p. 129).

Our second research question asked what specific interactive practices the participant and the other undertook that aided in stereotype revision. Our findings indicated that stereotype change involved cognitive, emotional, social and communicative components for our participants, sometimes in that order. Stereotype change therefore involved not just engaging in a cognitive revision but also socially manifesting a sense of equality. In effect, participants were *performing* equality in order to display that they no longer held a stereotype about the other. Many of these communicative- and relational moves that participants engaged in to bridge the perceived power differential between themselves (the one who held a stereotype) and the other (who was stereotyped) have been identified with quality interpersonal relations. For instance, empathy and taking the other's perspective has been linked to lasting intimate friendships (Selman, 1971) and to better produce listener-adapted messages (Delia, Kline & Burleson, 1979). Focusing on similarities has been shown to lead to interpersonal attraction (Byrne, 1971) and to increase liking for out-group members (Chen & Kenrick, 2002).

Many of the aforementioned communicative and relational moves are also acts that we typically associate with dialogue. Gesturing at the inhibition of a stereotype, the participants described several moves to co-create an I-Thou relationship with the other. These same qualities, of openness to (the other's) mystery, the lack of hierarchy between conversation partners, creating space for the other, are also frequently invoked as characteristic of dialogue and dialogic communication. Open communication, the ability to express themselves freely without being judged, and the other's ability to listen and contribute to the conversation are similar to what Rogers (1959) described as empathic listening. Language proficiency, which was initially a concern, was overcome when common ground (Clark, 1996) was established during the course of the interaction. Asking questions was another important communicative activity that participants mentioned, which has been previously been linked to perspective-taking (Quirk, 2006) and listening (Littlejohn & Domenici, 2000). In sum, stereotype review for our participants was encouraged by engaging the other in a set of communicative and relational acts that has characterized dialogue, both as a particular kind of communication and as an adverb/adjective (Pearce & Pearce, 2004).

CONTRIBUTIONS OF THE STUDY

Perhaps our findings are significant not only because they are consistent with prior research but also because they extend our knowledge about stereotype review in at least five ways. First, our findings respond to the call for identifying processes in intercultural contact situations (Pettigrew, 1998). As a methodology designed to examine gaps in thinking, SMM made it possible for participants situate themselves within the gap and to articulate the interpretive activities that led to stereotype change.

Our findings support other researchers (e.g., Semin, 2008; Yzerbyt & Carnaghi, 2008), who have noted how stereotype change is influenced by interpersonal communication processes. Second, by focusing on process, we were able to tap into the role of social interaction and communication in stereotype change. Our participants' accounts illustrate how both interpretive and communicative practices work in tandem to help participants make, handle and modify meaning. Cognitive processes such as subgrouping and conversion that are usually discussed in psychological terms were embedded within communicative activity for our participants.

A third contribution, which may have implications for contact theory, pertains to the notion of equality among participants. Contact theory has long held that equal status among groups is a prerequisite for a reduction in prejudice. However, equality, for the participants, was not a pre-existing condition that facilitated a change. Instead, *participants who initially presumed a difference in power communicatively constructed and performed equality* between themselves and the other.

A fourth contribution was that participants' construal of themselves as having egalitarian values was significant in changing their stereotypes. Our participants were self-professed, compulsive seekers of multicultural experiences and were able to stop themselves from stereotyping the other. Participants were thus "unprejudiced" in that despite holding stereotypes, they were extremely attentive to disconfirming evidence. Wyer (2004) has noted that research on prejudice and stereotyping has been preoccupied with demonstrating the degree to which the prejudiced individuals are likely to use information-processing strategies that are stereotype confirming. We agree with Wyer (2010) that unprejudiced individuals' information-processing strategies are just as important and yet understudied, but, of course, our participants do more than process information. Both the disconfirming evidence they pointed to in their contact with the other and the relational moves they themselves made after encountering their stereotypes were grounded in communication.

Finally, and most importantly for communication and social interaction scholars, our participants repeatedly invoked aspects of dialogue and dialogic communication, such as openness to the other, equality between partners, the ability to ask question and listen without judgment, appreciating difference and creating common ground, as being instrumental to their in-situ review of the held stereotype.

FUTURE DIRECTIONS

Although the study had strengths with respect to its methodological contributions, several aspects of the design invite further research to solidify the findings obtained here. The participants selected for the study had to fulfill certain criteria to be eligible for participation and so, the findings may not be applicable to the general population. The design was also based on an intensity sample of only ten people. However, the study was exploratory in nature and the findings warrant that further research with a larger sample is worthwhile. One possible avenue for further research is to include elicitations of instances where participants see the other in a more negative way than they did previously. The strength of our findings is in the participants' own accounts of experiences with stereotype change. We do not know however if the participants shed their stereotypes altogether or if this was an exceptional contact situation. While cognitive processes in stereotype change were reflected in encountering the stereotype and in perceiving an inconsistency in one's construction of the self as tolerant, the emotion accompanying this inconsistency pointed to the affective component of the change. The next activity was social in nature as there was a felt need to perform equality through communicative and relational moves. The final two moves were a return to cognitive reconstructions of the other but these were once again embedded in social interaction; especially within communication of a dialogic nature and process that led participants to reexamine their stereotype in situ and make moves to treat the other as "Thou". The intersection of cognitive, emotional, social and communicative activities in stereotype change that occurred for our participants is rarely documented in contact and stereotype literature and would be a productive direction for future research on prejudice.

APPENDIX

1. The Critical Entry

Think about a time when you interacted with or were in conversation with a person from a culture different from yours, which led you to change your views about what you had previously believed to be true about people of this culture. Start with a brief description of the situation.

2. Level 1 Triangulation Questions

a) What questions, confusions or muddles did you have at this point?
b) What conclusions, thoughts or ideas did you have?
c) How did you see power in society as related to this situation?
d) How did this situation relate to your sense of self?

e) How did this situation help you?

f) How did this situation hurt you?

g) If you had a magic wand at this point, what would you do and how would it have helped?

3. An Example of Level 2 Triangulation Questions

a) You had a negative association with arranged marriage... what happened that led you to that conclusion?

b) How did your conclusion connect with your life and past?

c) Did your conclusion about arranged marriage raise questions or muddles for you?

d) How does having a negative association with arranged marriage relate to power in society?

e) How does having a negative association with arranged marriage relate to your sense of self?

REFERENCES

Allport, G. W. (1954). *The nature of prejudice.* Cambridge, Mass: Addison-Wesley Pub.

Augoustinos, M., & Walker, I. (1998). The construction of stereotypes within social psychology: from social cognition to ideology. *Theory and Psychology, 8 (5), 629-652.*

Bohman, J. (2000). *Public deliberation: Pluralism, complexity, and democracy.* Cambridge, MA: The MIT Press.

Blumer, H. (1969). *Symbolic interactionism; perspective and method.* Englewood Cliffs, N.J.: Prentice-Hall.

Brewer, M. B. & Gaertner, S. L. (2004). Toward reduction of prejudice: Intergroup contact and social categorization. In M. B. Brewer, & M. Hewstone (Eds.), *Self and social identity. Perspectives on social psychology* (pp. 298–314). Malden, MA: Blackwell Pub.

Buber, M. (2000). *I and Thou.* New York: N.Y.: Scribner. (Original work published 1958).

Byrne, D. (1971). *The attraction paradigm.* New York: Academic Press.

Charmaz, K. (2006). *Constructing grounded theory: A practical guide through qualitative analysis.* Los Angeles, CA: Sage Publications.

Chen, F. F., & Kenrick, D. T. (2002). Interpersonal relations and group processes - Repulsion or attraction? Group membership and assumed attitude similarity. *Journal of Personality and Social Psychology, 83 (1),* 111-125.

Clark, H. H. (1996). *Using language.* Cambridge [England]: Cambridge University Press.

Connolly, P. (2000). What now for the contact hypothesis? Towards a new research agenda. *Race, Ethnicity and Education, 3 (2),* 169-193.

Cooperrider, D. L., & Whitney, D. K. (2005). *Appreciative inquiry: A positive revolution in change.* San Francisco, CA: Berrett-Koehler.

Corbin, J., & Strauss, A. (2008). *Basics of qualitative research: Techniques and procedures for developing grounded theory.* Los Angeles, CA: Sage Publications.

Delia, J. G., Kline, S. L., & Burleson, B. R. (1979). The development of persuasive communication strategies in kindergartners through twelfth-graders. *Communication Monographs, 46,* 241-256.

Denzin, N. K. (1989). *Interpretive interactionism. Applied social research methods series,* v. 16. Newbury Park, CA: Sage Publications.

Dervin, B. (2003). Comparative theory reconceptualized: From entities and states to processes and dynamics. In B. Dervin & L. Foreman-Wernet (with E. Lauterbach) (Eds.). *Sense- Making Methodology reader: Selected writings of Brenda Dervin* (pp. 61-72). Cresskill, NJ: Hampton Press.

Dervin, B. (2008). *Interviewing as dialectical practice: Sense-making methodology as exemplar.* Paper presented at the Annual Meeting of the International Association for Media and Communication Research. Stockholm: Sweden.

Dixon, J, Durrheim, K, & Tredoux, C. (2005). Beyond the optimal contact strategy: a reality check for the contact hypothesis. *The American Psychologist, 60 (7),* 697-711.

Foreman-Wernet, L. (2003). Rethinking communication: Introducing the sense-making methodology. In B. Dervin, L. Foreman-Wernet, & E. Lauterbach (Eds.), *Sense-making methodology reader: Selected writings of Brenda Dervin* (pp. 3-16). Cresskill, N.J.: Hampton Press.

Isaacs, W. (1999). *Dialogue and the art of thinking together.* New York: Currency.

Kashima, Y., Fiedler, K., & Freytag, P. (Eds.) (2008). *Stereotype dynamics: Language-based approaches to the formation, maintenance, and transformation of stereotypes.* New York: Lawrence Erlbaum Associates.

Kelly, G. (1955). *The psychology of personal constructs.* New York: Norton.

Littlejohn, S. W., & Domenici, K. (2000). *The systemic practitioner: Engaging communication in conflict.* London: SAGE.

Naumer, C., K. Fisher., & B. Dervin. *Sense-Making: A Methodological Perspective.* In Computer Human Interactions 2008. Florence, Italy: ACM.

Noelle-Neumann, E. (1974). Spiral of silence: A theory of public opinion. *Journal of Communication, 24,* 43-51.

Paik, J., MacDougall, B., Fabrigar, L., Peach, J., & Jellous, K. (2009). Altering Category-Level Beliefs: The Impact of Level of Representation at Belief Formation and Belief Disconfirmation. *Personality and Social Psychology Bulletin, 35, 8,* 1112-1125.

Patton, M. Q. (2004). *Qualitative research & evaluation methods.* Thousand Oaks, Calif.:Sage.

Pettigrew, T. F. (1998). Intergroup contact theory. *Annual Review of Psychology, 49,* 65.

Pettigrew, T. (2008). Future directions for intergroup contact theory and research. *International Journal of Intercultural Relations, 32 (*3) 187-199.

Pettigrew, T. F., & Tropp, L. R. (2008). How does intergroup contact reduce prejudice? Meta-analytic tests of three mediators. *European Journal of Social Psychology, 38 (6),* 922-934.

Quirk, M. E. (2006*). Intuition and metacognition in medical education: Keys to developing expertise.* New York, NY: Springer Pub.

Richards, Z., & Hewstone, M. (2001). Subtyping and subgrouping: Processes for the prevention and promotion of stereotype change. *Personality & Social Psychology Review, 5,* 52-73.

Rogers, C. R. (1959). A theory of therapy, personality and interpersonal relationships, as developed in the client-centered framework. In S. Koch (Ed.), *Psychology: A study of science,* 3, (pp. 184-256). New York: Mc Graw Hill.

Semin, G. R. (2008). Stereotypes in the wild. In Y. Kashima, K. Fiedler, & P. Freytag (Eds.), *Stereotype dynamics: Language-based approaches to the formation, maintenance, and transformation of stereotypes* (pp. 11-28). New York: Lawrence Erlbaum Associates.

Selman, R. L. (1971). Taking another's perspective: Role-taking development in early childhood. *Child Development, 42 (6),* 1721-34.

Stangor, C. (2000). *Stereotypes and prejudice: Essential readings. Key readings in social psychology.* Philadelphia, PA: Psychology Press.

Stewart, J. (1995). *Language as articulate contact: Toward a post-semiotic philosophy of communication.* Albany, NY: State University of New York Press.

Strauss, A. L., & Corbin, J. M. (1990). *Basics of qualitative research: Grounded theory procedures and techniques.* Newbury Park, CA: Sage Publications.

Maher, Felber & Feldman. (September 26, 2014). Season 12, Episode 28, Real Time with Bill Maher: Fellate Show. Los Angeles, CA: Home Box Office.

Wyer, N.A. (2004). Not all stereotypic biases are created equal: Evidence for a stereotype disconfirming bias. *Personality & Social Psychology Bulletin, 30(6),* 706-720.

Wyer, N. (2010). Salient egalitarian norms moderate activation of out-group approach and avoidance. *Group Processes and Intergroup Relations, 13,* 2, 151-165.

Yzerbyt, V. & Carnaghi, A. (2008). Stereotype change in the social context. In Y. Kashima,K. Fiedler, & P. Freytag (Eds.), *Stereotype dynamics: Language-based approaches to the formation, maintenance, and transformation of stereotypes* (pp. 29-58). New York: Lawrence Erlbaum Associates.

In: Communicating Prejudice   ISBN: 978-1-53610-167-6
Editors: S. Camara and D. Drummond   © 2016 Nova Science Publishers, Inc.

Chapter 2

THE INVITATION OF INTERGROUP DIALOGUE: SHOWING UP FOR SOCIAL JUSTICE EDUCATION

Karla D. Scott
Saint Louis University, Saint Louis, MO, US

ABSTRACT

On October 9, 2014 community activists and students "occupied" the campus of Saint Louis University—a Catholic, Jesuit institution 20 minutes away from Ferguson, Missouri. In response to the occupation support for intergroup dialogue on the SLU campus grew as the university community recognized the value of a pedagogy designed to bridge understanding across social and cultural identities. Intergroup dialogue emphasizes a sharing of lived experiences with listening to understand, not reply or defend. The study of human communication prepares many of us to facilitate interaction that leads to understanding; listening that creates connection and connection that creates compassion. Compassion allows one to sit with the discomfort of knowing someone else is in pain—and even though you may be complicit in it, remain with them as they share that reality and then stand with them in solidarity to dismantle that which created it.

INTRODUCTION

On October 9, 2014 community activists and students "occupied" the campus of Saint Louis University—a Catholic, Jesuit institution 20 minutes away from Ferguson, Missouri. The seven-day protest, known as Occupy SLU, ended when university president Dr. Fred Pestello signed the Clocktower Accords, a 13-point agreement to improve community engagement efforts and increase student diversity. OccupySLU was contentious for obvious reasons, and for our students preparing for midterm week it compounded anxiety. The university library was a busy place that late Sunday evening when protestors arrived and many students were frightened; they had never seen so many Black faces on campus before—despite the fact SLU is located in "midtown" of a city with a large African American population. Soon after the protest began administration set up phone banks to take calls from irate students, parents, and alumni. Comments on the SLU Facebook page were painful reminders of how systemic oppression, racism and White privilege operate daily. And the social media site YikYak illustrated just how freely one can disseminate hate and dehumanize others when anonymity is offered. Yes, even at a Catholic university.

During the occupation I was away visiting Santa Clara University, also a Jesuit institution, presenting on Intergroup Dialogue as social justice education—an initiative that I believe supports the distinctive Jesuit tradition of education. From afar I watched events unfold via a webcam installed at the SLU clocktower and wondered about the reactions of students in my Introduction to Communication and Culture class. The 100-level course required for Communication majors had 34 students, 21 of them first-year; it was predominantly White, with 6 students identified as Asian, 6 as Black and one as Mexican American. Several were second and third year students and for most, I was the first Black faculty member they had encountered.

I grew up in the St. Louis metropolitan area so I had not avoided class discussion of the "Black Lives Matter" protests after the August 9 Michael Brown killing in nearby Ferguson. At the start of the term I told them one of my goals was to help them better understand the challenge of communication across identity differences and divisions. They had just completed a social identity activity and submitted a paper—a seed had been planted and I thought this was quite a teachable moment.

When I arrived to class, my first day after the occupation ended, the students had arranged desks in a circle—early in the term we had found a way to configure them despite limited space. I remained silent until the class settled down.

"Well, a lot happened while I was away—huh?" I began. Most of them smiled and nodded, some eyes avoided me.

I asked a confounding question, "So, what was good about Occupy SLU?

"Nothing was good, they just disrupted midterms," yelled Peter, a White student who always contributed an answer to any question asked.

"I don't know why they said White students were privileged—my parents worked hard for me to get here," offered Billy, another White male from a small town nearby.

Students of color remained silent, looking at me, waiting—but I wanted to create space for more to be shared and heard.

"That's not what privilege is about," said Kim, a Black student, as she rolled her eyes.

"Well I just don't know what they want, with all this protesting, racism doesn't exist anymore," Peter offered in his authoritarian voice.

"Well it does on YikYak!"—the white feminist practically yelled at him.

I jumped in. "Ok so for a week, you all passed protestors, right out there by the clocktower," I pointed out the class window. "As you walked to class, you heard what they were saying, what they asked for, you maybe even stayed to hear some of the conversations they had with administrators."

"So if this was the first time you heard—in real time, what it is like for Black people in this city, this country, this campus; the problems, prejudice, pain—remember, not on you tube, a rap video or movie but up close and personal, heard real pain—raise your hand."

The Black students, Mexican American and White feminist student crossed their arms defiantly and looked around at all their other classmates with hands in the air.

Intergroup Dialogue at SLU

Universities are ideal locations for social justice education, especially now with changing demographics of race, gender and class and the globalization of campuses in the United States. Where else will students learn how to interact with others rather than the "other." How will they learn to tackle tough topics of the isms when their parents did/could not teach them because they never learned how? Many of us in the discipline of Communication can facilitate this learning—if there is a willingness and commitment.

I believe intergroup dialogue can create a space and place to speak and listen; can help facilitate shared understanding of the experience of another who is different, rather than "othering" one who is "Different." It is transformative, addressing the reality of 21st century communicative contexts and promoting the practice of equality and social justice in human interaction. It integrates educational theory and research to bridge understanding—a model the University of Michigan has used since the mid-80s after racial tensions gave administrators a "wake up call" to think deeply about the role of higher education in constructively addressing issues of diversity and democracy. The result was the Program for Intergroup Relations—an initiative based on commitments to dialogic and empowering education to engage students to learn about intergroup conflict in constructive ways and develop capacities to be responsible participants in building socially just communities (https://igr.umich.edu/article/igr-history).

Intergroup dialogue pedagogy includes three important features: 1) Content that engages students intellectually through readings and written assignments; 2) Structured interaction that intentionally creates learning across group differences with dialogues comprised of equal (best possible) numbers of students from each identity group; 3) Facilitative guidance to avoid students replicating the dynamics that exist (and they see) in wider society; relating to high and low power groups—student peer facilitators have to know how to recognize such dynamics and guide students to recognize and alter them as well (Zuniga, Nagda, Chesler & Cytron-Walker, 2007).

Since graduate school I have been interested in helping students learn about racial differences in communicative contexts and, as a Black woman, I have always understood social justice education as such a path. After my masters' program I taught my first race and communication class as a one-week summer workshop. We began on Monday at 8 a.m., met each day from 8-5pm and ended on Friday. The class of 50 included an almost equal number of Black and White students ranging in age from 19-62. It was physically and emotionally taxing but it showed me how creating a space and place to discuss racial differences can better understanding of "others."

I accepted my current faculty position at SLU 22 years ago because of the university mission to transform society through the "development of men and women with and for others"—a mission further supported by the Jesuit tradition of educating the whole person mind, body, heart, and spirit. Jesuit education also aims to develop students with the:

> intellectual wherewithal to think clearly, argue pointedly and...evolve as a leader, acquiring the ethical and moral underpinning necessary to make sound judgments. Through class, service learning and learning to appreciate cultural difference, you will come to see the world—and your place in it—as a wondrous opportunity for growth and good works." (http://www.slu.edu/jesuit-tradition-and-mission)

At SLU I created a race and communication course for a summer intersession format that met for a half day, every day for three weeks; I taught the course for 18 years. In that class I use the transactional model of communication to illustrate how, where, and why communication across racial divisions is problematic:

> The transactional model of communication is a graphic representation of the collaborative and ongoing message exchange between individuals, or an individual and a group of individuals, with the goal of understanding each other. A communicator encodes (e.g., puts thoughts into words and gestures), then transmits the message via a channel (e.g., speaking, email, text message) to the other communicator(s) who then decode the message (e.g., take the words and apply meaning to them). The message may encounter noise (e.g., any physical, psychological, or physiological distraction or interference), which could prevent the message from being received or fully understood as the sender intended. (http://www.natcom.org/discipline/)

This process is visually represented in Figure 1 offering a compelling image to help better understand ongoing racial divisions. In the center of the model—an area in the middle encompassing the "message"—is an overlap indicating that both participants share the meaning of the message. But how does that happen when the lived experiences of participants—i.e., that which makes them who and how they are—is so profoundly different? Creating a context where participants can hear firsthand about the lived experiences of those who are "different"—as an additional component of social justice education—can facilitate that better understanding.

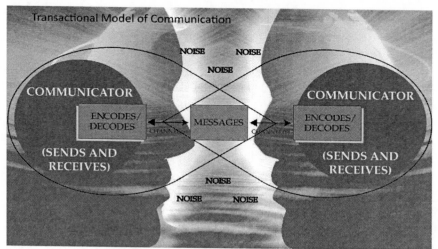

(http://www.natcom.org/Tertiary.aspx?id=511&terms=communication%20model).

Figure 1. Transactional model of communication.

In 2010 I attended the Summer Institute for Intergroup Relations at the University of Michigan and found my own course shared much with their model—supporting my belief in the value of dialogic pedagogy. Similar to the course I taught for many years the intergroup dialogue model creates opportunities to share and listen—a process critical in creating shared understanding. As noted cross-cultural dialogue facilitator and filmmaker Lee Mun Wah states, "In learning what makes each of us who we are, we can choose to transform that knowledge into compassion and understanding." (Mun Wah, 2004)

Michigan's four stage intergroup dialogue course begins with "creating the space:" interrogating dialogue, discussion and debate; active listening and social identity and ends with the sharing of testimonials—a reflection paper on racial identity. Stage two challenges that bonding with activities that divide the class by racial identity. Students of color share in a fishbowl while White students listen and observe. This is often the first time White students hear the lived experiences of students of color and it can create both discomfort and awareness. During the third stage there are discussions of systemic racism, oppression and privilege facilitate understanding and class activities vividly demonstrate lived experiences.

The final, "hot topic" stage creates opportunities to "do dialogue" on controversial issues with student peer facilitators assisting to support the process and monitor power dynamics. The end of term group project requires students to work collaboratively on a community or campus social justice initiative and a final paper offers a cumulative reflection on the course and personal growth. (Zuniga, et al. 2007).

Doing Dialogue Differently Takes Courage

Ongoing protests of racial inequality demonstrate how little is (still) known about those who are constructed as "different." What does communication offer to help change that and what can communication scholars do in their curriculum and classrooms to further social justice education? If we are to create a space for shared meaning, i.e., an area depicted in models of transactional communication as that place where the "stuff" we bring and the "stuff" the other brings overlap to create understanding, we need to create dialogue opportunities that allow each to see the humanity of the other as they share lived experiences.

Much "dialogue" lacks critical components needed for connection, compassion and solidarity but integrating them can help participants to see the humanity in others. Communication scholars have explored the work of philosopher Martin Buber who proposed the concept of *I and thou* as extending the invitation to another to be with you in the intimate human interaction of dialogue that transcends the differences (Arnett, 1986). But what does it mean to "be with another" when the other has been historically "othered"? How does one connect with the "other" especially when one who appears so different, shows up in ways that are even "foreign" and have been constructed as dangerous, deviant and even dehumanized? Ellen Langer's work on mindfulness challenges us to create more categories, construct alternate interpretations and definitions to replace habitual stereotypes. (Langer, 1989).

Buddhist principles of right speech, in the vernacular, mean not lying, not using speech in ways that create discord among people, not using swear words or a cynical, hostile or raised tone of voice, and not engaging in gossip. Re-framed in the positive, these guidelines urge us to say only what is true, to speak in ways that promote harmony among people, to use a tone of voice that is pleasing, kind, and gentle, and to speak mindfully in order that our speech is useful and purposeful (Roth, 2012). But do know I do not suggest invoking right speech to silence. Talking about race in mixed race groups is often contentious because we have so little practice doing it! Harsh tones, hostility, and anger are unavoidable as a reaction to not being heard. So to support right speech we need "right listening"—like any other mindfulness practice, both a skill and a way of being. In her book *The Zen of Listening: Mindful Communication in the Age of Distraction*, Rebecca Shariff writes that listening is one of our greatest personal natural resources, yet it is by far one of our most undeveloped abilities (Shariff, 2003).

The idea of the transformative nature of "I and thou" and right speech shares similarities with invitational rhetoric as a "request for the presence or participation of someone to engage in some activity with you" (Foss & Foss, 2003). This differs markedly from traditional forms of rhetoric aimed to persuade or change the other. The objective of invitational rhetoric "is understanding ... the goal is not to win or prove superiority but to clarify ideas—to achieve understanding for all participants involved in the interaction" (Foss & Foss, 2003, p. 7). Once we accept the invitation we must show up, fully present.

The Hebrew concept of Hineni captures what I believe is the most critical component of intergroup dialogue—we show up, ready. Hineni translates as "I am here for you fully, with the trust and vulnerability to do whatever it is you ask of me." Rabbi Ari Kaiman, Assistant Rabbi at Congregation B'nai Amoona and member of the St. Louis Rabbinical Association states:

> To be vulnerable to God is to allow for the possibility that you may be asked to sacrifice. No real relationship exists without vulnerability, no real relationship exists without some sacrifice. But without relationships, we may find ourselves alone. May we be blessed to find the strength to be vulnerable. (Kaiman, 2012)

Even without the reference to God, the message is still obvious—intergroup dialogue asks that we be in relationship and be vulnerable. Not easy for most of us according to scholar Brene Brown who studies vulnerability and defines it as "uncertainty, risk, and emotional exposure." (2012, p. 34). From two decades of teaching race and communication, I know that listening to Black pain often creates discomfort and White privilege can be a barrier to understanding. White guilt can become a stopping point as listening ceases and shame sets in. Again, from Brown—a definition: "Shame is the intensely painful feeling or experience of believing that we are flawed and therefore unworthy of love and belonging," (2012, p. 69). She identifies one of twelve shame categories as *being stereotyped or labeled*. This is a fear that often accompanies conversations and interactions about race and reconciliation—the shame of being labeled a racist. For many, how to avoid that label? Avoid the conversation.

We hear much about dismantling racism and the systems that sustain it. Communication scholars should recall that individuals make up those systems and structures so minds need to be dismantled as well. Perhaps a starting point for that is dialogue that emphasizes a sharing of lived experiences with listening to understand, not reply or defend. We who study and teach human communication are well situated to make critical contributions to narrowing racial divisions and cultivating understanding. Intergroup dialogue asks that we show up, exclaiming "Here I am" ready to participate in human interaction that facilitates a meeting in the middle for shared meaning and better understanding.

When I hear backlash to racial protest I think—often out loud—*What part of this do White folk still not understand? Why are we still here? What's missing? What's needed?* How can communication create the place for our students to learn something they have never, ever encountered in classrooms before? What can we do to facilitate progress? The study of human communication prepares many of us to facilitate the type of interaction that leads to understanding; listening that creates connection and connection that creates compassion. Compassion allows one to sit with the discomfort of knowing someone else is in pain—and even though you may be complicit in it, remain with them as they share that reality and then stand with them in solidarity to dismantle that which created it.

Intergroup Dialogue One Year After Occupy SLU

There are now additional options for an intergroup dialogue course at Saint Louis University. A First Year Dialogue experience is now offered through a partnership with the College of Arts and Sciences, Student Success Center and Housing and Residence Life. The format includes selected sections of the first year student retention program and a Learning Community. The curriculum introduces the concepts of personal, social and SLU identity, dialogic pedagogy and issues of social justice. My vision is that these students will then take the upper level intergroup dialogue course and in subsequent terms enroll in peer facilitation training and then co-facilitate an intergroup dialogue course. This is what social justice education "looks like."

It also develops a "practical skill" out of a liberal arts experience —an area of study many think has little value when college is viewed as a "commodity."

Twenty first century contexts of communication will continue to be challenged by differences that prohibit understanding "others." But if we are willing to show up, ready to be vulnerable in the spirit of "hineni," intergroup dialogue as social justice education can facilitate change. Yes we have had dialogue, even the "difficult" ones. But what we have not had enough of is dialogue that asks a student or colleague sitting right next to you: "What is it like for you to be Black on this campus?" And then listen; listen not to respond, but to understand… and believe what you hear.

REFERENCES

Arnett, R. C. (1986,) Communication and Community: Implications of Martin Buber's Dialogue. Southern Illinois University Press.

Brown, B. (2012). Daring greatly: How the courage to be vulnerable transforms the way we live, love, parent and lead. New York, Avery.

Foss, S. K & Foss, K. A. (2003). Inviting transformation: Presentational speaking for a changing world. Long Grove, IL, Waveland Press.

Kaiman A. (2012), January 4. Searching the meaning of 'Hineni - I am here.' The St. Louis Jewish Light. Retrieved from http://www. stljewishlight.com.

National Communication Association (n.d.) Transactional model of communication. Retrieved from http://www.natcom.org/Tertiary.aspx? id=511&terms=communication%20model.

Mun Wah, L. (2004). The Art of Mindful Facilitation. Berkely, CA. Stirfry Seminars.

Langer, E.J. (1989) Mindfulness. Reading, MA, Addison-Wesley.

Roth, B. (2012) Family Dharma: Right Speech Reconsidered. Retrieved from http://www.tricycle.com/web-exclusive/family-dharma-right-speech-reconsidered.

Saint Louis University. (n.d.)Mission Statement. Retrieved from http://www.slu.edu/mission-statement.

Saint Louis University. (n.d.). Jesuit Tradition and Mission. Retrieved from http://www.slu.edu/jesuit-tradition-and-mission.

Shariff, R. (2003). The Zen of Listening: Mindful Communication in the Age of Distraction. Quest Books.

University of Michigan, Program for Intergroup Relations, (n.d.) Retrieved from https://igr.umich.edu/about.

Zuniga, X, Nagda, A. B., Chesler, M. & Cytron Walker, A. (2007). Intergroup dialogue in higher education: Meaningful learning about social justice. ASHE Higher Education Report: Volume 32, Number 4.

In: Communicating Prejudice   ISBN: 978-1-53610-167-6
Editors: S. Camara and D. Drummond   © 2016 Nova Science Publishers, Inc.

Chapter 3

OUT WITH THE FAMILY: A DUOETHNOGRAPHY OF FAMILY, PREJUDICE, AND CRITICAL APPRECIATIVE INQUIRY

Liliana Herakova[1] and Ellen Correa[2]
[1]University of Maine, Orono, ME, US
[2]University of Massachusetts, Amherst, MA, US

ABSTRACT

In this duoethnographic narrative collage, we weave our voices to explore intersectional experiences of learning, responding to, and struggling with prejudice within and related to our families of origin and created families. In the context of family communication, we offer a critical analysis of Appreciative Inquiry (AI) through a social justice lens. We consider the family as a liminal site that connects public and private selves, commitments, and communication. Our stories and critical reflections seek to move the reader to consider the contributions AI can make to understanding our uses of communication to establish social and familial belonging and divisions, in relationship to hierarchical and structural systems of privilege and oppression.

INTRODUCTION

In this chapter we employ the method/genre of duoethnography to explore Appreciative Inquiry (AI) as a communication practice to establish social and familial belonging and divisions. We seek to do this within frameworks of Critical Cultural Theory (CCT), which uncover and work toward an end to socio-economic structures of inequality based on perceptions of social identity (Delgado & Stefancic, 2006), and to begin a dialogue regarding how precepts of AI and CCT may inform everyday family communication of prejudice, in hopes of finding the possibilities [within the family] for "positive change" (Cockell & McArthur-Blair, 2012, p. 52). This study seeks to build on Appreciative Inquiry research in three ways: 1) by moving the research from its usual context of business, nonprofits, and other formal organizational structures to discussion of everyday family life in its private and public dimensions; 2) building on nascent work exploring the efficacy of combining AI with CCT; and 3) employing the method/genre of duoethnography to "treat lived spaces as curricular text in order to evoke, interrupt, and create new perceptions and meanings in the process of interrogating such spaces" (Sawyer & Liggett, 2012, p. 629).

Critical Appreciative Inquiry (CAI)

Critical approaches to appreciative inquiry are fairly new in applications of AI as a transformative intervention. They are informed by the emancipatory commitments of critical theorists and activists (Grant & Humphries, 2006) and seek to explicitly engage and transform structures of inequality (Cockell & McArthur-Blair, 2012). Such critical approaches respond to criticisms that AI is too naively positive and can be homogenizing of multiple experiences (Grant & Humphries). Cockell and McArthur-Blair demonstrate, for example, that, as a specific intervention, CAI does not ignore issues of social justice, but rather engages them at several levels in designing community-building and transformative events - from planning through curriculum design to practices of discovery and sharing during the event itself. However, the authors insist that since the imagination of possibility is key to the transformation brought about by/in AI, the focus of engagement needs to be changed from a focus on issues to a focus on inquiry. Thus, for example, Cockell and McArthur-Blair discuss a case study of a community project with women who are experiencing addiction. Organizing the project in an *inquiry-focused* way around the theme of "using our influence" (p. 59), the "issue" of addiction is not glossed over, rather it is simultaneously explicitly and creatively acknowledged and disturbed through word-play (i.e., "influence" can mean both addiction and power).

According to Cockell and McArthur-Blair (2012), "[C]ritical Appreciative Inquiry seeks to recognize the impact of difference, power, and diversity" (p. 52). With this in mind, we suggest the following questions, to readers and ourselves. How do the family stories we share below demonstrate CAI's recognition (or lack thereof) of the impact of difference, power, and diversity? And given critical theory's "desire to fight oppression, injustice, and bigotry and create a fairer, more compassionate world" (Brookfield as cited in Cockell & McArthur-Blair, 2012, p. 52) what "critical" difference can CAI make when it comes to our family experiences with prejudice? What does/would a movement from issues to inquiry look like in the communication of prejudice in interactions involving our family members and us? What lessons about possibilities of and limitations to transformation can we take away from these stories? What frameworks are possible for CAI in the context of family experiences with prejudice?

Why Duoethnography?

Within the framework of social constructionism and post-colonial research methodology, duoethnography aims to construct meaning "in the process of interpretation" (Sawyer & Liggett, 2012, p.629). This is similar to the collaborative, future-creating, story-telling process described by Cockell and McArthur-Blair (2012) in their organizational applications of CAI, making duoethnography suitable in a CAI exploration of the communication of prejudice within the family. In one sense, duoethnography may be characterized as a form or subgenre of Collaborative Ethnography, which may involve two or more professional researchers gathering data from the same or different field sites "thereby highlighting more than one perspective of the complex social world" (May & Patillo-McCoy, 2000, p. 67). Sometimes referred to as Reciprocal Ethnography, it is also defined as an approach in which research participants play a more or less equal role with the professional researcher in conducting and writing up the research (Lassiter, 2005). These definitions fit our purposes in that here we may be regarded as both the researchers and the research participants, collaboratively defining the project, acting as participant/observers, and writing up the research.

Duoethnography also emerges from a tradition of autoethnography that Stacy Holman Jones (2005) defines as "a performance that asks how our personal accounts count" (p. 764). In their triple autoethnography exploring experiences of fatherhood, manhood, and patriarchy, Alexander, Moreira, and kumar (2012) explain that, "the collective effort builds a case study of how the traditions of sharing personal narrative, biography, and autoethnography provide an opportunity for critical personal scrutiny in a larger cultural context" (p. 122). More broadly, duoethnographic texts are dialogic research in process, where the readers are invited into the active meaning-making (Norris & Sawyer, 2012). According to Norris and Sawyer, "duoethnographers are the sites of research, not the topics" (p. 13). Furthermore, rather than analyzing personal experience using discrete categories, in duoethnography, "[A]lthough autobiographical, the focus is on how individuals experienced and gave meaning to a specific phenomenon, how these meanings transformed over time, and how the research continued the process of reconceptualization" (Norris & Sawyer, p. 13).

Such a process of reconceptualization is ongoing for us and particularly so when our family members - and we, ourselves, as members of our families - are intimately present in our research and activism. As friends and colleagues, we (Lily and Ellen) often compare and seek to bridge the strengths and limitations of critical theory with those of dialogic approaches, to generate, as the editors for this volume said in their call for chapters, "practical emancipatory frameworks . . . [with] the potential for creating opportunities for inclusivity, transformation, growth and social justice." We have shared family stories with each other as part of our personal struggles to better understand and respond to the communication of prejudice within our own families, particularly in our families of origin and in parent-child interactions. Applying duoethnography as a means to share and explore the role of CAI in some of these stories is an opportunity to enact writing as a method of inquiry (Richardson & St. Pierre, 2005). Duoethnography provides the opportunity for us to practice reflexivity, as we both appreciate and challenge our own and each other's ways of thinking about family interactions when performing and confronting prejudice, and in so doing "promote more complex and inclusive social constructions and re-conceptualizations of experience" (Sawyer & Liggett, 2012, p. 631).

In this text, we undertake (or rather, continue) a journey of transformation and meaning-making in relation to interactions that involved us and our family members and where the communication of prejudice heightened our self-reflexivity vis-a-vis social and familial structures. To date, we have found no duoethnographers who have considered Critical AI (CAI) as a lens on personal experience, nor AI scholars who have undertaken duoethnography as a method. Moreover, though the communication of prejudice within personal relationships has been considered in prior research (for summary, see Gaines Jr., Chalfin, Kim, and Taing, 1998), the family context, particularly the family of origin, seems to be more rarely explored in complex ways with regards to communicating prejudice. Finally, AI and CAI approaches, having been situated primarily in business, institutional, and educational contexts, are also not typical for family communication research. Yet, all these strands of research and methodologies are interested in transformations over the course of time and the roles of communication and storytelling in such transformations. Here, we seek to build on this shared interest in new ways: engaging and complicating our commitments to family, social justice, and inclusive communication.

Lily: Learning with Children

I always learn a lot from my son Sammie and from the questions posed by parenting – questions I thought I had the answers to, but are profoundly reshaped by our child's responses, experiences, applications. Sammie's favorite color is pink, still, at almost 5 years of age. This is a minor thing, but is something that has drawn the attention of strangers since he was almost two and picked pink ribbons at the craft store. Now, he goes to camp. He is supposed to bring with him a water bottle and the one he picked is a present from a close friend of mine - it's pink and it has colorful sharks and dolphins painted on it. After two days at camp, I noticed the bottle stayed in the backpack where I packed it and was completely full. I insisted that Sammie needed to drink his water, because it is hot and he needs to stay hydrated. I assumed he forgets about it. And then he told me that the other kids said this was a "girl's bottle," so he didn't want to be seen drinking from it. We, Remi and I, tried to coach him how to respond. We asked him if he likes his bottle, if it matters what others say, etc..

Then, he wanted to go to camp with a pink t-shirt he had picked and I was worried that he'd be made fun of. So, before camp that morning, I coached him again: "If someone says something about your shirt, you tell them there is no such thing as 'girl' colors and 'boy' colors and that you're the same person as yesterday and they can play with you the same way as they did yesterday." But in the car, I thought this - how artificial something like this must seem to him or the other kids, these are not their interactions... and what would happen if he said instead something like, "Yes, I'm wearing a pink t-shirt because pink is my favorite color. What is your favorite color?"

How often do we close conversations before they have even begun? And do we teach children to do the same? To guard against learning about another? How does the above translate to situations where more is at stake than a favorite color?

Lily: That Question

I remember one situation from the training you [Ellen] and I attended - the Lee Mun Wah diversity seminar. There was a woman in a wheel chair at one of the sessions and she said something like this:

> What do you think kids say when they see me in this wheel chair? Do they say 'How horrible!' or 'I'm sorry!' or 'Our world so needs to change and be more accommodating to you'... do they say any such thing? No, most of the time they want to sit on my lap, they ask me what happened, they ask me if having wheels gives me superpowers, they ask...

This little anecdote has stayed with me and now it comes back as I'm thinking about how my partner and I parent our child. We want him to be curious and respectful and caring, but when it comes to matters of identity, we teach him to make (assertive) statements, to guard the self, if you will... We don't teach him to ask questions, to open conversations. We don't teach him vulnerability. We teach him how to build walls.

And then I think about my own guardedness to mostly well-intentioned and smile-accompanied questions, such as "Where are you from?" and even more "Oh, I hear an accent, where is it from?" How can such conversations be transformative? How can I contribute to transformation? To break walls rather than reinforce the one I've circled myself in? For in answering these questions in one way or another, I don't only answer for myself in front of strangers - I answer for and with and about my family/families. Family members and kinship communities, broadly, don't ask me that question, though it was central to both my family and Remi's when we became a couple (our families of origin are of different nationalities from each other).

When I enter the classroom at the beginning of the semester, the question of my accented origin is inevitably the first one students ask. And I have noticed, though I want to be prepared to answer in some smart, engaging way, that it always produces two things for me. Firstly, a sort of a retreat - even after all these years, this is the question that sends me into the mode of "I have to be careful how I answer here, I'd rather not have to answer at all." Secondly, when I do answer in the classroom, I begin with my birth-place in Bulgaria and say my loved ones still live there; I continue by saying I also have family here and talk of my spouse's background in Poland and Germany and of our son's birth and life in the U.S. My family ties are an inescapable part of the tale of difference, prompted by what should be a simple question.

Ellen: Guarding the Self

Reading this leads me to think about how I deal with what has until recently been the ubiquitous question in *my* life: "What are you?" As a light skinned 3rd generation Puerto Rican who speaks English unaccented by Spanish, people – especially White people -- have trouble figuring out "what" I am, ethnically/racially speaking, so they ask. Or they used to ask until I began pronouncing my last name in Spanish – I grew up knowing/using the Anglo pronunciation (rhymes with Korea we'd say). But now I'm careful to roll my r's and people usually get that I am some kind of Latina. And it's one of the first things I say on the first day teaching a new class: "I identify as a Latina of Puerto Rican descent." Of course, that's appropriate, as the Communication and Service-Learning courses I teach all have an emphasis in intercultural communication; all deal with issues of inequality in a society stratified by social identity.

But I realize now these are also strategies I use to *avoid* the "What are you?" question. I know that my relatively light skin and my cultural assimilation into white mainstream society afford me a not so trivial measure of unearned privilege (including an ability to avoid that question). But there's also pain associated with not being recognized as a Puerto Rican; with knowing that this is due at least partially to my family's *quest* for the privilege associated with whiteness. But Lily, your story makes me wonder what the similarities and differences are between your "Where are you from?" question and my "What are you?" question. Where does the pain come from for you? If we're each exploring ways to use CAI in response to those questions, might those responses look/sound different because the pain comes from different places for each of us?

Here's my story of an encounter with expressed prejudice that happened many years ago but that pops up in my consciousness frequently.

Ellen: A Lesson from My Mother

My mother and I were sitting in my youngest brother's kitchen visiting with him and a close friend/mentor of his who had dropped by, and who we were meeting for the first time. I understood Joe[1], a White Italian American, to be a kind of father figure for my brother – a personal and professional mentor to whom Mike owed his new job as the youngest and first Latino fire chief in his city. We were talking about the job – about Joe's experiences as a fireman and battalion chief. And then he said it – he used the N word. He referred to those N****'s, I don't remember the exact context, more than once. He was on a tirade and the object of his derision was "those N***'s." Joe, my mother, and I were sitting at the dining room table. I remember seeing my brother's shoulders tighten as he stood at the kitchen sink with his back to us. I had gone back to school at 40 to earn a degree in Communication, with an emphasis in Multicultural Conflict Resolution. As far as my family was concerned I was the stereotypical bleeding heart liberal. Mike knew I would be outraged and I read his fear of what I would say in those tensed shoulders.

My mind was racing. This was my baby brother's mentor – perhaps the greatest influence on his professional life and at the time a substitute for the father he had lost at age 18. What do I do? What do I say? How do I respond to Joe in a way that lived up to my anti-racist commitments, to my friends of color, and to my newly emerging sense of myself as a person of color? How do I avoid harming my brother's relationship with this man who is so important to him? How do I avoid harming *my* relationship with my brother?

As I struggled with all this my mother spoke. "Joe, do you think all Black people are N****s?" There was a short pause and then he said, "No. There are good Black people out there. In fact, I've met some White people who are N*****'s." It went on like that for a while. Joe talking about and giving examples of bad White people as N****'s and good Black people as . . . well, good Black people. I think my mother did finally say that she didn't like the word N***. I'm not sure. What stays with me is that she was the one who intervened. Not the daughter who was rapidly becoming "overeducated" but the mother who didn't know what Critical Race Theory was – at least on an

---

[1] I've changed names in these stories to maintain the privacy of the individuals.

academic level -- and really didn't care to know. It was my mother who didn't hesitate to speak up when she heard a racist epithet and who was also intent on preserving the important relationships at stake – on making sure neither of her children was adversely impacted by the encounter.

The question my mother posed and the ensuing conversation was . . . not free from racist assumptions. But for me the point is that my mother did *something*. She asked a question. And I think, at least in part, she really wanted to know the answer to that question.

Lily: Surprises

The other day at the lake a guy asked me, as it often happens, "Where are you from?" I always assume that this question means one thing only - where have I come from to the U.S. Ok, but this was a nice guy and his kids had helped mine getting out of the water... The question - and my answer - gets more complicated when I am together with Sammie, who, I know, hears it all - I answer it just for myself, assuming "you" is second person, singular... I suppose Sammie's answer would/could be different from mine. So, I said, "I was born in Bulgaria" and then the guy started laughing. "No," he said, "I meant where do you live around here?"

Frankly, I have learned from critical theory that I should be suspicious of the "where are you from?" question - as it marks me as "different." But then so many people here have told me that it's just an ice-breaker question that even people with the standard accents ask each other as a way to learn about one another. So, is it my sense of vulnerability that the question raises that actually marks me as different? Is it my discomfort with the question? Or am I different in this context because *I* simply *don't* think that this piece of information – "I'm from Bulgaria" – alone, without continuation, says much about me, but I fear that *others* will make it say everything about me?

How do I see this as related to your very powerful story, Ellen? - I'm not sure, it's a really uncomfortable line to walk, but I think it has everything to do with transformation . . . So, if we assume that the mentor's use of the N-word says everything about him (i.e., he's racist) and are so put off by it that we don't interact, what change have we accomplished? For whom? Your mother's response is so interesting... not only because she dared ask and because she shared her feelings about the word, but also because her question seems to negotiate meaning and maybe ask the person using the word to think about it . . . Well, it doesn't sound like he saw anything wrong with it, but it sure does sound like he sensed the possible implications and guarded against them. Who do I identify with here? Where will I go with this story? You know . . . I do think I get defensive when asked the question of origin. Is this like the defensiveness of your brother's mentor? What does my defensiveness create differently? At the end, if the person asking thought my "origin" would tell him/her something about me, why should I think that me being "difficult" would tell him/her anything other than "she's a bitch" or better yet "Bulgarian women are bitches." What, if anything, is transformative here - for a person, for familial and social relations, for structures?

In our stories, what are those moments when transformation seemed (retrospectively?) possible or desired, but (at the time) seemed to fail? What are those moments that have stayed with us as question marks and even we are not sure how/if they have transformed us, let alone someone else who was in that interaction, or, even more grandly, transformed social inequality?

Lily: By the Fire with My Grandparents

It's quite idyllic, isn't it? Perhaps it's even fitting of imagining an "over there" that is not near-by. Yet, that's exactly how it was. It often is on the rare occasions when I'm back. My grandfather always grills, but not on a BBQ. Cooking on the small fire-pit that he built requires bending over or squatting - even at 80 years of age - to nourish the fire and nurture the cinders. I hang around, as I've always done. My grandmother is the sous-chef; she hands spiced meats or fish to my grandfather; she bends over next to my grandpa holding a plate where he puts the ready food. He always fusses around the fire and *skara*. While we're waiting and when our assistance is not needed, my grandma and I linger, sitting on very low, kids' chairs. And we talk.

I think this year is particularly important. They are painfully and frequently reflecting on "how long do we have left." And, I think, somehow everyone is sick of us – Remi, Sammie, and me – being away. There is an urgency in the sharing of worries that I haven't felt before. We begin talking about the time when my grandparents worked in Libya. It's a connecting point, it bonds us in the shared, recognized pain of being away from loved ones and in the shared, recognized understanding of chasing and staying with the opportunity of a "better, more secure" life.

I am familiar with the overall contours of my grandparents' narratives of life and work abroad. This time what stands out to me is a moral of hard work and the importance of work ethics. Both of my grandparents have high school educations, but are self-taught and have succeeded in life, by some measure. Beginning work as a teenager, my grandfather was a miner, but reached the ranks of a supervisor and manager in a factory making typewriters and parts. When he first went to Libya, he went alone and started working an exhausting night shift. His arrival there was not well received by the existing crew, but without complaining and with perseverance, he demonstrated he knew his stuff; he could get things done faster and of a better quality than previous workers. Soon, he rose up the ranks and my grandma joined him. Her tale is a little different, though it repeats some of the same themes of earning her chops professionally by drawing blueprints. She never forgets to tell me how hard it was to leave me, a six-month old baby at the time, and my mother; how she would look at our photo for hours and cry. Her sacrifice, lived and narrated, is in sepia, the color of that old photo. As I listen, I hear my own mother's grief at being, presently, away from *her* daughter and grandchild. Like me now, my mother was/is both a parent and a child, and now I recognize another familiar feeling, more elusively captured in the ironically lonely act of sending and looking at photos across geographic distances – a daughter's longing, my own.

My grandparents' life and work in Libya made a lot of things possible for us in Bulgaria in a time when a communist government controlled opportunity. And I recognize in the stories today not so much a need for gratitude, but various forms of bonding and belonging, of familiarity and care. I wouldn't want to risk them for anything, because in some way those bonds are also my lifelines. In that moment, I feel that it's a winding and multi-knotted path to turning a blind eye and a deaf ear to our loved ones communicating prejudice… and maybe it's a path of (self-) preservation; preserving roles and connections and respecting what holds us together.

For years, I have not known what to tell my family members when they make a joke or a comment that I find not simply politically incorrect, but offensive and prejudicial. For years, I have kept quiet. I never wanted to risk or lose my place at the table (Ahmed, 2010) – a possibility that seemed to me especially relevant after coming to the U.S. and becoming more educated. For a while, my political and social views were often responded to by words, such as "you're becoming too American." I was afraid of that; I didn't want that, because it also meant, again, difference – not like the rest of the family, perhaps not a part of the family… When I was away and alone, I needed to know I was a part of the family that cares for its members. This was our narrative. I couldn't risk not being present in it. But my position – as the youngest one, the daughter, and the one who left – was a precarious one. In the patterns of my family, had I been older, I could perhaps dispense tales and words of wisdom. As it were, mine were the words of dissent, of marking myself as liminally, if at all, belonging.

I realize my mind has drifted and I missed some part of my grandparents' story. But they are now talking—mostly my grandma actually, about what day-to-day life was like in Libya. The surprising and devastating rains. What foods tasted good and what foods they missed. About the gossip that marked life in a workers' compound. The conditions of their housing. The special group trips organized to the city market near-by. These are trips that my grandma made and she is the one talking about the fabrics and being able to buy jeans and corduroys (which were forbidden in Bulgaria). So it is my grandma who talks about the "Arabs" in their pure white clothes to shield them from the heat – how "dirty" the people are, garbage on the streets, and the smell in this place that is supposed to be an old civilization, but does not hold up at all to the hygiene standards my grandma grew up with and later instilled in my mother and me.

The words grip at me and I grip for words. In the context of preparing this text, we (Ellen and I) have been thinking and talking about CAI all summer it feels like. I've practiced CAI in identity dialogues with strangers (Correa, Herakova, & Jelaca, 2014). Yet, here I am again with someone I love in a want for words and a fear of (not) belonging . . .

So, I say something like "*Babo*, can you tell me what was good about living there, being in contact with these different people?" My grandma continues her stories and I continue to listen. There is no comment about me "thinking I know better" or "talking American again." And we continue to talk. It is so simple and so different from what usually happens. In fact, it is one of those touchy-feely communicative actions and interpretations that will likely be mocked as "typically American" in my Bulgarian home. I don't imagine this has been some profound transformative moment for me or for my grandmother, that we are now somehow "changed" (better?) individuals. I just have a different course of action; one that, at least in this situation, continued conversation rather than halted it. It is still warm by the fire.

Ellen: In the Car with My Brother

Lily, I'm deeply moved by your story. By the longing I hear for family, for belonging, even as, especially because, you are a half a world away from them. I am home with my family of origin now. Living with my mother and close by to my brothers. Doing research *with* them about our family history, about the meanings and effects of our family's process of becoming *Americanos*, as my mother says. And I revel in the ways this research has brought us closer, gets us talking about topics that before were either taboo or that resulted in dismissal, accusations and hurt feelings. But I still worry about the ways our "research talks" point up our differences. I worry that I am pointing my finger at their "internalized oppression," conveying a sense of the wrongness of the lives they've built and the people they have become, even as I grapple with my own wrongness/rightness. But lately I am trying hard to listen, really listen and not argue or criticize. After all it's not the role of the researcher to argue with her participants! But still I fear that despite the fact that this is supposed to be a dialogic ethnography, they get it. They're reading my dissertation drafts and as my brother once said to me, "You've drunk the liberal academic kool-aid."

It's 4th of July and I'm in the car with this brother. We're headed to our other brother's house to celebrate the holiday. We're doing our regular kidding and teasing, "brother/sister thing" when he says suddenly, "I need to tell you something. Something happened the other day that made me think of you and made me realize I'm a racist."

"Tell Me," I Say

My brother lives in what I jokingly refer to as a "one percenter neighborhood." On his salary as a state employee and his wife's as a nurse they were able to buy a relatively modest, but still very nice house, in a neighborhood of successful doctors and lawyers, and captains of industry. Most of the homes are mansions sitting on sprawling acreage. His is a medium sized ranch house with a small front and back yard in comparison to his neighbors. He's talked before about the irony of a Puerto Rican living in this almost exclusively white and upper class community and, especially since we've embarked on the family ethnography, he's told some stories where he's been the target of prejudice from his neighbors. But this story is different.

"I was looking out the living room window and saw two Black women walking on the road, and the first thing I thought was, 'What are they doing here?' It felt so out of place to see them, and to be honest it made me uncomfortable. And in the next minute I thought, 'Boy you really are a racist.' It's you and your liberal crap," he said looking at me and laughing. "You've ruined me. I'm getting to be liberal."

"Wow, that's powerful" I said, not sure how else to respond.

He went on quickly, "Later that day I was standing on the front lawn talking to Dr. Klavan (his neighbor) and I asked him, 'Did you see those women walking in the neighborhood this afternoon?' He knew right away who I was talking about. He'd seen them too and had the same reaction I had. I told him, 'Well you know, as soon as the Puerto Ricans move in the Blacks can't be far behind.'"

"What did he say to that?" I asked.

"He laughed and said, 'Yeah, but it started with the Estonians invading the neighborhood.'"

"Is he from Estonia?"

"No, he was born here but his heritage is Estonian."

"He was trying to connect with you, because he likes you. He was placing himself, with you, in the category of a member of an unwanted group."

"Yeah. Well I just wanted you to know that now you've ruined me," he said smiling. "Cause it's your fault that now I know I'm a racist."

We talked a little bit more about it. I think I said something pedantic like – 'to the extent we have racial privilege we can all be racist.' And I admitted I thought I'd have a similar reaction in that situation, and that's what I'm trying to explore, and change as I can, through my research. And I wondered aloud what Dr. Klavan's reaction would be if one of the Black women bought a home in the neighborhood. Or for that matter, what my brother's reaction would be.

He just said, "Yeah," and was silent after that until we moved on to another subject, going back to our regular kidding and teasing brother/sister thing.

So . . . for me, the "different course of action" you discuss above may be the new way my brother and I have begun to talk about prejudice. Perhaps the "appreciative" quality of my dialogic research methodology "created a space where [he] had the courage to share [his] story" (Cockell & McArthur-Blair, 2012, p. 60) and self-reflexively consider the ways our Puerto Rican family has been socialized to consider people of color as "them" and White people as "us." And as you say, this is not an example of a change for all time, but rather a moment of self-reflexivity and (always partial) insight that seems to me to be something we can build on to move to a better place.

Critical Dialogues/Appreciative Reflections

Lily: I'm thinking now that within our families, we experience the role and work of AI in much more protracted ways. Prior work using CAI, even such activist work, has been engaged in a process, usually using the 4Ds of discovery, dreaming, designing, and destiny (Cockell & McArthur-Blair, 2012; Michael, 2005). However, this process has been, at least in reporting it, somewhat bound by the deadlines of a planned and requested intervention. Interactions within the family rarely happen like that. They are dialogic (Baxter, 2011) not in the sense of talking with each other, but in the sense of each family member developing and including different voices and roles in various interactions over the lifespan. We have deep, dynamic, and on-going relational histories, spanning multiple generations and ways of connecting. To return, in a more concise way to our questions from the beginning, how is CAI relevant here? How do we, then, "assess" outcomes and transformations?

My awareness of the communication of prejudice in my family and my reactions to such communication increased as I became a (marginal) part of a society (in the U.S.), where I don't quite belong. At the same time, not belonging here makes my (and my created family's) belonging to our family networks (in Bulgaria, Poland, and Germany) that much more important; in some cases, it feels necessary for survival. So, I don't want to jeopardize these relationships, as fraught with levels of inclusion and exclusion as they might be. This makes writing autoethnographically about my family harder (including this text) ... I am strongly enculturated in a tradition of family members' obligations to protect the face of the whole family, to not air out our dirty laundry (which, in fact, may often not seem all that dirty to us either). But that's only part of the story – the other part is that if I'd be showing some dirty laundry, I also want to proudly be able to display the clean ones. They hang on the line together, warmed by the same sun, exchanging aromas... and I want my eyes, ears, and words to equally draw on and be drawn by both. This is not simply a task of balancing – one bad for one good – it's a task of engaging the complexity. I don't think this task is sufficiently served by critical theory alone, which is where I see the possible contributions of affect and AI-orientations to social (in)justice.

Trained in critical theory, I have learned to hear and recognize "problems" and problematic communication (Cockell & McArthur-Blair, 2012) and perhaps am to some degree equipped to write about them, but this is also an isolationist writing/thinking. I want to write appreciatively about communication of prejudice and/or inclusion that happens in my family, but it is hard for me, still, to overcome the tendency to focus on "what is wrong in what is said/done." The texts that, thus, come out are simplified and one-directional, failing to engage the complexities, possibilities, and limitations of relations and belonging.

Ellen: Yes. My dissertation may be characterized as airing family laundry as well – engaging, as you say, the complexity of family communication of prejudice. And it's also important to me to create a context to do this helpfully, in a way that preserves and deepens these most important relationships. But, Lily, perhaps I am at this moment closer to the other end of the appreciative-critical spectrum. Mine and my family's experience of assimilation into dominant white norms has required a kind of "appreciation" that I now wish to see more clearly. I want to understand the ways we have been socialized/pressured to express and even internalize "appreciation" for what Marilyn Frye (1992) calls "whiteliness," and in so doing inflict harm on ourselves and others. *My* introduction to critical theory came later in life – when I returned to college in middle age. But my introduction to an insidious kind of appreciation came much earlier – its roots are with my grandparents who came to the mainland and even my ancestors before that. These roots are deep and do not surface for inspection easily. So, as I know that a kind of CAI can be helpful to do this work with my family, I also want to avoid, as I can, falling into a kind of appreciation that precludes self-reflexivity and critical assessment of the social and historical structures that influence how we've come to the places we are.

Lily: At this time, I want to think that I have changed how I talk with my family members – that I try not to "accuse" them or "teach" them from my high horse, that instead I speak of my experiences here, away from them. I hope appreciative questioning and my own storytelling with my family would foster an interaction of "discovery," in a way much akin to that in which Sarah Michael (2005) describes the potential of AI as an interview-guiding research methodology. At the same time, family interactions are also different – they are on-going and mixing depths of relational histories with breadths of personal experiences and variations. In this context, does an orientation to "discovering" linkages and possibilities make a difference in communicating prejudice? Does it provoke a new level of "care" and relationality?

Aimee Carillo Rowe (2005) reminds me that movements toward and/or passivity of belonging are also always political. Belonging is a mode of participation in social structures that is, at least to a degree, a matter of choice, the very enactment of which is in response to one's perceived relation to such structures. Writes Carillo Rowe,

... the presumption of belonging that undergirds dominant identity formations, such as whiteness and heterosexuality, erases the choices that we make around our belongings which are constitutive of our identities. This erasure fixes identity, however unintentionally, in individualistic terms: "I am." The transformative possibilities of a "politics of location" are limited by such oversights. The absence of critical interrogations of the conditions of possibility for hegemonic modes of belonging produces two erasures *critical to forging resistive or transformative modes of belonging: agency and accountability.* (p. 32, emphasis added)

Appreciative inquiry (AI) is about transformation, the "generative" (Bushe, 2007), the possibilities (Sutherland, 2012). Although AI is optimistic, a wishy-washy focus on the positive in AI has been criticized (Bushe, 2007). Similarly, a particular turn to affect in cultural studies has been seen both as optimistically reparative (e.g., Sedgwick, 2003) and as too naively optimistic - as affect that is ignorant and independent of materiality and of the postcolonial possibilities of cultural theories from the margins (Hemmings, 2005). Ellen, can optimisms be insidious, as your criticism of AI in the context of "whiteliness" above suggests?

Ellen: Yes, I think they can and as I said above, I join those critics in a concern that AI has the potential to reinscribe "appreciation" for ideas and ways of thinking/being that contribute to injustice and oppression. I know that you agree that it's important not to dismiss these concerns too quickly, as any theory/method can be misused. But now I'm thinking about how AI's emphasis on inquiry may be salient in one of my family stories. Cockell and McArthur-Blair (2012) say that "Appreciative Inquiry works to find the possibilities within an organization for positive change" (p. 52). Perhaps my mother's question to Joe about the "N" word could be viewed as a means to find the possibilities within *that interaction* for positive change. In my view she used her question, "Do you think all Black people are N***s?" to reframe the conversation. She employed Joe's racist term to ask him, in a way he could hear, to think/talk about how he was stereotyping and vilifying African Americans as a group. I don't mean to characterize this particular response as an antiracist model. Rather, I want to suggest that this response used Joe's own words, not to appreciate his racist invective, but rather to inquire into life experiences that negated his prejudiced depiction of African Americans. This did indeed happen, as he responded to my mother's question with stories of positive interactions with Black people (now no longer using the racist epithet). I have no doubt that this conversation would have been/ended differently if she (or more likely I) had said something like "I don't like that word. We don't use that word in our family!" There's a reason why I remember this exchange so many years after the fact. And now, as I think of the potential for CAI in family communication, remembering and thinking takes my breath away.

Lily: Can we also add listening to the mix, because our stories above are as much about listening to/with the multiple voices in the family and what they make (im) possible as it is about the content of the event itself? What we hear in the voices and stories of our relatives, but also what we hear in our own stories and responses – which do we allow in, through the process of listening, in various interactions. Is the critical scholar there together with the granddaughter, the mother, and the foreigner, when we sit by the fire with my grandparents? Do we listen for the complex co-presence of a sister, woman, Latina, researcher, social activist, and educator when we drive with your brother in the car? The question of sitting "by the table of happiness" (Ahmed, 2010), the question of inclusion does not only refer to "who can speak," but also to "for whom does our listening make room?" This listening/dialogic (Baxter, 2011) question of inclusion is also not only constitutive of our relationship to an-other, but also our relationships to ourselves within the context of social and familial structures. Sometimes, the multiplicity of voices/selves comes from quite the same mouth, the same body, making a process of ascribing "location" (Carillo Rowe, 2005) difficult. As with the promises of the critical focus on affect, the critical focus on questions, and the critical practice of AI, listening, too, promises possibility – it is a relational opening, "a process of contraction, of stepping back and creating a void into which the other may enter" (Lipari, 2004, p. 137). In Communication Studies, listening can also be posited to be "an other" – "The Other Side of Language," as is titled Fiumara's book (1990).

Lily and Ellen: Why bring all this together – AI, affect, questions, and listening? We can see them all as connective tissues – not in an overly optimistic way, as connective tissues may painfully deteriorate, mutate, stagnate. And yet, connective tissues also make some movements possible, while maybe making other movements impossible. Connective tissues are multi-directional, multi-locational, and multi-chronemic. When thinking about and living their possibilities and their limitations, structures, histories, (re-) training, promises, our unique chemistries, and the environmental influences on that chemistry are all in dialogue and are connected. They are also transformed. The generative/transformative ideal of AI does not blindly lie in imagining the beautiful possible, but in connecting structures to possibilities, since imagination, as a communicative act that is made visible in intervention AI practices, is part of the "chain of speech communion" (Bakhtin, 1984). It, thus, links cultural and relational discourses and selves of past and present with their (transformed) future possibilities (Baxter, 2011). The questions and threats raised in the presence of prejudice (even when *we* might be the perpetrators) are questions of variably fitting in a set of social structures and relations. Reflexivity here is not so much of/on the self and an individual, as it is of/on structures and our becomings in them. This is what makes it potentially transformative.

We are sometimes bound – assimilated, perhaps – through others' wills, recognitions, and actions, while certain affects (and bodies!) can expel us from normativity (Lorde, 1984), unseat us from "the table of happiness" (Ahmed, 2010). In a paradoxical way, prejudice is connective, as well – delineating the contours and boundaries of belonging as they exist macro- and micro-socially (e.g., family belonging). And where do we stand in relation to these contours and boundaries? And how, where, with whom do we move? What moves/movements seem possible and of those, what are doable? What are the "alien affects," who are the "affect aliens" (Ahmed, 2010) in the particular context? If we move from a focus on making statements to a focus on asking questions and listening within a CAI framework, not whose voices are included, but for whom and for what affects are the spaces/voids of listening open? How do we open them?

As stated above, connective tissue mutates and it is changeable. Trauma may change it. Frictions may change it. Deliberate interventions - such as surgery - may change it. Bodily processes and nutrition may change it. Our belonging and affiliations – even those that social norms decree as ideally most stable, such as our families of origin and the bonds of love and affection we choosingly create – are similarly change-able, transformative and transformation-able. And it is also perhaps in our closest belongings[2] that the multiplicity of our selves is most often (invoked) at play out in the open – when we are daughters, mothers, women, scholars, sisters, spouses, teachers, wage-earners, wage-spenders, little girls, etc. all at once in the weave of the fabric that is being made. Yes, certain selves may be highlighted, made central, while others deliberately left like shadows on the sidelines of the interaction. And yet, they are there, always – as social norms, as lived realities, as rebellions, as affects, as expectations. They do the imaginings, the

---

[2] Not as "things that I own" but as the multiple form of "belonging" to a community, family, place, etc.

transformations – together with others with whom we belong and often "long to belong" (Carillo Rowe, 2005). Are transformations always to be celebrated? We end with a disclaimer. We do not consider CAI to be the best or only means of understanding/addressing family communication of prejudice, but rather view it as a practical theory and strategy that has important potential to create spaces for movement towards "a society of freedom and justice" (Brookfield as cited in Cockell & McArthur-Blair, 2012, p. 74). As Michael Hecht (1998) avers, "It is clear that, like most societal problems, prejudice must be addressed across different layers and through multiple tactics and strategies" (p. 20). We concur, and offer this duoethnography to begin to explore the efficacy of CAI as one means to understand and transform family communication on prejudice.

REFERENCES

Ahmed, S. (2010). Feminist killjoys (and other willful subjects). *The Scholar & Feminist Online, 8.3.*, n.p.

Alexander, B. K., Moreira, C., & Kumar, H.S. (2012). Resisting (resistance) stories: A tri-autoethnographic exploration of father narratives across shades of difference. *Qualitative Inquiry,* 18. 121-133.

Bakhtin, M. (1984). *Problems of Dostoyevsky's poetics.* Minneapolis, MN: University of Minnesota Press.

Baxter, L. A. (2011). *Voicing relationships: A dialogic perspective.* Thousand Oaks, CA: SAGE.

Brookfield, S. (2005). *The power of critical theory: Liberating adult learning and teaching.* San Francisco: Jossey-Bass.

Bushe, G. R. (2007). Appreciative inquiry is not (just) about the positive. *OD Practitioner, 39* (4), 30-35.

Carillo Rowe, A. (2005). Be Longing: Toward a feminist politics of relation. *NWSA Journal, 17,* 15-46.

Cockell, J., & McArthur-Blair, J. (2009). Critical appreciative inquiry. In J. Cockell, & J. McArthur-Blair, *Appreciative inquiry in higher educaiton: A transformative force* (pp. 51-75). Hoboken, NJ: Wiley Press.

Correa, E., Herakova, L., & Jelaca, D (2014). Racing (for) social justice: Performing apologia and accountability in dialogues about race. *Forum Qualitative Sozialforschung / Forum: Qualitative Social Research,* 15(3). http://nbn-resolving.de/urn:nbn:de:0114-fqs1403120.

Delgado, R. & Stefancic, J. (2006). Critical race theory: An introduction. *NYU Press.* Retrieved from http://www.odec.umd.edu/CD/RACE/CRT.PDF.

Fiumara, G. C. (1990). *The other side of language: A philosophy of listening.* London & New York: Routledge.

Frye, Marilyn. 1992. "White Woman Feminist." In *Willful Virgin: Essays in Feminism, 1976–1992,* 147–169. Freedom, Calif.: Crossing Press.

Gaines Jr., S. O., Chalfin, J., Kim, M., & Taing, P. (1998). Communicating prejudice in personal relationships. In M. Hecht (Ed.), *Communicating Prejudice* (pp. 163-186). Thousand Oaks CA: Sage.

Grant, S., & Humphries, M. (2006). Critical evaluation of appreciative inquiry: Bridging an apparent paradox. Action Research, 4, 401-418.

Hecht, M.L. (Ed.). (1998). *Communicating prejudice.* Thousand Oaks, CA: Sage.

Hemmings, C. (2005). Invoking affect: Cultural theory and the ontological turn. *Cultural Studies, 19,* 548-567.

Holman Jones, S. (2005). Autoethnography: Making the personal political. In N.K. Denzin, & Y.S. Lincoln (Eds.), *The Sage handbook of qualitative research* (3rd ed.). (pp. 763-791) Thousand Oaks, CA: Sage.

Lassiter, L.E. (2005). *The Chicago guide to collaborative ethnography.* Chicago: The University of Chicago Press.

Lipari, L. (2004). Listening for the other: Ethical implications of the Buber-Levinas encounter. *Communication Theory, 14,* 122-141.

Lorde, A. (1982). *Zami: A new spelling of my name.* Freedom, CA: The Crossing Press.

May, R.B. & Patillo-McCoy, M. (2000). Do you see what I see? Examining a collaborative ethnography. *Qualitative Inquiry,* 6(1), 65-87.

Michael, S. (2005). The promise of appreciative inquiry as an interview tool for field research. *Development in Practice, 15,* 222-230.

Norris, J., & Sawyer, R. D. (2012). Toward a dialogic methodology. In J. Norris, R. D. Sawyer, & D. E. Lunds (Eds.), *Duethography: Dialogic methods for social, health, and educational research* (pp. 9-40). Walnut Creek: Leftcoast Press.

Richardson, L. & St. Pierre, E.A. (2005). Writing: A method of inquiry. In N.K. Denzin & Y.S. Lincoln (Eds.), *The Sage handbook of qualitative research* (3rd ed.). (pp. 959-978) Thousand Oaks, CA: Sage.

Sawyer, R.D. & Liggett, T. (2012). Shifting positionalities: A critical discussion of duoethnographic inquiry of a personal curriculum of post/colonialism. *International Journal of Qualitative Methods, 1,* 628-651. Retrieved from http://web.b.ebscohost.com.silk.library.umass.edu/

ehost/pdfviewer/pdfviewer?sid=61548e9b-4ea3-48ce-a696-52e5311b72d0%40sessionmgr111&vid=1&hid=107.

Sedgwick, E. K. (2003). *Touching Feeling: Affect, Pedagogy, Performativity.* Durham, NC: Duke UP.

Sutherland, K. R. (2012). *Make light work in groups: 10 tools to transform meetings, companies, and communities.* New York: Incite Press.

In: Communicating Prejudice   ISBN: 978-1-53610-167-6
Editors: S. Camara and D. Drummond   © 2016 Nova Science Publishers, Inc.

Chapter 4

TEACHING TOWARD AN APPRECIATION OF DIFFERENCES: THE CHALLENGE FOR INTERCULTURAL COMMUNICATION COURSES

Darlene K. Drummond
Dartmouth College, Hanover, New Hampshire, US

ABSTRACT

In taking a diversity-affirming ethical orientation and prescriptively promoting diversity, community colleges suggest differences along the lines of race, ethnicity, gender, class, language, sexual orientation, and ability are positive assets to the functioning of society. However, while the majority of students at these colleges are people of color, eighty percent of the faculties are white, 50-year olds, who now must consider practicing a culturally responsive pedagogy to impact student learning and completion. Most often it is the few faculty of color who are called upon to provide the necessary diversity training. In this paper I reflect on the creation of a course developed specifically for faculty to enhance intercultural communication competence as a key component of a college's employee development program.

The face of "American culture" is changing with two-thirds of the world's immigrants coming to the United States. If this trend continues, by the year

2050, the proportion of White Americans will decrease to 53%, down from the current 72% (Roberts, 2004). The influx of people of color is changing the face of the American student. Although high school graduation rates for students of color are increasing, college graduation rates are dismal with only 11% of black students, 15% of Hispanic students, and 23% of white students who enrolled in 2-year colleges in 2004 graduating within three years (Mangan, 2009).

The community college is lauded as a minority-serving institution. However, eighty-three percent of the full-time teachers in community colleges are white 50-year olds. Only 17% of the faculties are categorized as faculty of color --specifically African American, Latino/Hispanic, Asian/Pacific Islander, and American Indian (Twombly & Townsend, 2008). Although campuses possess policies and practices that advocate diversity, faculty of color often view themselves as isolated with suppressed social and cultural identities and that are subordinated to their White colleagues (Levin, Haberler, Walker, & Jackson-Boothby, 2014).

In promoting themselves as minority-serving, community colleges are taking a diversity-affirming ethical orientation and prescriptively promoting diversity in decision-making. Diversity affirmation is premised on the notion that difference and multiplicity are positive, good, and beneficial to the institution, society, humanity, and the planet. Differences along the lines of race, ethnicity, gender, class, religion, language, sexual orientation, ability, nonconformity, though emotion and action are considered positive assets to the functioning of institutions and society. Most important, diversity integration and inclusive practices can foster a reconciliation process overcoming the legacy of past power differentials and privileges associated with race, gender, and class in the United States (Aragon & Brantmeier, 2009).

However, a diversity-affirming orientation requires a culturally responsive pedagogy in which faculty deconstruct the concept of "culture" and reflect on their own culture (Haviland & Rodriquez-Kiino, 2009) ultimately resulting in culturally responsive classrooms. These teachers recognize their own ethnocentrism, have knowledge of students' cultural backgrounds, understand broad social, economic, and political contexts, have the ability and willingness to use culturally appropriate management strategies, and have a commitment to building caring classrooms (Weinstein, Tomlinson-Clarke, & Curran, 2004). Ultimately, instructional knowledge involves the ability to enhance learning through designing environments to enhance learning. Through active learning, students are given opportunities to engage with faculty and classmates to test their thinking and take responsibility for their own learning (Rich, Gayle, & Priess, 2006).

One way that community colleges strive to improve learning conditions for both faculty and students is through employee development programs. A key component of faculty development is assisting faculty in becoming great teachers whose students learn, persist, and complete a certificate or degree program. The most effective faculty development programs include institutional support, formality, goal-direction, a reward structure for participation, faculty ownership, and an administration that values good teaching (Murray, 1999).

TAPPED

As an instructor at a community college, I was required to teach 12 classes a year. However, I taught public speaking which was an elective and unfortunately as a new faculty member "lacked the popularity to attract students to enroll in my sections" according to at least one of my colleagues. To fulfill my commitment, I was asked to teach an intercultural communication class through the college's employee development program. I was thrilled! Finally I would have the opportunity to utilize my education to teach something other than public speaking! With a publication and teaching record in intercultural communication and a PhD, I knew I was the most qualified person to teach such a course.

My joy was short-lived when my dean informed me that I would have to team teach the course with "a well-known and respected instructor." That "well-known and respected instructor" was one of the three of us responsible for teaching communication courses at the college. White, female and a teacher for over 40 years, she had no background teaching intercultural communication, no publication record and no PhD. I was told I should "be happy to be the instructor of record" and that "her name will lend credibility to the course" and "attract participants." However, the design of the course and the bulk of the teaching would be my responsibility.

I was insulted and angry! Why did I need to team teach a class with someone with little- to-no subject matter experience when I was an expert in it? This was just more evidence of the racist environment I existed. I felt I had been transported back into the 1950s. I was the Black woman that needed to be constrained to ensure no White folk were offended –the child that needed watching. Of course I objected but was informed that I should not be "so sensitive" and "didn't really have a choice if I wanted to continue teaching."

From my first day of work, it became clear to me that the Majority-White faculty did not think much of its "minorities" especially Black students. Terms like "deficient," "slow," "challenged," "disadvantaged," "not as bright as," "wild and loud" were normal vernacular in describing them. No one ever indicated that they were referring to a Black student. Everyone knew. This coded language suggesting Blacks are intellectually inferior to Whites was now extended to me. I was the one with the "least teaching experience" and the one with "little understanding of the institution's culture," and "unknown to the local community." In one instance I had moved from experiencing prejudice to full-blown discrimination as my dean's negative attitude toward Blacks was used to strip me of my dignity and force me to team teach (Marsiglia & Hecht, 1998). My dean and I had had several conversations about race and I knew his intentions were good and dictated by his superiors, but I was disappointed that he could not understand or voice the harm this decision caused me. At that moment, I vowed to teach the course exactly as I wanted regardless of the consequences.

CASE STUDY

A case study approach is useful for theoretical elaboration and/or analytic generalization (Yin, 1994). It employs a variety of methods (e.g., interviews, observations, and document analysis) to build an understanding of a phenomenon in context (Creswell, 2009). The phenomenon under study was teaching intercultural communication to community college instructors. The context was a team-taught 3-credit course, *Intercultural Communication Competence*, which met on three consecutive Saturdays from 9-5. All 20 participants were either staff or faculty. The majority were female, faculty and White. Four individuals were people of color. Course instructors, one Black female and one White female, served as facilitators. Qualitative course evaluations and unsolicited email messages were interview data, while key documents analyzed included personal experience papers and reflection papers. My purpose, as the designer and one of the instructors of the course, was to determine whether or not participants would be inspired to practice culturally responsive pedagogy to build culturally responsive classrooms by experiencing the strategy themselves.

THE COURSE

The primary objective was to assist participants in acquiring the knowledge and communication skills to effectively interact with strangers and individuals different from themselves with an emphasis on intercultural interactions within the United States. Participants explored the following questions: What is intercultural competence? What explanations are there for various interactions between people of different cultures? What comprises culture? How do varying cultural perspectives impact daily interactions? What verbal and nonverbal skills are consistent with effective communication? Participants were expected to achieve (1) a familiarization with the most contemporary theory in intercultural communication, (2) the ability to enumerate a set of inferences about effective communication in the context of co-cultural interactions, and (3) gain an appreciation for the value of narratives in understanding human behavior. I wanted them to understand intercultural communication explanations in the form of theories, but more importantly, to motivate them to assess and examine their own possible biases and prejudices that may impact communication with students and colleagues.

Instructional Design

This course was unique in its instructional design. It did not take a traditional *etic* approach that sees knowledge located in the interpretations of scientists who are *not* part of the culture(s) under investigation (Kottak, 2006) catering to members of the dominant group and neglecting inclusion of the voices of people of color (Aragon & Brantmeier, 2009). I took an *emic* approach in which knowledge and interpretations exist within cultures and are best described by members of those cultures (Headland, Pike, & Harris, 1990). The voices of a variety of cultural perspectives were privileged, including that of African, Asian, Bi-racial, Hispanic/Latino, Native, and Jewish Americans. Differences in sexual orientation, social class, and gender were addressed. I knew this approach could cause some to feel anxious and uncomfortable but believed it would positively impact the amount of learning that would take place. Discomfort and anxiety are often prerequisites to attitude change.

I employed the following instructional design (see figure): (1) Theory: Participants listened to a lecture on a widely accepted theory in communication, specifically uncertainty reduction theory, communication theory of identity, accommodation theory, and co-cultural theory. (2)

Readings: Then, they read selected narratives from Gonzalez, Houston, and Chen's (2011), *Our Voices: Essays in Culture, Ethnicity, and Communication*. This text employs narrative-style essays that share culturally-oriented personal experiences on ethnic identities, race, class, and gender that serve as examples making theories understandable and meaningful. (3) Reflection: Participants wrote a short paper addressing very specific questions to demonstrate their understanding of experiences and concepts addressed in a narrative and were challenged to engage in deeper analyses utilizing information from the theory lecture. (4) Activity: They participated in various activities like role-playing to assist them in focusing in on their own personal experiences and how those experiences were similar and/or different from those shared in the readings. (5) Discussion: Participants shared insights learned and challenged one another's conclusions. We ended each session by summarizing key points and practical skills that could be used in future intercultural encounters. (5) Assessment: For the final assignment, participants demonstrated their knowledge and understanding of course content by completing a personal experience paper. In the paper, they wrote a personal script of an actual intercultural experience, applied theory to explain why events happened in the way they did, and explained how the encounter could have been improved with the various communication skills learned.

From beginning to end, the course was designed to encourage participants to step out of their comfort zone, engage in deep meaningful dialogue, take the perspective of others, question themselves, face uncomfortable truths, and ultimately be motivated to try more appropriate and effective strategies in future intercultural encounters. Cognitive processing was ignited by activities based on ten active learning instructional strategies that require one to link one's own personal experiences to the "truth" of the experiences in the readings. Active learning instructional strategies (Bonwell & Eison, 1991) included interactive lectures, a guest lecturer, question and answer sessions, think/pair/share exercises, small-group discussion, puzzles, video critique, role-playing, and problem-based learning. The tie of theory to narratives then to personal experiences was meant to spark intense discussions resulting in "ah ha" moments. I wanted participants to engage in the highest-level of critical thinking possible in order to process information at a level higher than rote recall (Gayle, Preiss, & Allen, 2006).

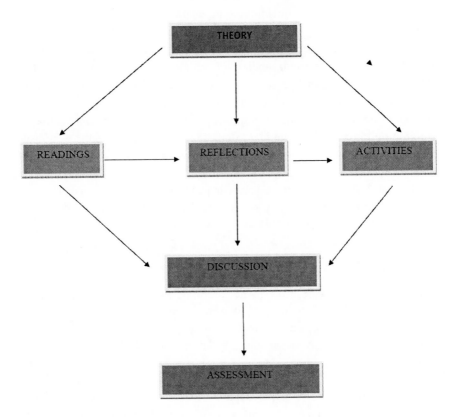

Figure 1. Instructional Design.

COURSE EVALUATION

Course evaluations and unsolicited email messages suggest that the class was successful. In analysis of both quantitative and qualitative responses, participants agreed that the instructors communicated ideas and concepts clearly, were knowledgeable about the subject, well-organized and fully prepared for class, accessible, encouraged participation, used good examples in presentations, noticed when they needed help, chose readings and assignments that were helpful for learning, demonstrated a passion for the subject, provided excellent resources, and responded timely to messages. All indicated they would recommend the course to others, that learning outcomes were provided, policies and grading methods were stated clearly, and that the course was definitely challenging but met expectations. Nineteen of the twenty participants were successful in completing this pass/fail course.

As previously noted, I designed the course utilizing a culturally responsive pedagogy inclusive of a culturally responsive classroom management style. I wanted participants to reflect on their own cultural orientations in the hope that that reflection would translate into the need to monitor their own behavior for more equitable treatment of others, lead to questioning of traditional assumptions about what works in a multicultural environment, and ultimately commit to building more caring classrooms. The following statements indicate that many are headed in the right direction. As one participant stated:

> I was so impressed with the class and text that I am going to use what I learned in my own classes. I have to say that I think this course should be mandatory for faculty, staff and students.

While yet another noted:

> It takes a full-scale effort on the part of the entire college community to create a warm welcoming environment where every student no matter where they come from and no matter the group with which they identify feels as though they're understood. A class like this creates a space for having those conversations.

In addition to desiring participants leave the class with a better understanding of the impact of cultures on our lives, I wanted them to gain an appreciation of narratives, communication theories and research that explain intercultural interactions. The degree to which these goals were met are evident by an examination of the reflection papers. For example, responses became progressively more sophisticated (connecting theory to experience to strategies they could employ) from the first assignment to last. In preparation for the first day of classes, they were asked to read a set of essays describing how Asian, Hispanic, Jewish, and Jamaican American ethnic identities are enacted through communication. Each essay utilized Hecht, Jackson, and Ribeau's (2003) communication theory of identity. Essay scores were extremely low indicating they did not thoroughly answer questions, nor drew conclusions or made connections across readings. For example, most responses were of the following type:

This particular author has to operate in two different cultures, both of which she has an extremely difficult time fitting into. She functions as an outcast in both. She faces social ramifications as a result and has to come to terms with living her life in two groups: a dominant culture and a minority.

This response was a simple summary of the essay. Participants did not connect the experiences of the authors with their own, apply theory, or discuss how instances highlighted by the authors fit or contradicted ideas from class discussions and activities. Several indicated they could not relate to a narrative with comments such as:

As I read the assignment, I kept looking for something I felt that I could respond to. The authors were very angry, using the word 'despicable' in several places. While I saw their point of view, I could not help but feel sadness for them. It is a terrible thing to be filled with such hatred.

However, by the last meeting, participants were able to see how Giles, Coupland and Coupland's (1991) accommodation theory explained effective and ineffective communication encounters impacted by class status, race and gender. Scores on these final reflection papers were very high indicating more thorough understanding, better analysis, and the ability to link theory to experiences articulating differences and similarities across cultures. Note the following sentiment expressed by some:

Sister-friends are probably more readily found among Black women than white women. White women tend to not associate with each other after life events make them move or situations become too complicated to take the energy to maintain a solid relationship because they do not want to get involved. After reading some of the articles associated with this theme, one could also tie in the idea of family as with the *La Familia* among Mexican Americans. Sometimes, blood runs thicker than water and Black women associate themselves as part of a family because of their shared heritage.

In addition, by the end of the course, most, if not all participants were able to generate their own stories and connect them with those of the authors in the articles read. The following is an example:

When the authors speak of 'alternating invisibility and hypervisibility,' I think of my own experience as principle of a majority Black and Mexican American elementary school. Being blonde haired and blue eyed, I immediately stood out from the crowd at PTA meetings. In fact, most of the time I could count only a few white faces in the crowd, and most of those were teachers. That was 'hypervisibility.' On the other hand, when I would approach a group of Black teachers having a conversation, I would feel as if I wasn't included. That feeling of 'invisibility' was even more uncomfortable than the feeling of being stared at in a 'hypervisible' mode. In the first case, it was just a matter of fact that I was different, but in the second, I felt intentionally ignored.... Interestingly, there were few teachers with Hispanic backgrounds at this school. I wonder if those few felt 'hypervisible' or 'invisible' in our faculty discussions.

Again, the course was designed to encourage students to step out of their comfort zone, to engage in deep meaningful dialogue, to take the perspective of others, to question themselves, face uncomfortable truths, and ultimately be motivated or inspired to try alternative strategies in future intercultural encounters. I wanted them to apply contemporary theory to instances of intercultural communication, to understand what behaviors are appropriate and effective communication in the context of co-cultural interactions, and acquire an appreciation for the value of narratives in understanding human behavior. I believe these objectives were met.

LESSONS LEARNED

Entrenched racist institutionalized practices are extremely difficult to change. Nevertheless, when an institution commits to change and announces such commitment through its mission statement and programming, we should be open to acknowledging and supporting that commitment instead of painting the entire organization as deceptive. Although the majority of those in decision-making roles may be prejudiced and engage in discriminatory practices, there are usually two or more individuals who are committed to the cause. Those are the people with whom we must interact to impact change.

I now acknowledge that there was strong institutional support for employee development. Support received from the dean's office and the Employee Development Program located within the Office of Institutional

Effectiveness was impressive. Our accommodations were top-notch with access to the highest quality technology at the institution. Breakfast and lunches were catered. Our meeting space was comfortable with both large and small intimate spaces to facilitate the various activities planned. Paranoia aside, our sessions remained private with no interruptions or unexpected visits from the administration. This institutional support for employee development was the open door needed for a few individuals to assist one another in not only tolerating differences but appreciating them.

To effectively teach an intercultural communication competence course, it is best to begin with the assumption that everyone present has good intentions, especially when they are electing to participate. Concentrate on what you have in common. We all valued good teaching and valued it enough to risk facing our own prejudices and those expressed by others. In order to face one's own prejudices, one must feel safe. We established rules of conduct so that everyone felt safe enough to be as honest and vocal as possible. We agreed to not discuss any details of actual college-related experiences with anyone outside of class. As a result of this safety pack, we shared extremely personal stories of failed and successful intercultural encounters involving race, gender, social class, regional distinctions and sexual orientation. As suggested by Lindsley (1998) the most successful organizational diversity interventions recognize the many layers, dimensions and interpenetrating identities of its workforce. We spoke to inclusiveness on as many levels as possible given time constraints; and helped each other through the difficult terrain of dealing with hurt. Comments were made and misunderstood. Voices were raised. We laughed and cried. Our interactions were emotionally draining, difficult but truly cathartic and worthwhile.

In speaking to inclusiveness, I learned another valuable lesson. We must meet people where they are and not where we want them to be. The most effective way to get others to appreciate racial differences is to first help them appreciate other, arguably, less threatening ones such as generational, regional and social class differences. When one can see the privilege one has in one or more of these areas, then the groundwork has been laid to assist him or her in understanding the privilege granted or denied through racial distinctions.

Finally, those of us who consider ourselves experts in intercultural communication can learn to appreciate differences too. I still believe this course was a result of a discriminatory act. At first, I felt resentment toward my co-facilitator, saw her as a watch-dog and wondered if she would feel the need to report back on my activities. Whether or not she did, I will never truly know. Nonetheless, I do know that she, in all her difference (i.e., age, race, educational level and experience) was instrumental to the success of the course. As both a facilitator and participant in the class, she did not hold back. When I lectured, she backed me up and never contradicted anything I said. We played to our strengths. She opened herself up to being the confidant of other Whites in the room who did not feel as comfortable with me; asked for my advice and used it. Her support of me in addition to her connection to the local community, respect, and similarity to the majority of our participants in age, class and upbringing aided in perceptions of credibility in me. As a team, we moved effortlessly through activities with a silent understanding and communication between us that demonstrated that we were on the same page. We wanted the same thing –for our participants to appreciate difference.

REFERENCES

Aragon, A. & Brantmeier, E. J. (2009). Diversity-affirming ethics and critical epistemology: Institutional decision making in community colleges. *New Directions for Community Colleges, 148*, 39-51.

Bonwell, C. C., & Eison, J. A. (1991). *Active learning: Creating excitement in the classroom.* 1991 ASHE-ERIC Higher Education Reports. Office of Educational Research and Improvement: Washington, DC.

Creswell, J. W. (2009). *Research design: Qualitative, quantitative, and mixed methods approaches, 3rd ed.* Thousand Oaks, CA: Sage.

Gayle, B. M., Priess, R. W., Allen, M. (2006). How effective are teacher-initiated classroom questions in enhancing student learning? In B. M. Gayle, R. W. Preiss, N. Burrell, & M. Allen (Eds.), *Classroom communication and instructional processes: Advances through meta-analysis* (pp. 279-293). Mahway, NJ: Lawrence Erlbaum Associates.

Giles, H., Coupland, N., & Coupland, J. (1991). Contexts of accommodation: Developments in applied sociolinguistics. Cambridge: Cambridge University Press.

Gonzalez, A., Houston, M., & Chen, V. (2011). *Our voices: Essays in culture, ethnicity, and communication 5th Ed.* New York, NY: Oxford University Press.

Haviland, D. & Rodriguez-Kiino (2009). Closing the gap: The impact of professional development on faculty attitudes toward culturally responsive pedagogy. *Journal of Hispanic Higher Education, 8*(2), 197-212.

Headland, T., Pike, K., & Harris, M. (1990). *Emics and etics: The insider/outsider debate.* Thousand Oaks, CA: Sage.

Hecht, M. L., Jackson, R. L., & Ribeau, S. A. (2003). African American communication: Exploring identity and culture. Mahwah, NJ: Lawrence Erlbaum Associates.

Kottak, C. (2006). *Mirror of humanity*. McGraw-Hill: New York.

Levin, J. S., Haberler, Z., Walker, L., & Jackson-Boothby, A. (2014). Community college culture and faculty of color. *Community College Review, 42*(1), 55-74.

Lindsley, S. L. (1998). Organizational interventions to prejudice. In M. L. Hecht (Ed.), *Communicating prejudice* (pp. 302-310). Thousand Oaks, CA: Sage.

Mangan, K. (2009, August 24). High enrollments and low graduation rates challenge struggling states. *The Chronicle of Higher Education Special Reports*. Retrieved from https://chronicle.com/article/Demographics-Challenge/48147/.

Marsiglia, F. F., & Hecht, M. L. (1998). Personal and interpersonal interventions. In M. L. Hecht (Ed.), *Communicating prejudice* (pp. 287-301). Thousand Oaks, CA: Sage.

Murray, J. P. (1999). Faculty development in a national sample of community colleges. *Community College Review, 27*(3), 47-64.

Murray, J. P. (2002). Faculty development in SACs-accredited community colleges. *Community College Review, 29*(4), 50-66.

Rich, C., Gayle, B. M., & Preiss, R. W. (2006). Pedagogical issues underlying classroom learning techniques. In B.M. Gayle, R. W. Preiss, N. Burrell, & M. Allen (Eds.), *Classroom communication and instructional processes: Advances through meta-analysis* (pp. 31-42). Mahway, NJ: Lawrence Erlbaum Associates.

Roberts, S. (2004). *Who are we now: The changing face of America in the twenty first century*. New York: Henry Holt and Company.

Twombly, S., & Townsend, B. K. (2008). Community college faculty what we know and need to know. *Community College Review, 36*(1), 5-24.

Weinstein, C. S., Tomlinson-Clarke, S., & Curran, M. (2004). Toward a conception of culturally responsive classroom management. *Journal of Teacher Education, 55*(1), 25-38.

Yin, R. (1994). *Case study research*, 2nd ed. Thousand Oaks, CA: Sage.

In: Communicating Prejudice   ISBN: 978-1-53610-167-6
Editors: S. Camara and D. Drummond   © 2016 Nova Science Publishers, Inc.

Chapter 5

IDENTIFYING STEREOTYPES: THE STORIES NIELSEN AND NICKELODEON TELL BLACK CHILDREN AND HOW TO "APPRECIATE" THEM

Dianah Wynter

California State University, Northridge, CA, US

ABSTRACT

This paper examines the way in which post-millennial programming on the Nickelodeon Channel assigns consumerist labels and stereotypical roles to its Black adolescent characters, and, in turn, to its Black adolescent viewers, and the consequences that can occur when shows stereotype Black characters.

By examining *True Jackson VP* (2008-2011), the animated series *NFL Guardians of the Core* and *The Haunted Hathaways* (2011-2016), we explore the role that statistical data from Nielsen media research and consumer expenditure surveys play in the perpetuation of stereotypes in children's programming.

This paper further seeks to articulate the problems of stereotypes in children's television programming and consider solutions by describing some of Nielsen's and Nickelodeon's past practices that served as a platform for social change using Srivastva, Fry and Cooperrider's 4-D Model of Appreciative Inquiry.

Keywords: children's programming, network television, Nielsen, stereotyping, Consumer data, Nickelodeon, Appreciative Inquiry, 4-D Model, *True Jackson, Haunted Hathaways*

INTRODUCTION

This paper presents an examination of how post-millennial programming on the Nickelodeon Channel assigns consumerist labels and stereotypical roles to its Black adolescent characters, and, in turn, to its Black adolescent viewers. Studies have shown that stereotypical portrayals and media invisibility can damage the social and emotional development of children and adolescents (Campbell, 2011), but few articulate what we can do to appreciate the portrayals and facilitate peak learning in children when shows stereotype Black characters.

To illustrate this point, this paper discusses three Nickelodeon programs in which stereotypes are identified, that meet the following criteria: (1) The shows premiered in 2008 or later; (2) The programs feature Black talent and/or leading characters; and (3) The shows' targeted demographics were 6–11, 9-14, or 14-17 age range. The three programs that serve as the focus of this paper are hit sitcoms *True Jackson VP* (2008-2011), the animated series *NFL Guardians of the Core* and *The Haunted Hathaways* (2011-2016). As a backdrop, we also explore the role that statistical data from Nielsen media research and consumer expenditure surveys play in the perpetuation of these practices in children's programming.

This paper further seeks to articulate the problems of stereotypes in children's television programming and consider solutions by describing some of Nielsen's and Nickelodeon's past practices that served as a platform for social change using Srivastva, Fry and Cooperrider's 4-D Model of Appreciative Inquiry (Srivastava, 1999). Furthermore, Wynter's Stereotype Metric is based on the Appreciative Inquiry 4-D Model, and is designed to help parents of black children assess children's programming.

DISCOVERY PHASE: NIELSEN'S DATA AND OTHER STATISTICS

Discovery is the first phase in the 4D model, which is intended to deal with capturing *what works* within specific communities (Conklin, 2014). Nielsen's 2005 report, "TV Audience Special Study: African American Audience," analyzed viewing habits of Black households in general, including data on Black viewers under the age of 18. Nickelodeon emerged on top as the channel most viewed by this demographic. Significantly, Nickelodeon's African-American viewership outpaced—by 42%—the Disney Channel, the second most watched channel viewed by African-Americans under 18 at the time of the study (Steadman, 2005). The report further revealed that Viacom's *America's Top Model* developed a decidedly African-American following, with African-Americans under 18 constituting 45% of its viewers, ranking the show among the top six programs they regularly watched (Steadman, 2005). The Consumer Expenditure Survey of 2005 showed that, while African-American consumers spent less than the other groups in most consumer categories, they spent *more* on apparel than the US overall average and more than other groups (DOL, 2007). Armed with the foregoing intelligence, Nickelodeon developed *TRUE JACKSON, VP* to cater to its retail advertisers and to demonstrate an interest in the Black viewing audience.

However, the "discovery" was lacking in important details. Empirical data support that Black households watch more television (7.12 hrs./day) than the national average (5.11 hrs./day) in the United States (Nielsen, 2011). This trend applies to all age demographics. Black households also enjoy an uncommonly higher percentage of television-set ownership than the national average. Moreover, Black children under the age of 18, "watch more Nickelodeon than any other broadcast affiliate or network." Clearly, Nielsen's meticulous research addresses *what* children and adolescents are watching, and *when* they are watching it. However, what remains unaddressed is *why* they are watching, which is to "model" the social roles they see as they strive to create their own self-identity (Stroman, 1984).

THE DREAM PHASE

The second stage is called Dream, which focuses on our imagination and what we desire things to be or what we think or hope could be possible

(Conklin, 2014). In Nickelodeon's animated series *NFL Rush Zone: Guardians of the Core* Ishmael (or "Ish"), a pintsized African-American boy, receives powers from an intergalactic mentor, and regularly springs into action using his intellect and videogame prowess (aided by the NFL) to save football and the planet from the evil extra-terrestrials. Animated versions of real NFL players and coaches give Ish advice and encouragement. Our "underdog" protagonist rises to every test before him, as wise adults tout the benefits of teamwork, and a caring mom supports and loves our hero. In season two, Ishmael is redrawn as a buff 15-year-old to appeal to an older target audience. He is no longer "the one," but is instead the quarterback of a *team* of Guardians of the Core. The wonderfully diverse team includes a Latino, a heavyset Pacific Islander named Tua, two Caucasian males, and a Caucasian female. Season two also transforms Ishmael's mother into a tall and curvaceous beauty. Her role is expanded to include being a scientist who becomes integral to some of the storylines.

The Nickelodeon of the 1990's carried several programs with this possibility in mind. Nickelodeon cast Black children in leading roles, and not merely as token supporting roles. The portrayal of Black and Asian children in leading roles allowed the primary viewing audience to imagine a world in TV that mirrored the world they lived in and experienced every day (for example, *Cousin Skeeter* (1998); *The Journey of Allen Strange* (1997); and *The Mystery Files of Shelby Woo* (1996)). The Nickelodeon of the 1990's surfed the "inclusion" wave by drawing attention to the more invisible sectors of society and doing so with imaginative and creative programming. No doubt, it continued the trend started by NBC president Brandon Tartikoff in the 1980's with Black family programming such as *The Cosby Show* and *The Fresh Prince of Bel Air*. *The Cosby Show* ranked number one in its timeslot its first seven years (Budd, 1992).

However, since 2000, Nickelodeon has reversed this trend and it has not acted alone. According to the Screen Actors Guild 2008 Casting Data Reports, casting of African-American talent "showed the largest drop in proportion to total roles... Each category showed a decrease... falling from" 15.5% in 2002 to "14.8% in 2007 to 13.3% of total roles in 2008" (SAG, 2008). Many broadcast networks have reduced Black characters to one or two per series. Half-hour broadcast family sitcoms (e.g., *Modern Family, Parenthood, Mom, Last Man Standing)* no longer featured Black families (Braxton, 2012). In 2014, the ABC network stepped out alone to premiere a new series ironically titled "*Blackish,*" about a Black family whose profoundly bourgeois trappings yield existential dilemmas about their Blackness. The series features film actor

Laurence Fishburn as the patriarch. The show's ironic title *Blackish* —i.e., sort of but not quite Black— comes across to some as an attempt to minimize the characters' African heritage. NBC's *The Carmichael Show* starring comedian Jerrod Carmichael, has won a third season, but only after the network raised its order of ten episodes to the standard minimum of thirteen (Andreeve, 2016).

In contrast to broadcast channels, cable channels offer a more Black-themed family shows, albeit in non-primetime hours. TV Land's *Soul Man* (2012), starring Cedric the Entertainer, depicts an R & B singer who gives up the glamorous life to become a church minister. BET, a Viacom channel actively develops and produces content featuring Black casts, among them *The First Family* (2012), an apolitical sitcom about a Black president and his eccentric relatives. Nickelodeon itself added a new Black sitcom *Instant Mom* (2013), on its late-night block of shows on Nick, Jr. named "NickMom." Clearly, its name is its target audience.

Undeniably, the changes to the television landscape are most critical when they impact programming served to children and adolescents. Are the changes at Nickelodeon's children's programming purely data-driven? Is consumer data playing a larger role in the creative process and influencing the portrayals of African-Americans? How are these portrayals impacting the perceptions of African-Americans on Nick's children's shows? The purpose of this study is to address these crucial questions, not to indict Nickelodeon; The fact the network touted three millennial shows starring African-American actors, running concurrently, displays its commitment to diversity. However, it is important to pinpoint the challenges that stereotypes present for young black viewers.

True Jackson, VP

TRUE JACKSON, VP (2008-2011) was developed for a target audience of girls nine to 14. The show revolves around a 15-year-old Black high school student named True Jackson (delightfully played by Keke Palmer) with a flair for fashion, who is given the chance to run her own fashion line. The show does not focus on the creativity, industriousness, or even the talent of this "whiz kid" protagonist, but rather, on her self-doubt, aversion to school and traditional pedagogy. The show saddles its Black male adolescents with the stereotypical roles of angry jock, rapper, or criminal and plagues other Black characters —and consequently, its adolescent viewers— with an assortment of other stereotypes.

True's "backstory" is a positive narrative to share with young viewers. The main character is a beautiful, confident, industrious, principled self-starter and go-getter. Before she enters the world of fashion, True sells sandwiches on the sidewalk to make extra money. She is not afraid of hard work. The program's premise started out promoting creativity and initiative; and granted, because of its milieu, it also celebrates materialism (Van Boven, 2011), self-objectification, and unhealthy body images. But a closer look at *True Jackson, VP* reveals a narrative created using the techniques of racial stereotyping, subtyping and race-gender invisibility, choices possibly driven by consumer data that sacrifice the quality of the Black adolescent's viewing experience in order to cater to mainstream sensibilities.

True Jackson is a high-school student who conspicuously doesn't attend school, at least for the first nine months of the show, from November 8, 2008 to July 25, 2009. In most television comedies about adolescence, school is an integral part of the story. Not only does True *forego* school for the first eighteen episodes, there are few references to school at all. As the second season approached, a high school location was added. To introduce the high school and justify its lengthy absence, dialogue about the "summer vacation being over" was sprinkled throughout an episode titled "Back to School."

The establishing shots of True's high school in New York City show diverse teenagers milling about. Once inside, however, True emerges as the only Black girl in the whole school. Black girls or girls of color are rendered invisible. True Jackson herself was the only Black female on the show for almost the entire first season. Except for the "sassy" gay Black secretary, True is the "token" in her own show. Also conspicuously absent are True parents. Her father appears once during the entire series, as does her mother (played by Vivica A. Fox) who appears in the thirty-fifth episode (of fifty-eight), along with True's only Black friend. The invisibility of other Black girls is disturbing, as visibility *in* the media is an indicator of value *by* the media, which in turn creates and maintains the perception of value for our mediated society. Conversely, media invisibility indicates vulnerability and devaluation (Gerbner, 1980).

As shown by the following examples, stereotypes burden the Black male adolescent characters in many of the show's episodes. In "Flirting with Fame," True develops a crush on the new guy in school. She later discovers that her crush, played by Tyler James William of *Everybody Hates Chris*, is an international teen rapper who is only attending school between tours. In "My Boss Ate My Homework," True's boss has to spend the day in detention, where he encounters the second stereotype, the angry, oversized Black football player. In "Little Buddies," True's friend Ryan mentors a pintsized Black freshman that attends school only to commit crimes. In the climax of the storyline, Ryan wears a "wire" to entrap his charge and has him arrested. Furthermore, these prevailing stereotypes of the rapper, the dumb athlete, and the criminal appear in the first six episodes of the high school setting's debut.

Such disparaging depictions of Black male adolescents serve to reinforce negative perceptions to *all* of its viewers. But they can be more damaging for the Black adolescent viewers, because it undermines their efforts to establish their own self-identity and model social roles, at a time when they are most endeavoring to do so (Stroman,1984). Donning a "social role" implies participation in society, whereas wearing an imposed stereotype/label deems one as broken and useless to society (Dyer, 1999). Stereotypes that are relentlessly foisted upon targeted groups can cause some victims of stereotyping to eventually embrace the goals of the stereotyped group and abandon their own authentic hopes and aspirations (Campbell, 2011).

True Jackson, VP affords few opportunities for female adolescent viewers to model credible social roles. In fact, the hi-jinx of the storylines often undermines the main character's "special gift," i.e., her creativity. In "True Takes Iceland," True comes down with "designer's block" when she competes in a design contest. When her dog bites a hole in her design, True wins the competition -- for her uniqueness. True sees her victory as an ill-gotten gain, and so does the audience. She doubts herself and fears that she is not talented, just lucky. Self-doubt is a wonderful issue to address in a series about adolescence. However, the series rarely gives True's actual creative abilities any moments to shine. Viewers never see her cutting any fabric or stitching an actual garment. The plethora of teens on YouTube, demonstrating how they made their prom dresses, highlights the absence of this activity on the series. The program's premise promotes creativity and initiative; however, its execution often fails to portray the work required to succeed in the exciting world of fashion. Albert Bandura's social learning theory has articulated that if one *believes* [he or she] can [succeed] at a vocation or job, that belief will provide the inspiration to pursue it (Bandura, 2001). *True Jackson VP,* however, was seems to have been developed as total "fantasy," and not "inspiration." The absence of any realistic portrayal of creativity makes the fashion world and its lifestyle seem unattainable, which diminishes the appeal of the show.

Historically, shows with "whiz kid" protagonists had plots that were resolved by the exceptional application of their protagonist's talent (e.g., *Doogie Howser MD, Jimmy Neutron, Mathilde* and the Harry Potter franchise). The makers of *True Jackson VP* set the bar low for True and her viewers. The implications are that (a) there was no serious consideration or expectation that this audience would aspire to succeed in the world of fashion, and (b) there was no serious consideration of this audience in any way other than as consumers, as evidenced by the series' merchandise tie-in with Wal-Mart. The brand 'Mad Styles by True Jackson' was an actual fashion line for tweens created for the show, and available exclusively at Wal-Mart during its run (Adweek 1). While the characteristics of the show correlate to consumer data, they do not correlate to the desires of young girls to imagine themselves in someone else's life.

Bandura's research on motivation articulates that, "the higher people's perceived efficacy to fulfill educational requirements and occupational roles, the wider the career options they seriously consider pursuing, the greater the interest they have in them, the better they prepare themselves educationally for different occupational careers, and the greater their staying power in challenging career pursuits" (Bandura, 2001). Subsequently, the "perceived efficacy to fulfill educational requirements" as presented by *True Jackson VP* to its Black viewers would be low indeed. As pure fantasy, the show did not give its the viewers enough to believe in or to model. True Jackson herself is a stereotype, or more specifically, a 'subtype' within a stereotyped group (Blaine, 2007); this means she is the *exception* to the accepted stereotypical perception of Black girls. She is thin, good-natured, smart, ambitious, attends a predominantly White school and has grown up as an only child in a bourgeois household. And yet, at other times, True is a "sassy black woman," who regularly lapses into Ebonics with her pithy catch phrase, "He said what now?" reminiscent of the ever popular, "Say what?" and "What you talkin' 'bout, Willis?" from *Different Strokes*.

True Jackson VP exploits stereotypes, subtypes, tokenism, and race-gender invisibility. Empirical data overwhelming indicate that such techniques of media representation promote feelings of "devaluation" among young Black viewers (Gerbner, 1980), and undermine the efforts of impressionable young viewers to establish their own self-identity and model social roles at a time when they are most trying to do so (Peterson, 1983).

NFL Rush Zone: Guardians of the Core

NFL RUSH ZONE: GUARDIANS OF THE CORE (2010-2014) was developed by Nickelodeon and NFL Productions for a target audience of children aged six to 11, and was subsequently tweaked for an older demographic (aged nine to 14). The season first featured an undersized ten-year-old Black male protagonist (Ishmael or "Ish") who is chosen by an intergalactic mentor to save football, and the earth's core from the destructive powers of evil aliens. The show's sole purpose is to produce the next generation of NFL viewers.

Nickelodeon's animated series *NFL Rush Zone: Guardians Of The Core* addressed one of the key concerns for television producers and executives in the millennium, i.e., the need for content across the various digital platforms. The series debuted in 2010 on the NFL and NickToons websites as short 'webisodes,' and as interstitial programming on NickToons during football season. It was also made available on iTunes. The websites received over 1.2 million hits in the age 6 – 11 demographic. The second season premiered as full half-hour episodes on NickToons in the summer of 2012.

Nickelodeon and NFL Productions created the program to target demographic groups that did not watch football-centered programming. In season one, the protagonist of *NFL Rush Zone: Guardians Of The Core* was a ten-year-old, even though the data indicated that children and adolescents were largely disinterested in NFL programming. The NFL served both as a production entity and an integrated brand product (Flint, 2012). The show's singular ulterior motive means that the show itself is first and foremost, strategic communication, not children's storytelling. Nickelodeon provided the NFL with viewers to be indoctrinated. Sports industries have used children's cartoons as public relations vehicles for decades, e.g., *Speed Racer* (1967), *Hot Wheels* (1969), *Where's Huddles?* (1970), and *The Harlem Globetrotters* (1972).

Strikingly absent is Ish's father, who is only mentioned in the dialogue. In the first episode, it is Ish's mother who takes him to the football games, not his father. To justify Ish being fatherless for the entire series, the writers added dialogue in the second season that cast Ish's father as an officer stationed overseas. With this rhetoric, the writers created a heroic rationale for the father's absence, while reinforcing the stereotype of the Black family with no father. Coaches are often portrayed in the media as the only father young black males have (e.g., *Glory Road, Coach Carter, Remember the Titans, Hoop Dreams*), and this stereotype is perpetuated in *NFL Rush Zone*.

Drastic changes were made in season two, *NFL Rush Zone: Season of the Guardians*, with Ishmael redrawn as a 15-year-old to appeal to an older target audience. Additionally, when the Guardians do battle with the evil aliens, Ish and his team don "Power Ranger" type body armor that completely obscures their identities and the storylines are resolved by fight sequences. The show deftly interweaves high-definition live-action NFL game footage with animated versions of entire NFL teams. Because the series exalts the "ideals" of the NFL, i.e., teamwork, sportsmanship and diversity. *NFL Rush Zone: Season of the Guardians*, is not unhealthy programming for this demographic. The show fosters an appreciation for the game as a symbol of American values. The show's mission is not to fill to viewers' minds with unattainable aspirations of playing in the NFL, but rather to cultivate NFL consumers, i.e., season ticket holders, buyers of ancillary products, and broadcast viewers. In so doing, NFL Productions and Nickelodeon intentionally assigned a consumerist label to its lead character and hence to its viewers. Still, the show placed its motives squarely in the foreground and consequently, has a sense of integrity.

NFL Rush Zone: Season of the Guardians' abrupt change in target audiences illustrates the unflinching use of segmentation that Nielsen advocates: "The world is a fragmented place, we can help you hone in on the segments that matter to you" (Nielsen, 2013). The implication of this statement is that there are segments that matter and segments that don't matter, and the narrower the focus the better. Nielsen's report on advertising for millennials stresses that female viewers prefer "aspirational" themes and "happy situations" where the female viewer can "imagine herself" (Gender, 2012). Additionally, "silly, off-beat humor that's not mean-spirited tickles the funny bones of young women." These appear to be key ingredients in the half-hour sitcom, *The Haunted Hathaways.*

The Haunted Hathaways

THE HAUNTED HATHAWAYS (2013-present) was developed for a six-to-11, and nine-to-14. Similar to the heroine in the 1947 film *The Ghost and Mrs. Muir,* single mom Michele Hathaway moves into a new house with her two daughters, and discover it is haunted by the ghosts of its previous residents— in this iteration, a Black jazz musician Ray Preston and his two young sons, Miles, 13, and Louis, 9. With *The Haunted Hathaways*, Nickelodeon unintentionally perpetuates tacit indifference toward the deaths of young, Black males. *The Haunted Hathaways* series premiered on July 13, 2013, the acquittal date of Trayvon Martin's murderer, an irony overwhelmingly noticed by various Black communities. The auspicious premiere date may have been one reason for the abundant internet inquiries:

How did Miles' and Louis's die? Where is their mother? Is she dead, too? Why isn't *she* haunting the house? etc.

Created as a vehicle for ten-year-old rapper, Lil P Nut, *The Haunted Hathaways* unfortunately trivializes the deaths of young Black males and tacitly portrays child mortality in a comedic and casual manner. Parents can help their children to recode the series as a metaphor for the young, Black male's quest for respect and understanding in a world that fears him: Miles is the appeaser, who wants to make friends with the people that are afraid of him. "Please, don't be scared... Relax. I'm a *good* ghost," Miles tells Taylor Hathaway, who is his age. "The name's Miles, rhymes with smiles," he says, desperate to ingratiate himself. In contrast, little Louis (played by Benjamin "Lil P-Nut" Flores, Jr.) is the righteous ghost, refusing to hide his gifts just to assuage other people's prejudiced fear. Louis wants nothing less than to be his true, authentic self, i.e., a scary ghost.

The comic premise of the show, however, is that Louis is not a very powerful ghost. Significantly, even in death, Louis is powerless. Repeated media representations of "even sympathetically presented or accidental victims in an underrepresented population," without balancing them with images of them being powerful and effective, "diminishes and degrades that group" (Gerbner, 1980). The image of young Black males are nonchalantly degraded, as the show emphasizes how fun and cool it is to be a ghost. The endless display of pranks, punch-lines, and magical powers, fails to mention the pre-requisite for such hi-jinx– that one must be dead.

Assuming that the show's demographic is young children between the ages of 6 and 11, we can further assume that the viewers understand death as an irreversible and permanent phenomenon (NIHCC, 2006). But Miles and Louis look the same as they did when they were alive, indicating that their deaths *lack* permanence. Children across different ethnic groups will have different experiences of death and subsequently, will have different reactions to this representation. For example, the "risk of mortality was 33-75% higher among black children than white children" (Singh, 2010). Taking this statistic into consideration, *The Haunted Hathaways* is highly insensitive; the show portrays a highly vulnerable group, i.e., African-American boys, in the most feared and dreaded condition, (dead), and then mocks of them. Little boys seem to appreciate the show less than girls do, as the members of the "I Hate Haunted Hathaways" Facebook page are predominantly boys. It is not surprising, since the only characters that boy viewers have to relate to are the two dead characters whose desires are thwarted in most episodes.

Showtime's *Dead Like Me* and Syfy Channel's *Being Human* depicted young ghosts using a more dignified approach; moreover, the ghosts were not children. Uniquely, ABC's *Moe's World* featured the ghost of a black child and, in 1990, was the most talked about pilot in Hollywood (Rosenberg, 1991). The opening sequence showed Moe, a young Black boy playing basketball in the schoolyard, displaying Michael-Jordan-esque moves. Then his voiceover is heard, "Dying really helped my game. I was good before, but now... I'm unstoppable" (Sullivan, 1990). *Moe's World* featured thoughtful humor and a daring premise: struck down by a car, Moe haunts his neighborhood and appears to his loved ones in their dreams.

The show was ahead of its time and very controversial. ABC Television, even after paying for the pilot and the first four episodes, shied away from producing the series. In the 25 years since *Moe's World*, violent news stories, TV series like *Cops,* police dramas, music videos, and videogames have provided a relentless stream of images of young Black males dying. These images have become so pervasive that they have ceased to appall, as evidenced by *The Haunted Hathaways*.

The increased mortality rate of young Black males in America correlates with the introduction of television in the United States. In fact, the murder rate "of young black males rose 300% during the three decades after television's introduction in the United States" (Media Violence, 2001). Gerbner verifies the correlation between the aforementioned "kill rate" and "victimization rate" in various Black communities. Killings disproportionately involve Black victims (Gerbner, 1980). Victimization (of violent crimes) likewise disproportionately involves Black victims – children and youth (Gibbs, 1988). But media rarely portray the Black victims with empathy or compassion, but instead, paint both victim and aggressor with the same unsympathetic brush.

Statistical data, consumer reports, and Nielsen reports and techniques (e.g., segmentation) seem to drive creative choices for Nickelodeon's children programming. The consequence of stereotyping and other narrow depictions is the emotional scarring of their own young viewers. Young viewers run the risk of internalizing these inadequate models (Stroman, 1984), because adolescents watch television for the purpose of "trying on" and modeling the social roles they see portrayed on TV. Imposed stereotypes can potentially undermine and replace their authentic positive goals.

THE DESIGN PHASE: NICK'S PAST ACHIEVEMENT IN DIVERSE PROGRAMMING

The third phase is Design. This phase is for the contemplation of all elements in order to gain clarity (Conklin, 2014). This phase answers the question: what can be done to facilitate optimal change and growth? In this phase we consider Nickelodeon's recent achievements in diverse programming. We start with the animated series *Fairly Odd Parents,* which for years was the number one cable show in African-American households and second most popular cable show among *all* U.S. households. *Fairly Odd Parents* revolves around little Timmy Turner, a neglected young boy harassed by his dastardly older sister. His two wacky fairy godparents and trio of goofy friends come to his aid. One of Timmy's most effective buddies is A. J., an African-American boy genius that invariably invents the appropriate super-gadget to get them out of tight jams. *Fairly Odd Parents* debuted in 2001 and is still in production. The show's creators added this adorable Black genius in season three. Between 2001 and 2013, A.J. appeared in 59 of the 109 episodes. His label as a "genius" allowed all children to see themselves in that role. Studies on "self-labeling" and "stereotype threat" have shown that media portrayals and media inclusion have a direct impact on cognitive performance (Scott, 2012).

Nielsen's 2011 report "State of the African American Consumer" revealed that increased Black income and education levels *exceeded* expectations, despite the national economic slump. Notwithstanding, their viewing patterns remained unchanged. Flawed expectations of reduced purchasing power from this demographic may be behind the elimination of Black-oriented programming in broadcast and cable, and reduction in the casting of Black actors. Nielsen found "unchanged viewing patterns" among Black households, which suggests that Nickelodeon might still hold onto this demographic, as Black households may continue to watch shows despite the absence of Black characters. The continued drop in Nickelodeon's ratings indicates otherwise.

History reveals that media often derive confidence from other media. In the 1980's and 1990's, the Hudlin Brothers' *House Party* movies, independent films of Spike Lee such as *School Daze*, *Do the Right Thing* and *Jungle Fever,* and Paramount's Eddie Murphy comedies such as *Coming to America* and *Boomerang* with Halle Berry, introduced the world to the Black middle class (Rhines, 1996). Bill Cosby's crossover appeal gave Brandon Tartikoff and NBC the confidence to present an upper middle class Black family over the airwaves. And America welcomed them. Its success inspired a succession of family sitcoms with diverse minority casts that has yet to abate; from *The George Lopez Show*, *All-American Girl* starring Margaret Cho, and *My Wife & Kids* with Damon Wayans, to *Fresh of the Boat*, *The Goldbergs,* and *Modern Family* which features a gay, married couple raising a daughter.

With the unparalleled popularity of hip-hop and gangster rap culture at the end of the twentieth century, disproportionate media portrayals of black violence, aberrant sexuality, and poverty became ubiquitous, and theoretically might have triggered advertisers' loss of faith in the buying power of Black America. As stated before, media follow other media. In reality, more than half of Black households are middle class and above, and consumer spending for this group is expected "to reach $1.3 trillion by the year 2017," according to the Selig Center for Economic Growth (Nielsen, 2012). With this buying power, and emerging Black-owned television networks with programming that does not traffic in negative stereotypes of black children (e.g., TV One, Gospel Channel, Aspire), Black viewers may be the true beneficiaries from the network "blackout" after all. But can the solution to the hyper-segmentation of the television simply be more segmentation?

In 2012-2013, the Disney Channel, which has demonstrated a gift for diverse programming (e.g., *Doc McStuffins*, *K.C. Undercover, The Proud Family*, myriad Tia and Tamara Mowrie shows, etc.), surpassed Nickelodeon in the ratings (Molloy, 2012). There has been controversy between Viacom and Nielsen, with the former questioning the accuracy data received from the latter (Lieberman, 2011). Such tensions appear to confirm the powerful influence of Nielsen data on the creation of television content.

American television has always been a contradiction. It is an art medium that reflects the splendor of American culture and the talent of American writers, performers, and producers. At the same time, it is the primary instrument for advertisers that view culture strictly as a commodity (Smythe, 2009). Television poses an even greater contradiction in the lives of African-Americans. On one hand, television's coverage of the civil rights movement helped to bring about great advancements for African-Americans. On the other hand, during the first three decades of television, the rate at which African-American males were murdered rose 300% (Media Violence, 2001). Today's target marketing and consumer fragmentation yield visual segregation, which in turn creates a distorted perception of the world, one where everyone is the same.

THE DESTINY PHASE: WYNTER'S STEREOTYPE METRIC FOR BLACK CHILDREN'S VIEWING

The final phase is Destiny. This step requires that one to commit energy to facilitate peak learning experiences around programming (Conklin, 2014). Wynter's Stereotype Metric for Black Children's Viewing is a 4-D appreciative inquiry tool to empower parents to help their children have a learning experience with the content presented in the shows their children watch. It provides not only hands-on monitoring of their children's television consumption, but also ways in which parents can engage their children to think critically about the content they are viewing. Furthermore, the metric allows parents to analyze and assess television content for what could be different (see Appendix).

All networks can benefit from finding ways to profit without in selling distorted self-perceptions to young people. The solution lies in broadcast and cable networks, both mainstream and niche, committing to the ideals of inclusion, and representing the true fabric of America, especially when the children are watching.

APPENDIX

Wynter's Stereotype Metric for Black Children's Viewing [Live Action & Animated Shows with Ethnic Characters]	
Q1 Discovery	+ 1 for every black character identified
What black characters exist in the *story*? What contributions do black characters make to the story?	+ 1 for every contribution identified.
Q2 Dream	+ 1 for each smart Black character
What did you hope to learn from these characters?	- 1 for each dumb or ignorant character of color

Appendix (Continued)

Q3 Design What other choices could this character have made? Who will be affected by his/her choices? How? How were you impacted by the actions of the character? How?	+ 1 for each character whose thoughts and actions affect the outcome.
Q4 Destiny What is next for this character? What can you do to be different from any negative characters in the show?	+ 1 for every act of help or kindness per black character (PBC)
	+ 2 for every heroic act per black character (PBC)
	− 1 for every negative acts or statement PBC
	− 2 for each act of violence and intimidation PBC
If you could make one wish for any unlucky or negative character, what would it be?	+ 1 for any *character, place* or *thing* in the show, that you can "re-code" in a more positive way; (for example, give a secret meaning to or a hidden identity) _____ _____
	TOTAL

Wynter Stereotype Metric Score		
14 to 21	★★★★	Binge-worthy!
8 to13	★★★	Get the popcorn.
2 to 8	★★	Not bad.
1	★	Last resort.
0 or less		Pass the remote

REFERENCES

Aarts, H., Chartrand, T. L., Custers, R., Danner, U., Dik, G., Jefferis, V. E., & Cheng, C. M. (2005). Social Stereotypes and Automatic Goal Pursuit. *Social Cognition*, 23(6), 465-490. doi:10.1521/soco.2005.23.6.465.

AdWeek Staff. (2009, August 13). Wal-Mart stays True with apparel line. *AdWeek*. Retrieved October 13, 2013, from http://www.adweek.com /news/advertising-branding/walmart-stays-true-apparel-line-106290.

Andreeve, N. (2016, May 15). 'The Carmichael Show' Renewed For Season 3 By NBC. Retrieved June 01, 2016, from http://deadline.com/2016/05/the-carmichael-show-renewed-season-3-nbc-1201756781/.

Back to School. [Television series episode]. (2009, January 25). In *True Jackson VP*. Los Angeles, CA: Nickelodeon.

Bandura, A., Barbaranelli, C., Caprara, G. V., & Pastorelli, C. (2001). Self-Efficacy Beliefs as Shapers of Children's Aspirations and Career Trajectories. *Child Development*, 72(1), 187-206. doi:10.1111/1467-8624.00273.

Being Human [Television series]. (2011, January 17). Los Angeles, CA: Syfy Channel.

Blaine, B. E. (2007). *Understanding the psychology of diversity*. Los Angeles: SAGE.

Braxton, G. (2012, October 13). Not quite primetime for black families on network shows. *Los Angeles Times*.

Budd, M., & Steinman, C. (1992, July). White racism and The Cosby Show. *Jump Cut: A Review of Contemporary Media,* 5-12.

Campbell, M. C., & Mohr, G. S. (2011). Seeing Is Eating: How and When Activation of a Negative Stereotype Increases Stereotype-Conducive Behavior. *Journal of Consumer Research*, 38(3), 431-444. doi:10.1086/659754.

Change of Plans. [Television series episode]. (2012, November 11). In *NFL Rush Zone Season of the Guardians*. Los Angeles, CA: NickToons.

Conklin, T. A., & Hartman, N. S. (2013). Appreciative Inquiry and Autonomy-Supportive Classes in Business Education: A Semi-longitudinal Study of AI in the Classroom. *Journal of Experiential Education,* 37(3), 285-309. doi:10.1177/1053825913514732.

Dead Like Me. [Television series]. (2003, June 27). Los Angeles, CA: Showtime Network.

Department of Labor (DOL), Bureau of Labor Statistics. (2007). *Consumer expenditures in 2005*. Washington, DC: U.S. Dept. of Labor, Bureau of Labor Statistics.

Dyer, R. (1999). Stereotyping. In *College Reader on Lesbians and Gays in Media, Society and Politics* (pp. 297-300). New York, NY: Columbia University Press.

Faber, R. J., McLeod, J. M., & Brown, J. D. (1979). Coming of age in the global Village. In E. Wartella (Ed.), *Children Communicating* (pp. 215-249). Beverly Hills, CA: Sage.

Flint, J. (2012, March 9) Kids are watching more television, not less, report says. *Los Angeles Times*.

Flint, J. (2012, September 5). NFL and NickToons hope to score touchdown with cartoon. *Los Angeles Times*.

Flirting with Fame. [Television series episode]. (2009, November 21). In *True Jackson VP*. Los Angeles, CA: Nickelodeon.

Gender Divide Reaching Male vs. Female Millennials. (2012, September 14). Nielsen Newswire.

Gerbner, G., Gross, L., Signorielli, N., & Morgan, M. (1980). Aging with Television: Images on Television Drama and Conceptions of Social Reality. Journal of Communication, 30(1), 37-47. doi:10.1111/j.1460-2466.1980.tb01766.x.

Gerbner, G. (1980). Children and Power on Television: The Other Side of the Picture. In G. Gerbner, C. Ross, & E. Ziegler (Eds.), *Child Abuse: An Analysis and Agenda for Action*. New York, NY: Oxford University Press.

The Ghost and Mrs. Muir [Motion picture]. (1947). United States: Twentieth Century Fox.

The Ghost and Mrs. Muir [Television series]. (1968, September 21). Los Angeles, CA: ABC Television.

Gibbs, J. T. (1988). *Young, black, and male in America: An endangered species*. Dover, MA: Auburn House Pub.

Juenger, T. (2013). Why the Internet Won't Kill TV (Rep.). New York, NY: Sanford C. Bernstein.

Lieberman, D. (2011, November 29) Nickelodeon's Ratings Decline Is No "Blip"; Is Viacom Or Nielsen To Blame? Retrieved June 01, 2016, from http://deadline.com/2011/11/nickelodeons-ratings-decline-is-no-blip-is-viacom-or-nielsen-to-blame-199006/.

Little Buddies. [Television series episode]. (2010, January 30). In *True Jackson VP*. Los Angeles, CA: Nickelodeon.

Media Violence. (2001). In *Pediatrics*. Elk Grove Village, IL: Committee on Public Education.

Molloy, T. (2012, March 12). Disney knocks Nick from top ratings perch. Retrieved April 4, 2014, from *Thewrap.com*.

My Boss Ate My Homework. [Television series episode]. (2010, January 16). In *True Jackson VP*. Los Angeles, CA: Nickelodeon.

Nielsen. (2011, March 30). State of the Media: U.S. TV Trends by Ethnicity (Rep.). Nielsen Reports. doi:http://www.nielsen.com/us/en/insights/reports/2011/tv-trends-by-ethnicity.html.

Nielsen Media Research. (2012). African American Consumers: Still Vital, Still Growing (Rep.). Retrieved November 8, 2013. From Nielsen.com website: http://www.nielsen.com/content/dam/corporate/us/en/microsites/publicaffairs/StateOfTheAfricanAmericanConsumer2012.pdf.

Nielsen.com (2013, October 1) Solutions: Segmentation Strategy. Retrieved June 01, 2014, from http://www.nielsen.com/us/en/solutions/segmentation.html

Nielsen.com. (2013, September 19) African-American Consumers Are More Relevant Than Ever. Retrieved November 8, 2013, from http://www.nielsen.com/us/en/insights/news/2013/african-american-consumers-are-more-relevant-than-ever.html.

Peterson, G. W., & Peters, D. F. (1983). Adolescents' Construction of Social Reality: The Impact of Television and Peers. *Youth & Society*, 15(1), 67-85. doi:10.1177/0044118x83015001005.

Pilot. [Television series episode]. (2013, July 13). In *The Haunted Hathaways*. Los Angeles, CA: Nickelodeon.

Pilot. [Television series episode]. (1990). In *Moe's World*. Los Angeles, CA: ABC Television.

Pilot. [Television series episode]. (1994, October 15). In *My Brother and Me*. Los Angeles, CA: Nickelodeon.

Pilot. [Internet Television series episode]. (2010, Sept). In *NFL Rush Zone Guardians of the Core*. Los Angeles, CA: iTunes.

Poling, D. A., & Hupp, J. M. (2008). Death Sentences: A Content Analysis of Children's Death Literature. *The Journal of Genetic Psychology*, 169(2), 165-176. doi:10.3200/gntp.169.2.165-176.

Poussaint, A. (2008). Why Is TV So Segregated? Retrieved October 14, 2013, from http://fun.familyeducation.com/television/african-americans/35259.html.

Radsken, J. (2013, July 13). Ghosts Busted: Nickelodeon's 'Hathaways' is so Bad, it's Scary. *McClatchy Tribune Business News*. Retrieved October 13, 2013.

Rhines, J. A. (1996). *Black film, white money*. New Brunswick, NJ: Rutgers University Press.

Rosenberg, H. (1991, 3 May). *Moe's World* Deserves a Network Shot. *Los Angeles Times*. Retrieved October 9, 2013.

Scott, G. L. (2011). *The role of media portrayals on the activation of stereotype threat: A study of African American test performance*. Charleston, SC: BiblioBazaar.

Screen Actors Guild. (2008). Affirmative Action and Diversity. *Casting Data Reports*. Retrieved August 31, 2013, from https://www.sagaftra.org/files/sag/documents/2007-2008_CastingDataReports.pdf.

Singh, G. K. (2010). *Child mortality in the United States, 1935-2007: Large racial and socioeconomic disparities have persisted over time*. Rockville, MD: U.S. Dept. of Health and Human Services, Health Resources and Services Administration.

Smythe, D. (2001). On the Audience Commodity and its Work. In M. G. Durham & D. Kellner (Eds.), Media and cultural studies: Keyworks. Malden, MA: Blackwell.

Spaced Out. Transparents. [Television series episode]. (2001, April 6). In *Fairly Odd Parents*. Los Angeles, CA: NickToons.

Srivastva, S., & Cooperrider, D. L. (1999). *Appreciative management and leadership: The power of positive thought and action in organizations*. Euclid, OH: Williams Custom Pub.

State Of The African-American Consumer. (2011). *Nielsen Media Research*. National Newspaper Publishers Association. Retrieved June 01, 2016, from http://www.nielsen.com/us/en/insights/reports/2011/state-of-the-african-american-consumer.html.

Steadman, J. (2005). *TV Audience Special Study: African-American Audience* (Rep.). Los Angeles, CA: Nielsen Media Research.

Stroman, C. A. (1984). The Socialization Influence of Television on Black Children. *Journal of Black Studies*, 15(1), 79-100. doi:10.1177/002193478401500108.

Sullivan, K. R., & Nickerson, N. (Writers). (1990). Moe's World [Television broadcast]. In Moe's World. Los Angeles, CA: ABC Television.

National Institutes of Health Clinical Center (NIHCC). (2006). Talking to Children about Death. Bethesda, MD.

The Secret gets out. [Television series episode]. (2014, September 20). In *Henry Danger*. Los Angeles, CA: Nickelodeon.

True Takes Iceland. [Television series episode]. (2009, January 25). In *True Jackson, VP*. Los Angeles, CA: Nickelodeon.

Van Boven, L., Campbell, M. C., & Gilovich, T. (2010). Stigmatizing Materialism: On Stereotypes and Impressions of Materialistic and Experiential Pursuits. *Personality and Social Psychology Bulletin*, 36(4), 551-563. doi:10.1177/0146167210362790.

In: Communicating Prejudice   ISBN: 978-1-53610-167-6
Editors: S. Camara and D. Drummond   © 2016 Nova Science Publishers, Inc.

Chapter 6

COMMUNICATING THROUGH PREJUDICE: AN INNOVATIVE CRITICAL-CULTURAL AUTOETHNOGRAPHY OF APPRECIATIVE RELATIONSHIPS

Mark P. Orbe[1], Robert Razzante[2]
and Victoria H. Orbe[3]
[1]Western Michigan University, Kalamazoo, MI, US
[2]Arizona State University, Tempe, AZ, US
[3]University of Michigan, East Lansing, MI, US

ABSTRACT

This co-authored book chapter utilizes autoethnographic data as a means to explore what co-cultural practices individuals use in response to prejudicial communication in a variety of contexts. Using a co-cultural theoretical framework, our thematic analysis of prejudgments based on race, gender, age, and/or sexuality reveals how particular co-cultural communication orientations – and the specific practices associated them – can work to transform interactions containing prejudice toward relationships that are defined by mutual understanding, respect, and self-efficacy. The chapter concludes with a discussion of theoretical, conceptual, and practical implications.

Fueled by human attitudes and supported by institutional systems (van Dijk, 1989), different forms of oppression have long been a constant existence in the U.S. (Hardiman & Jackson, 1997). Yet, over time, these harmful forms have become increasingly subtle, ambiguous, nebulous – and consequently difficult to manage (Dovidio et al., 2002; Sue et al., 2007). Considerable research exists that investigates the forms and consequences of, as well as individual responses to, discriminatory communication (for summary, see Camara & Orbe, 2010). This current study takes a novel approach to studying the topic, in that it explores how prejudice and difference can be an integral part of appreciative relationships (Hecht, 1998). Specifically, we draw from self-generated autoethnographic narratives that allow for in-depth analysis of how communicative practices can work through the prejudice toward an appreciative relationship. Within this context, we focus on instances of communicating prejudice – "inaccurate and/or negative beliefs that espouse or support the superiority of one cultural group" (Orbe & Harris, 2015, p. 10).

Our research is motivated by Hecht's (1998) call for research that values the "appreciation of difference" in relationships, including those which contain moments of, or sustained, prejudice. In particular, the study summarized in this chapter reflects three aspects of Hecht's implications for future research. First, by focusing on mutually satisfying relationships we assume a "positive or proactive approach toward understanding appreciation and how to create it" (p. 337). Second, our analysis does not "isolate racism from other 'isms' (p. 337); instead we examine communication contexts which are informed by prejudices based on age, gender, race, sexuality, and/or socioeconomic status. Third, and finally, we respond to the challenge of incorporating appreciation "in our theories and our methods" (p. 338) by utilizing co-cultural theory as a means to explore relationships where "difference was appreciated and valued" (p. 338).

EXTANT LITERATURE REVIEW: COMMUNICATIVE RESPONSES TO PREJUDICE

Much work on prejudice has been generated since Hecht's (1998) ground-breaking edited volume, *Communicating prejudice*. Scholarship, in and outside of the communication discipline, has examined the manifestation of various forms of cultural prejudice and discrimination across contexts. For instance, we have gained significant understanding of how prejudgments based on race (Sue et al., 2007; Utsey et al., 2000), age (e.g., Hajek & Giles, 2002), gender (Swim & Heyers, 1999; Woodricka & LaFrance, 2001), sexuality (e.g., Muraco, 2005), and disability (e.g., Braithwaite & Thompson, 2000; Ryan, Anas, & Gruneir, 2006) are reflected in everyday interactions. According to Camara and Orbe (2010), the vast majority of this research has explored the communication of "isms" (Hecht, 1998) while very few examine the complex ways that people respond to such discourse.

When faced with acts of prejudice, individuals respond in different ways based on a myriad of factors (Swim, Cohen & Heyers, 1998). According to Major, Quinton, and McCoy (2002), some of these strategic responses involve non-confrontational coping strategies that reflect cognitive avoidance, blunting, denial or mental disengagement (Ruggiero, Taylor & Lydon, 1997). This appears to be the case especially when existing power dynamics make more assertive and direct alternatives dangerous to one's livelihood (Stanback & Pearce, 1981). A smaller, but growing number of studies report that individuals also employ direct confrontation, reporting to authorities, and mediation (Camara & Orbe, 2010; Stokoe & Edwards, 2007). But the question remains unexplored: How do these responses impact the nature of relationships? Decisions on how to respond to prejudice depend largely on a number of factors including situational context and the existence of social support (Miller & Kaiser, 2001). Co-cultural theory (Camara, Katznelson, Hildebrandt-Sterling, & Parker, 2012) is a communication framework that provides significant insight into the ways that individuals communicate when situated in traditionally marginalized social locations. Consequently, we provide an in-depth description of the theory next.

Co-Cultural Theory

According to Orbe and colleagues (Orbe, 1998; Orbe & Spellers, 2005; Orbe & Roberts, 2012), co-cultural theory promotes increased understanding of how persons who are traditionally marginalized in dominant societal structures communicate in their everyday lives. Grounded in the power of exploring lived experiences through phenomenology (Husserl, 1964; Lanigan, 1988), co-cultural theory emerged from the experiences of a variety of co-cultural groups, including members of racial and ethnic groups, women, persons with disabilities, gays/lesbians/bisexuals, and those with a lower socioeconomic status (Orbe, 1998). Some scholars (e.g., Todd-Mancillas, 2000) have argued that given power dynamics exist on multiple fronts, consequently, co-cultural theory can apply both to traditionally marginalized group members as well as individuals whose life experiences reflect situational subordinate status (e.g., lower level employees).

The initial work in co-cultural theory centered on the emergence of a co-cultural communication model; the focus was on specific practices that individuals from traditionally marginalized groups enact during their interactions with dominant group members (Orbe & Roberts, 2012). Once these communicative practices were established (Orbe, 1996), the focal point shifted to understanding how people came to select certain practices over others (Orbe & Spellers, 2005) – with a particular focus on six interrelated factors that influenced co-cultural strategic choices. Each of these factors, in italics below, is central to the core idea of co-cultural theory.

> Situated within a particular *field of experience* that governs their perceptions of the *costs and rewards* associated with, as well as their *capability* to engage in, various communicative practices, co-cultural group members will adopt certain communication orientations--based on their *preferred outcomes* and *communication approaches*--to fit the circumstances of a specific *situation*. (Orbe, 1998, p. 129)

Of particular interest to this study is communication orientation, a concept that refers to a specific stance that is assumed as co-cultural group members interact with others. Communication orientation, as described by Orbe (1998), is primarily influenced by two components: communication approach and preferred outcome. Conceptualized as the communication stance with which one interacts with dominant group members, communication approach can be nonassertive (prioritizing other's needs and desires above one's own), assertive (balancing attention to both self and other's needs), or aggressive (putting one's needs and desires above others). Preferred outcome centers on the co-cultural group members' consideration of the eventual impact of their communication with others. Three options exist: assimilation (working to blend in with dominant culture), accommodation (working within dominant structures toward change), and separation (creating and maintaining distance between self and dominant group members). Focusing on the nine co-cultural communication orientations, and the various co-cultural practices associated with each (summarized in Table 1), this study aims to answer the following research question:

RQ1: Utilizing the concepts of co-cultural theory, how do relational partners use strategies to overcome prejudice and work toward mutual understanding, respect, and self-efficacy?

Table 1. Summary of Co-Cultural Practices Associated with each Orientation

Examples of Practices	Brief Description
Nonassertive Assimilation	
Emphasizing commonalities	Focusing on human similarities while downplaying or ignoring co-cultural differences
Developing positive face	Assuming a gracious communicator stance where one is more considerate, polite, and attentive to dominant group members
Censoring self	Remaining silent when comments from dominant group members are inappropriate, indirectly insulting, or highly offensive
Averting controversy	Averting communication away from controversial or potentially dangerous subject areas
Assertive Assimilation	
Extensive preparation	Engaging in an extensive amount of detailed (mental/concrete) groundwork prior to interactions with dominant group members
Overcompensating	Conscious attempts—consistently enacted in response to a pervasive fear of discrimination—to become a "superstar"
Manipulating stereotypes	Conforming to commonly accepted beliefs about group members as a strategic means to exploit them for personal gain
Bargaining	Striking a covert or overt arrangement with dominant group members where both parties agree to ignore co-cultural differences
Aggressive Assimilation	
Dissociating	Making a concerted effort to elude any connection with behaviors typically associated with one's co-cultural group
Mirroring	Adopting dominant group codes in attempt to make one's co-cultural identity more (or totally) invisible
Strategic distancing	Avoiding any association with other co-cultural group members in attempts to be perceived as a distinct individual
Ridiculing self	Invoking or participating in discourse, either passively or actively, that is demeaning to co-cultural group members
Nonassertive Accommodation	
Increasing visibility	Covertly, yet strategically, maintaining a co-cultural presence within dominant structures
Dispelling stereotypes	Myths of generalized group characteristics and behaviors are countered through the process of just being one's self
Assertive Accommodation	
Communicating self*	Interacting with dominant group members in an authentic, open, and genuine manner; used by those with strong self-concepts
Intragroup networking	Identifying and working with other co-cultural group members who share common philosophies, convictions, goals
Utilizing liaisons	Identifying specific dominant group members who can be trusted for support, guidance, and assistance
Educating others	Taking the role of teacher in co-cultural interactions; enlightening dominant group members of co-cultural norms, values, etc.
Aggressive Accommodation	
Confronting	Using the necessary aggressive methods, including ones that seemingly violate the "rights" of others, to assert one's voice
Gaining advantage	Inserting references to co-cultural oppression as a means to provoke dominant group reactions and gain advantage
Nonassertive Separation	
Avoiding	Maintaining a distance from dominant group members; refraining from activities and/or locations where interaction is likely
Maintaining barriers	Imposing, through the use of verbal and nonverbal cues, a psychological distance from dominant group members
Assertive Separation	
Exemplifying strength	Promoting the recognition of co-cultural group strengths, past accomplishments, and contributions to society
Embracing stereotypes	Applying a negotiated reading to dominant group perceptions and merging them into a positive co-cultural self-concept
Aggressive Separation	
Attacking	Inflicting psychological pain through personal attacks on dominant group members' self-concept
Sabotaging others	Undermining the ability of dominant group members to take full advantage of their privilege inherent in dominant structures

* Note: These communicative practices are examples of tactics enacted to promote each orientation. It is important to recognize that some tactics can be used innovatively to promote more than one communication orientation. For example, communicating self, intragroup networking, and educating others can also work together toward an assertive separation communication orientation.

METHODOLOGICAL FRAMEWORK

Autoethnograpy

This research project builds upon, and simultaneously extends critical-cultural autoethnography as articulated by Boylorn and Orbe (2012). In particular, we use autoethnographic data to collectively explore interpersonal and/or intercultural manifestations of communicative episodes that featured moments of, or sustained, prejudice. This decision to focus on autoethnographic narratives is in direct response to criticisms that quantitative data, like that collected via surveys, fail to capture the interactional subtleties of any given situation (Speer & Potter, 2000).

According to Denzin (1997), autoethnography involves the "turning of the ethnographic gaze inward on the self (auto), while maintaining the outward gaze of ethnography, looking at the larger context wherein self experiences occur" (p. 227). Such an approach encourages a multidimensional exploration of a phenomenon (Mumby, 1993), and when done within a diverse research team, can provide multiple opportunities to engage self- and other-generated perceptions of the same lived experience. Autoethnography has been the method of choice for a number of communication inquiries including those exploring interpersonal and intercultural relationships across a variety of contexts (e.g., Allen, Orbe, & Olivas, 1999; Bochner, Ellis, & Tillmann-Healy, 1996; Geist & Gates, 1996). In this particular project, we drew from existing research that featured the synergistic energies of collective autoethnographies (e.g., Orbe, Groscurth, Jeffries, & Prater, 2007; Orbe, Smith, Groscurth, & Crawley, 2010). Consulting these pieces, we found that such a collective autoethnographic approach was especially fitting for our scholarly inquiry, given our interest in examining the interactions between self and others in contexts where a myriad of cultural identity markers were negotiated in various ways. In short, this methodological framework allowed us to engage in autoethnographic explorations (Allen et al., 1999) where narratives of self (Communication Studies 298, 1997) were engaged through personal and collaborative reflections.

Process of Discovery

After receiving the call for proposal for the edited book project, Mark approached two graduate students at different universities, Victoria and Rob, to collaborate on a project. While Victoria and Rob had never met prior to the project, both were interested in exploring issues of culture, power, and communication. Via email, we began our project by self-generating 30 different case scenarios that contained negotiations of prejudice. In particular, each of the co-authors were asked to:

> Think of 10 past and/or current interactions/relationships that you perceive as involving prejudice. In other words, you felt prejudged by some aspect(s) of your cultural identity (e.g., age, gender, race/ethnicity, socioeconomic status, spirituality, etc.). These can be interactions with family members, friends, neighbors, co-workers, strangers, etc.

Within each description, we used a number of prompts that guided autoethnographic descriptions with significant depth: (A) What is/was the relationship that you are describing? Who is the person to you?; (B) How did/do you feel prejudged by the other person?; Did/do you feel discriminated against (was/is the person's prejudice acted upon)?; (C) How did/do you respond to the person's prejudice?; and (D) How, if at all, did your relationship develop/change over time? Specific attention was paid to generating case scenarios that reflected a wide variety of cultural identity markers, relationships, and situational contexts. This initial process resulted in 21 pages of single-spaced autoethnographic descriptions of personal encounters with prejudice. The 30 case scenarios, as summarized in Tables 2, 3, and 4, reflected a substantial range of bases and sources of prejudgment, as well as situational context. Eleven case studies featured appreciative relationships.

Table 2. Basis of Prejudgment*

	All Case Scenarios (N = 30)	Appreciative Case Scenarios (N = 11)
Race	N = 15 (50%)	N = 4 (36%)
Gender	N = 7 (23%)	N = 3 (27%)
Age	N = 7 (23%)	N = 3 (27%)
Class	N = 5 (16%)	N = 1 (9%)
Sexuality	N = 4 (13%)	N = 1 (9%)
Spirituality	N = 3 (10%)	N = 1 (9%)
Nationality	N = 3 (10%)	N = 0 (0%)
Abilities	N = 1 (3%)	N = 0 (0%)
Political Affiliation	N = 1 (3%)	N = 0 (0%)

* Several case scenarios involved more than one basis of prejudice (e.g., both race and class were salient issues).

Table 3. Source of Prejudgment

	All Case Scenarios N = 30	Appreciative Case Scenarios N = 11
Close Friend/Significant Other	N = 7 (23%)	N = 3 (27%)
Stranger	N = 7 (23%)	N = 3 (27%)
Professor/Administrator	N = 4 (13%)	N = 0 (0%)
Co-worker/Classmate	N = 4 (13%)	N = 2 (18%)
Acquaintance	N = 3 (10%)	N = 1 (9%)
Supervisor	N = 2 (6%)	N = 1 (9%)
Student/Subordinate	N = 2 (6%)	N = 1 (9%)
Family Member	N = 1 (3%)	N = 0 (0%)

Table 4. Situational Context

	All Case Scenarios N = 30	Appreciative Case Scenarios N = 11
School	N = 11 (36%)	N = 4 (36%)
Public	N = 8 (26%)	N = 3 (27%)
Professional Conference	N = 3 (10%)	N = 3 (27%)
Home/Private	N = 3 (10%)	N = 0 (0%)
Work	N = 2 (6%)	N = 0 (0%)
Church	N = 2 (6%)	N = 1 (9%)
On-line	N = 1 (3%)	N = 0 (0%)

Once the initial autoethnographic case scenarios were generated, we each individually read through the data and made notes regarding four elements. First, each of us determined the source(s) of prejudgment, identifying which aspect of identity was at the core in terms of the prejudgment? (see summary in Table 2). Second, using the descriptive list generated by Orbe and Roberts (2012), each co-author identified the: (a) co-cultural practices, (b) co-cultural communication orientations, and (c) co-cultural factors contained in each case scenario. This process was enacted so that each person could become familiar with all of the case scenarios and offer their perceptions. All perceptions were compiled into tables that differentiated each person's coding and then we met to discuss the similarities and differences. Specifically, we focused on the 11 case scenarios that reflected instances of prejudice within contexts where appreciative relationships existed or emerged. This represented an important aspect of our collective autoethnography because we were able to more fully discuss the perceptions of our own lived experiences in the context of two external interpretations. At times, perceptions were consistent across the board; however, a number of case scenarios generated considerable discussions regarding the narratives as lived, as recorded, and as ultimately understood in a larger context. These discussions were useful – not to establish any sort of intercoder reliability but – to provide a self-reflexive process whereby each co-author could gain additional perspectives of their interpretation of the lived experience. Field notes were recorded in writing from this meeting and used to further inform the ultimate writing of each of our autoethnographic reflections. Our next section highlights our collective narratives, organized around three thematic insights.

THEMATIC-ANALYTIC FINDINGS: CO-CULTURAL RESPONSES TO PREJUDICE

Contemplating, authoring, analyzing, and constantly reflecting on the 30 case scenarios of communicating prejudice provided a powerful means to understand how prejudice impacts relationships with strangers, peers, subordinates, supervisors, as well as family and friends. Almost two-thirds of the case scenarios reflected instances where prejudice seemed to doom the relationship. Within in this section, we utilize eleven of our individual autoethnographic narratives to illustrate three thematic points of insight that help to understand how prejudice is negotiated within appreciative relationships. Specifically, we illustrate: (1) field of experience as solid foundation, (2) the importance of accommodation as preferred outcome, and (3) situational contextualization of nonassertiveness and assertiveness.

Field of Experience as Solid Foundation

Our autoethnographic analysis demonstrated how all six co-cultural factors impacted how our responses to prejudgments manifested in various aspects of our lives. However, field of experience emerged as especially important in the eleven case scenarios that reflected descriptions of appreciative relationships. Our first autoethnographic narrative, authored by Victoria, demonstrates the important role that field of experience played in an interaction with a childhood friend regarding her sexual identity.

* * *

Coming out and being one of the only "out" queer people in your high school comes with a lot of judgment, support and curiosity. As one of the first or only gay person a lot of my friends have known I was open to a lot of the questions. "Farrah" is a childhood friend, she is Lebanese...she has an outgoing personality and has no filter in her interactions with others. That's something I enjoyed about her company, her "realness." At the end of my junior year in high school I started coming to terms with my sexuality and coming out to close friends bit by bit. All reactions had been positive thus far and nothing but love and support had been voiced, but there was a reoccurring element of "shock."

Farrah and I were going out to breakfast in town and I decided I would tell her of my same-sex sexuality. When I told her "I'm gay," she sort of choked on her food and immediately brought up my ex-boyfriend. Then quickly moved to "You're too pretty to be a lesbian, you are just so girly!"

I had to explain to her how sexuality evolves and how at a young age I felt I was supposed to follow gendered sexual scripts and date boys. I went on to say "Do you just think all lesbians are ugly, Farrah?" I spent most of the breakfast making her aware of basic principles of sexuality and gender identity, even showing her some examples of fem lesbians from Showtime's "The L Word" – explaining that lesbians can have a myriad of different "looks," some being "femmy" and others maybe "butchy" and everywhere in between. Farrah was very engaged and interested in what I was saying, but it was clear she had never at a conversation breaking this down before.

There was an endearing tone from Farrah's confusion and I did not feel offended. I was the only lesbian Farrah knew at the time and she had no other archetype, except of the stereotypical "butch" lesbian, to compare me to. Over the years Farrah has most certainly become more acquainted with my sexual identity and her nativity has not wedged itself in our friendship. I do not hangout with Farrah as much in the most recent years because we go to different universities across the state. Yet, in our most recent encounter she revealed to me that "I always thought you would just go back to guys." If any stranger or peer would judge me by their pre-conceived notions on what a lesbian should look like or that this whole thing was a "phase," I would be deeply offended and run through a laundry list of how/why they are wrong. Since Farrah is a childhood friend I still decide to let it slide and not take her ignorance personally.

* * *

Within this narrative, Victoria's affinity towards an established relationship with Farrah framed her response to prejudice. Instead of being offended, she understood the preconceived stereotypes as a reflection of Farrah's uncensored honest ignorance about same-sex attracted individuals. Consequently, Victoria focused her response on educating others – specifically teaching her about "basic principles of sexuality and gender identity" and including some popular culture media images to help solidify her points. By being open and honest with Farrah, she also enacted co-cultural practices of communicating self and dispelling stereotypes. Combining nonassertive and assertive accommodation orientations, Victoria was able to maintain a relationship with her close friend while simultaneously expressing her sexuality.

In Victoria's example, the co-cultural factor of field of experience was most salient with her established relationship with Farrah, something that informed a keen awareness of her particular personality and communicative style. For the example provided by Mark below, the solid foundation of field of experience reflected an emerging professor-student relationship but also a conscious awareness of how faculty of color are perceived in predominately white universities.

* * *

Tom was an undergraduate student of mine who was interested in staying at our university to get his master's degree. He was extremely bright, articulate, and hardworking – someone who I would have loved to work with. I first met him when he was a student in my interracial communication class – one of the few students who reflected dominant group status (white, male, middle class, heterosexual, able-bodied, etc.). During this class, I got the impression that it was one of the first times where he was expected to acknowledge, and constantly manage, his privileged societal positions.

Tom visited me during office hours several times throughout the semester. We talked about class assignments and his interest in graduate school. Toward the end of the semester, he asked me if I would be open to working with (mentoring) him if he decided to stay for graduate school. When I responded affirmatively without hesitation, he seemed surprised. When I asked him about his reaction, he shared that he had talked with a few current graduate students (all of whom were white) who had told him that "Dr. Orbe only works with black students." While I disagreed with this perception, I immediately understood it given that I had a strong record of mentoring underrepresented students in our department.

My initial reaction was anger and frustration that some majority students had this (mis)perception of me. However, this was overwhelmed by Tom's comfort in sharing the information with me and his desire to seek out a mentoring relationship with someone who would clearly challenge him and some of his ideologies.

Tom and I worked collaboratively together during his master's program and we developed a close relationship, including both professional and personal connections, which remains intact today. During his graduate programs – including a PhD at another university – we navigated a number of situations which required an awareness and openness to cultural difference. However, we've both gotten to know a lot about one another that has allowed us to see one another in multidimensional ways that resist simplistic cultural stereotypes.

* * *

Within this professional workplace context, Mark enacted a nonassertive accommodation orientation as he negotiated the racial dynamics of a predominately white department. Although he felt some anger and frustration about being misunderstood by some white students and could have decided to adopt a separation preferred outcome, he opted to embrace the opportunity to work with Tom. By doing so, he enacted co-cultural practices – dispelling stereotypes and increasing visibility – that worked to alter existing perceptions of faculty of color in his school. He could have been more assertive and/or aggressive in his approach (e.g., educating others or confronting), but his past experiences had taught him that *showing* others is sometimes a more powerful tool than *telling* others. In this example, his response allowed for the development of a close relationship and demonstrated his commitment to working with students from all backgrounds.

The Importance of Accommodation as Preferred Outcome

Without exception, all of the self-generated narratives of communicating prejudice that involved appreciative relationships contained co-cultural practices that reflected the preferred outcome of accommodation. Responding in ways that solely worked toward assimilation and/or separation seemed to block the type of authentic communication that fostered appreciative relationships. Interestingly, as illustrated in Mark's narrative below, cases that involved strong relational ties often times reflected combinations of accommodation and assimilation.

* * *

"Jamal" was a fellow communication professor who I met at our annual national conference. An African American man about the same age as I, he was an officer in one of the association's groups dedicated to the study of African American communication. As someone who participated with this group for a several years, we were friendly with one another each year during the conference but never had any substantive conversations. We did, however, have several friends in common.

At the close of one conference meeting, Jamal asked what I was doing for dinner; shortly thereafter we decided to walk to a restaurant nearby and eat together. During dinner, in his role of association officer, Jamal asked me about my interests in running for an office. I responded by saying that I might be interested in the future, but that it wasn't something that I wanted to do before I got my publications off the ground. The conversation then moved to my interest/motivation, as a non-African American, in being a part of a group that studies African American communication issues. As Jamal raised this issue, I got the feeling that this was one of the reasons why he initiated the dinner in the first place. I explained that I was a bi-racial person who had been raised in a predominately Black and Puerto Rican neighborhood, and my scholarly interests reflected that set of lived experiences. His response was point-blank: "You can describe yourself as bi-racial, but I'm always going to see you as a white man." I was taken aback by his comment, and thought about invoking the importance of agency in self-definition; instead I allowed the conversation to flow to different topics without responding directly to his comment. I didn't think that I needed to persuade him to see me differently than I saw myself, but I did feel that he had prejudged me in terms of his own racialized categories.

Given the history, both in terms of society at large and this particular group, I felt like I could understand Jamal's concern about my involvement in the group. So, my response was not to confront his perceptions but to show him my commitment to the group and African American communication scholarship through my work (e.g., service to the group, publishing, mentoring, etc.). I was confident that his perception of me would change by simply getting to know me, as me. As such, this one interaction didn't define our relationship; instead it brought to the surface an issue that existed implicitly.

Over the years, Jamal and I developed a relationship that went beyond that of professional colleagues. We became friends who looked forward to hanging out during our annual meeting and keeping in touch the rest of the year. The more that we got to know one another, the more he was able to see my interest as genuine and invested. In many ways, and in several instances, he became one of my biggest supporters in the academy.

* * *

In this example, Mark articulates a keen awareness of a historical distrust of non-African Americans in this particular organization (field of experience). Accordingly, he strategically enacted practices associated with nonassertive accommodation – namely increasing visibility and dispelling stereotypes – in his interactions with Jamal. While these were his intentions, his co-authors helped him to question if he wasn't in fact, averting controversy and practicing overcompensation. Reflectively, he questions his behaviors and wonders how his actions were perceived by Jamal and others in the organization: Was he simply being himself, or was he working extra hard to prove that he was not like other non-African Americans? This leads to the possibility that his behaviors might be perceived by others as more assimilation rather than accommodation. In either case, his response to prejudgments based on race fostered a long-time meaningful relationship.

Just as Mark was able to enact nonassertive accommodation with Jamal in the example above, Rob's example below shares another instance of how one can practice nonassertive accommodation in order to build healthy, authentic relationships. Rob's example highlights prejudgments based on gender (and possibly age) and demonstrates how communicating one's honest feelings between supervisor and supervisee can ultimately bring both parties closer together.

* * *

"Zoe" and "Caitlin" are the director and assistant director of a student affairs office at my undergraduate university. I had been working closely with Zoe and Caitlin for about a year as one of two student coordinators that works year round in the office. The other student coordinator, Ryan, was also a white male who was a year older than me. Of the four of us, I felt that my communication style was the most androgynous/feminine. Whenever Zoe and

Caitlin needed to make a decision, I sometimes felt like my perspective went unnoticed.

At the end of my second year, Ryan and I graduated so it was time for Zoe and Caitlin to hire two new student coordinators. During a morning meeting, Zoe encouraged more females to apply for the positions because she felt women who are more qualified than men usually decide not to apply for higher positions (That year 74% of our leaders were female). In the next couple of days, Zoe, Caitlin, Ryan and I interviewed each candidate for the new coordinator positions and I regret having to miss the last interview to go meet up with my first-year students. I left my final interview feeling like we all agreed on the two people to hire, one male and one female; both very qualified for the position. The interview I missed happened to be a female that ultimately was hired as a student coordinator. Zoe and Caitlin made their decision right after the interview without me in the room, and they happened to decide on two females. Ryan and I both agreed that the male advocated for was the more qualified individual for the position. However, the bottom line is that Zoe and Caitlin thought otherwise. Once again, I felt like my opinion didn't matter.

I found out about the student coordinator hirings from Ryan, and I immediately called Caitlin to ask her why she didn't run the two coordinators by me before she finalized the decision. She told me that she and Zoe felt that they hired the two people they were looking for. After the phone call I tried to take a nap to sleep my frustration away but I wasn't able to. I then tried to read my frustration away, but that didn't work either. I finally decided to write a letter to Caitlin about why I disagreed with her choice, but I never had any intention of actually sending it. That night at the last session of the day, I asked to speak with Caitlin about what had transpired, and in a personal yet professional way I told her how I felt about not being included in the final decision. Empathetically, she understood where I was coming from and told me her reasoning behind her choice.

After our talk, I feel Caitlin realized how I felt about my opinions being overlooked. She pointed out that there was nothing we could do about the decision that was already made, but she also asked how we could improve the hiring process going forward. I felt that she made an effort to include my thoughts and opinions moving into the next year. I also let Zoe know how I felt, and she agreed that she might have rushed a decision without hearing all points of view. I feel my relationships with Zoe and Caitlin reached a deeper personal level after articulating how we all felt.

* * *

This example demonstrates how Rob utilized an assertive accommodation orientation in order maintain a healthy work relationship with Caitlin and Zoe. Considering the space and time of the decision, Rob could have practiced nonassertive separation by using the co-cultural responses of avoiding or maintaining barrier to conceal how he felt. Instead, he considered the perceived costs and rewards of his communication approach and decided to communicate self by asking to meet with Caitlin and Zoe to share how he felt. By interacting in an open and genuine manner, both sides grew together in better understanding of how to make communal decisions in the future.

Situational Contextualization: Nonassertiveness and/or Assertiveness

Consistent with the tenets of co-cultural theory (Orbe, 1998), a hyperconsciousness for strategic practices exists when individuals feel the tensions of ingroup/outgroup positioning. A final thematic insight that emerged from the autoethnographic data related to the importance of situational context in discerning a particular communication approach. As demonstrated with the two examples in this final section, both nonassertive and assertive approaches appeared most conducive to the development and maintenance of appreciative relationships. The first case scenario illustrating this point of thematic insight was generated by Rob.

* * *

"Tammi" was a black middle age woman who I met at a diversity training conference. The first night of the conference I decided to sit next to Tammi, two other black women, and one white woman. I didn't know anyone at the table so I naturally felt a little uncomfortable.

During the first night, I tried breaking the ice so I asked one of the ladies at the table if she was a student at a nearby college. She corrected me and said that she actually worked at the college as a fulltime employee. I told her I was sorry because I thought she was a student because of how young she looked. Tammi overheard my reasoning and she quickly questioned me why I didn't think she was young enough to be a student herself. Everyone busted into laughter and I turned beet red for making prejudgments of my own (it didn't help that this was at a diversity conference of all places). I felt I was being attacked for my comment which I regretted making.

On the second day of the conference, I purposefully sat next to Tammi so I could right my wrong from the day before. During one of the breaks I asked Tammi what kind of music she listened to, but she thought her music was too "old" for me. Before she told me her favorite artists, she asked me who some of my favorite artists were. I told her that my top three artists/bands were Sam Cooke, Al Green, and The Beatles. She quickly responded by asking if I was, "an old black man stuck in white man's body." I thought that was hilarious, and she went on to share some of her favorite artists that she thought I would like.

As the conference went along, Tammi and I grew closer together. I began to understand her humor and I realized she would never let me live down that comment I made on the first night. However, at the end of the conference she told me I was like a son that she never had. That comment alone made my week.

* * *

This scenario provides an example of how Rob emphasized commonalities between Tammi and himself in order to develop a better understanding of each other across differences based on race and age. After the first night of the conference, Rob could have practiced nonassertive assimilation by censoring his comments in order to avert any more controversy. He also could have practiced nonassertive separation by avoiding any activities or locations where interaction was likely to occur. Instead, the situational context of the conference and his field of experience influenced him to continue to develop a positive relationship through sharing common interests in music (emphasizing commonalties). Next, Victoria provides another example of how situational context informs a balance of co-cultural communication orientations practice in order to build an authentic relationship.

* * *

"Tayo" is a male college friend from Nigeria who I have bonded with over sports. I was captain of an Intramural (IM) Co-Ed soccer team and asked if he would be interested in playing and he was enthusiastic about the league. We had a fun season but were not very victorious; another male player from Africa scored all but one of our goals. One night at a bar after a game Tayo and I were talking about our performances, other teams and IM rules. One of the co-ed league rules revolving gender was that goals scored by women are worth two points versus one point for goals scored by men.

I expressed my disapproval of this logic, how it was a sexist microaggression often found in sporting institutions. Tayo responded saying that the rule was necessary to make it fair, just like in tennis matches. He claims it's proven that women have inferior physical skill sets, and body make-up, compared to men.

I interjected saying that we have been conditioned to believe this and I didn't feel supported as a woman because of the rule. Tayo joked saying I thought "girls" would be happy about that. Here Tayo made the assumption that I enjoy or "appreciate" this covert act of sexism and take it as a "privilege." I told him obviously I don't care about the rule that much since I still take part in the league, but it is something that has bothered me.

This was one of the first incidents that my feminist identity was salient in my friendship with Tayo. Our friendship has flourished and we still often play sports together. Although I may have ruffled his perceived "truth" of women and men in sports, I don't think the conversation made him an objector of the rule or swayed him on women's sporting competence.

* * *

Victoria's autoethnographic case scenario with Tayo reflects a classic example of two friends who ultimately "agree to disagree" about an issue. In this particular interaction, Victoria engages in educating others by explaining her perception of – and disagreement with – rules based on gender stereotypes (communicating self). Her friend, Tayo, seemingly refuses to accept her perspective and maintains his gendered perceptions of female athletes. Despite this difference, the friendship continues to flourish. Through our co-cultural analysis, we can understand how Victoria has enacted bargaining whereby she and Tayo create an unspoken rule to ignore their competing views on the issue and focus on the other enjoyable aspects of their friendship. This case scenario demonstrates the reality that appreciative relationships typically involve the negotiation of difference on some level.

SUMMARY AND CONCLUSION

Responding to Hecht's (1998) call for more research on the positive aspects of relational difference, this research study uses autoethnographic data to explore how individuals negotiate prejudice in appreciative relationships. Through collective critical autoethnography (Boylorn & Orbe, 2014), we engaged in a self-reflective process through which we were able to understand how prejudgments based on race, gender, age, and sexuality could enhance – and not necessarily deter – relational development. Co-cultural theory (Orbe & Roberts, 2012) served as a productive theoretical framework for our analysis. In particular, it prompted three important findings regarding the negotiation of cultural difference, in the form of prejudice, that exists in various stages of relationship development.

First, field of experience serves as an important foundation and helps to situate prejudicial communication within larger contexts. As demonstrated within our analysis, drawing from one's complex set of lived experiences and the particular interactions of a specific relationship inform how individuals interpret and respond to being prejudged. Accordingly, instances of prejudice steeped within cultural difference are negotiated differently within established relationships than with strangers or acquaintances. Second, the co-cultural preferred outcome of accommodation is most associated with the development of appreciative relationships. The vast majority of our autoethnographic narratives of prejudice were *not* a part of appreciative relationships; instead the prejudgments seemed to doom the development of any meaningful interaction. In these scenarios, we enacted co-cultural practices that were associated with the preferred outcomes of assimilation and separation. These responses did not permit for any sort of authentic communication. However, accommodation-based practices promoted the type of honest and open interactions whereby relationships could productively negotiate the prejudice of difference. Our third, and final, conclusion is that both nonassertive and assertive communication approaches are instrumental in creating and sustaining appreciative relationships. Earlier conceptualizations of co-cultural theory (Orbe, 1998) emphasized that no one communication orientation is ideal; strategic responses must reflect a negotiation of various factors. Our self-study demonstrates how several different co-cultural factors (e.g., situational context, field of experience, preferred outcome) lead to practices that reflect different communication approaches. For instance, negotiating relational prejudice productively involved both nonassertive (e.g., increasing visibility) and assertive accommodation (e.g., communicating self, educating others) orientations.

The study makes significant contributions to how cultural difference, in the form of prejudice, can be negotiated in positive, mutually satisfying relationships. As such, it makes valuable contributions to the study of communicating prejudice (Hecht, 1998) and the utility of co-cultural theory (Orbe & Roberts, 2012) in research that explores the inextricable relationship between culture, power, and communication. Additional research is warranted to continue this line of inquiry. First, we call for scholars to embrace the intercultural dialectics of similarities↔differences and privilege↔disadvantage (Martin & Nakayama, 1999) in their examinations of relational communication. A dialectical framework provides insight into the ways that opposing poles exist and require constant attention; it advocates for a "both/and" rather than an "either/or" approach. In terms of appreciative relationships, this requires scholars to explore how individuals negotiate ways in which they are *both* similar and different, as well as how they *both* experience various forms of cultural privilege and disadvantage. Second, we urge intercultural communication researchers to draw from other theoretical frameworks to deepen our understanding of appreciative relationships. For instance, even within our analysis summarized in this chapter, we saw direct applications of communication theory of identity (Hecht, Warren, Jung & Krieger, 2005) that could add to our analysis in terms of how personal identities are enacted within various relational contexts. This is one of many theories that could be applied to this area of research. In closing, our innovative cultural autoethnography provides an excellent foundation for future studies that look to examine how individuals negotiate multiple aspects of themselves in relational contexts with others who reflect a similar set of complex identity markers.

REFERENCES

Allen, B. J., Orbe, M., & Olivas, M. R. (1999). The complexity of our tears: Dis/enchantment and (in)difference in the academy. *Communication Theory, 9*(4), 402-429.

Bochner, A. P., Ellis, C., & Tillmann-Healy, L. M. (1996). Relationship as stories. In S. Duck (Ed.), *Handbook of personal relationships* (pp. 307-324). Sussex, UK: John Wiley.

Boylorn, R. M., & Orbe, M. (Eds.) (2014). *Critical autoethnography: Intersecting cultural identities in everyday life.* Walnut, CA: Left Coast Press.

Braithwaite, D. O., & Thompson, T. L. (Eds.) (2000). *Handbook of communication and people with disabilities: Research and application.* Mahwah, NJ: Lawrence Erlbaum Associates.

Camara, S. K., Katznelson, A., Hildebrandt-Sterling, J., & Parker, T. (2012). Heterosexism in context: Qualitative interaction effects of co-cultural responses. *Howard Journal of Communications, 23*(4), 312-331.

Camara, S. K., & Orbe, M. (2010). Analyzing strategic responses to discriminatory acts: A co-cultural communicative investigation. *Journal of International and Intercultural Communication, 3(2)*, 83-113.

Communication Studies 298 (1997). Fragments of self at the postmodern bar. *Journal of Contemporary Ethnography, 26*, 251-292.

Denzin, N. K. (1997). *Interpretive ethnography: Ethnographic practices for the 21st century.* Thousand Oaks, CA: Sage.

Geist, P., & Gates, L. (1996). The poetics and politics of re-covering identities in health communication. *Communication Studies, 47*, 218-228.

Dovidio, J. F., Gaertner, S. L., Kawakami, K., & Hodson, G. (2002). Why can't we all just get along? Interpersonal biases and interracial distrust. *Cultural Diversity and Ethnic Minority Psychology, 8*, 88-102.

Hajek, C., & Giles, H. (2002). The old man out: An intergroup analysis of intergenerational communication among gay men. *Journal of Communication, 52*(4), 698-714.

Hardiman, R., & Jackson, B. (1997). Conceptual foundations for social justice courses. In M. Adams, L. A. Bell, P. Griffin (Eds.), *Teaching for diversity and social justice* (pp. 16-29). New York: Routledge.

Hecht, M. L. (Ed.) (1998). *Communicating prejudice.* Thousand Oaks, CA: Sage.

Hecht, M. L., Warren, J. R., Jung, E., & Krieger, J. L. (2005). The communication theory of identity: Development, theoretical perspective, and future directions. In W. B. Gudykunst (Ed.), *Theorizing about intercultural communication* (pp. 257-278). Thousand Oaks, CA: Sage.

Lanigan, R. L. (1988). *Phenomenology of communication: Merleau-Ponty's thematics in communicology and semiology.* Pittsburgh, PA: Duquense University Press.

Major, B., Quinton, W., & McCoy, S. K. (2002). Antecedents and consequences of attributions to discrimination: Theoretical and empirical advances. In M. Zanna (Ed.), *Advances in experimental social psychology* (pp. 251–330). New York: Academic.

Martin, J. N., & Nakayama, T. K. (1999). Thinking dialectically about culture and communication. *Communication Theory, 9*(1), 1-25.

Miller, C. T., & Kaiser, C. R. (2001). A theoretical perspective on coping with stigma. *Journal of Social Issues, 57,* 73–92.

Mumby, D. K. (1993). Critical organizational communication studies: The next 10 years. *Communication Monographs, 60*, 18-25.

Muraco, A. (2005). Heterosexual evaluations of hypothetical friendship behavior based on sex and sexual orientations. *Journal of Social and Personal Relationships, 22*(5), 587-605.

Orbe, M. (1996). Laying the foundation for co-cultural communication theory: An inductive approach to studying non-dominant communication strategies and the factors that influence them. *Communication Studies, 47*, 157-176.

Orbe, M. (1998). *Constructing co-cultural theory: An explication of culture, power, and communication.* Thousand Oaks, CA: Sage.

Orbe, M., Groscurth, C. R., Jeffries, T., & Prater, A. D. (2007). Locating whiteness across the communication curriculum: A collective autoethnographic analysis of pedagogy, cultural standpoints, and student/teacher interaction. In L. M. Cooks & J. S. Simpson (Eds.), *Whiteness, pedagogy, and performance* (pp. 27-48). New York: Lexington Books.

Orbe, M., & Harris, T. M. (2015). *Interracial communication: Theory into practice.* Thousand Oaks, CA: Sage.

Orbe, M., Smith, D. C., Groscurth, C. R., & Crawley, R. L. (2010). Exhaling so that we can catch our breath and sing: Reflections on issues inherent in publishing race-related communication research. *Southern Journal of Communication, 75*(2), 184-194.

Orbe, M., & Roberts, T. (2012). Co-cultural theorizing: Foundations, applications & extensions. *Howard Journal of Communications, 23*(4), 293-311.

Orbe, M., & Spellers, R. E. (2005). From the margins to the center: Utilizing co-cultural theory in diverse contexts. In W. B. Gudykunst (Ed.), *Theorizing about intercultural communication* (pp. 173-192). Thousand Oaks, CA: Sage.

Ruggiero, K. M., Taylor, D. M., & Lydon, J. E. (1997). How disadvantaged group members cope with discrimination when they perceive that social support is available. *Journal of Applied Social Psychology, 27*, 1581-1600.

Ryan, E. B., Anas, A. P., & Gruneir, A. J. S. (2006). Evaluations of overhelping and underhelping communication: Do old age and physical disability matter? *Journal of Language and Social Psychology, 25*(1), 97-107.

Speer, S. A., & Potter, J. (2000). The management of heterosexist talk: Conversational resources and prejudiced claims. *Discourse & Society, 11*(4), 543-572.

Stanback, M. H., & Pearce, W. B. (1981). Talking to "the man:" Some communication strategies used by members of "subordinate" social groups. *Quarterly Journal of Speech, 67*, 21-30.

Stokoe, E., & Edwards, D. (2007). 'Black this, black that:' Racial insults and reported speech in neighbour complaints and police interrogations. *Discourse and Society, 18*(3), 337-372.

Sue, D. W., Capodilupo, C. M., Torino, G. C., Bucceri, J. M., Holder, A. M. B., Nadal, K. L., & Esquilin, M. (2007). Racial microaggressions in everyday life. *American Pyschologist, 62*(4), 271-286.

Swim, J. K., & Hyers, L. L. 1999. Excuse me—what did you say?!: Women's public and private responses to sexist remarks. *Journal of Experimental Social Psychology, 35,* 68–88.

Swim, J. K., Cohen, L. L., & Hyers, L. L. (1998). Experiencing everyday prejudice and discrimination. In J. K. Swim & C. Stangor (Eds.), *Prejudice: The target's perspective* (pp. 37–60). San Diego, CA: Academic Press.

Todd-Mancillas, W. (2000). Constructing co-cultural theory by M. Orbe and Communication and identity across cultures edited by D. V. Tanno and A. Gonzalez [book review]. *Communication Theory, 10*(4), 475-480.

Utsey, S. D., Ponterotto, J. G., Reynolds, A. L., & Cancelli, A. A. (2000). Racial discrimination, coping, life satisfaction and self-esteem among African Americans. *Journal of Counseling and Development, 78,* 72-80.

Van Dijk, T. A. (1989). Structures of discourse and structures of power. *Communication Yearbook, 12,* 18-59.

Woodzicka, J. A., & LaFrance, M. (2001). Real versus imagined gender harassment. *Journal of Social Issues, 57,* 15–30.

In: Communicating Prejudice   ISBN: 978-1-53610-167-6
Editors: S. Camara and D. Drummond   © 2016 Nova Science Publishers, Inc.

Chapter 7

DIFFUSING PREJUDICE AND FEAR IN A GENDER AND COMMUNICATION CLASSROOM

Kevin T. Jones

George Fox University, Newberg, Oregon, US

ABSTRACT

This chapter will identify how the author confronted a community of prejudice and fear in a Gender and Communication classroom and turned it into a community of truth telling[1] and tolerance. Working from a theoretical framework of critical pedagogy and the work of Parker Palmer, this chapter explores how the classroom is often seen as a culture of fear and disrespect. This culture of fear needs to be confronted by identifying a community of truth tellers as found in two different models of truth telling. After exploring how to achieve a community of truth telling when faced with prejudice, the chapter will explain in great detail the application of a metaphor about "riding the bus" and how this metaphor has sustained a class when faced with prejudice and fear.

---

[1] The word "truth" is used here and in this essay, not as capital "T" Truth – an absolute singular truth – but for "truth telling" that represents a little "t" truth, which stands for engaging in dialogue on enlightenment, knowledge, ways of knowing, and pedagogical insight.

"I have come to the frightening conclusion that I am the decisive element in the classroom. It is my personal approach that creates the climate. It is my daily mood that makes the weather. As a teacher, I possess the power to make a student's life miserable or joyous. I can be a tool of torture or an instrument of inspiration. I can humiliate or humor, hurt or heal. In all situations, it is my response that decides whether a crisis will be escalated or de-escalated and a person humanized or dehumanized."

-Haim Ginott[2]

INTRODUCTION

When I first began my teaching career over 30 years ago I had a habit of committing a very bad joke. When my students would complain about an assignment or whine in class about schoolwork, I would jokingly hold up my grade book and say, "Who holds the grade book?" There might be a few murmurs but the act would generally quiet the class down and we could move on. My feeble attempt to diffuse the situation was not meant to be mean, but merely to allow me to move on to the next issue at hand.

I thought little of my actions until I received a student course evaluation one semester that declared, "Kevin is on a total power trip. He threatens us with bad grades if we don't do what he says." I was stunned and horrified. I realized I had mistakenly turned my classroom into a power struggle. That was the last thing I wanted to do but as a young graduate student starting his teaching career, I found myself in the middle of one of the many mistakes I have made in my career. I began to research issues of power in the classroom and found myself emerged in the literature of critical pedagogy. As I began to incorporate the works of people like Paulo Friere and Parker Palmer into my curriculum, I felt I had begun to remove much of the power differential from my classrooms. I no longer asked, "Who has the grade book?" and I began to see where I was making mistakes.

A little over 15 years ago, I began teaching a course titled "Gender and Communication." I lobbied successfully to have the course added as an upper division elective to the general education curriculum at the university where I taught. Imagine my horror during the first semester of teaching a section of Gender and Communication to a general education audience when one student

---

[2] Ginott, H. G. (1972). *Teacher and child: A book for parents and teachers.* New York: Macmillan. Page 15.

proclaimed in front of the entire class "this whole class is bullshit!" Once he spoke up, I found that this student was not alone. A few other students appeared to be so threatened by the course content and were so prejudice against it, that they were visibly angry.

I found myself wanting to yell at them, "Don't you understand that your gendered identity has been socially constructed by the dominant cultural norm!!!" But to do that, I would be returning to a power paradigm that I had worked very hard to remove. I needed to figure out how to remove prejudice in the classroom without force or power. To confront this challenge, I returned once again to critical pedagogy and the work of Parker Palmer and his insightful work *The Courage to Teach*. In critical pedagogy I found the challenge to eliminate power from the classroom and give a voice to every student. In Palmer I was reminded of how the classroom is a masked culture of fear and once I realized that, I could quickly turn my attention and energy to uncovering the culture of truth telling that was right in front of my eyes. My reading challenged me to confront the fear and prejudice in my class and find some way to discover the truth telling lying in wait. I also had to do this without creating a power struggle.

My brainstorming led me to create a metaphor that I began using in class that leveled the playing field for everyone involved. The metaphor involved using the concept of "riding a bus." We are all on the same bus ride when exploring our gendered identities. The challenge lies in understanding that where we sit on that bus affects our perception of what we see while riding the bus. Once the bus stops and we all exit the bus, we see that we have all been on the same journey together. Taking the ride allows students to share their version of the journey, which fosters a community of truth telling and defuses the community of prejudice and fear. This chapter will explore Critical Pedagogy and Palmer's cultures of fear and truth telling and will connect theory with practical anecdotes to provide relevant tools and strategies designed to confront prejudice and enhance the classroom experience for both student and teacher alike.

THEORETICAL FRAMEWORK

Theory informs practice. It is the habit of many to align themselves with one theory and to claim its elements as their own. While understanding the power of such alignments, I instead find myself claiming elements of several theorists. I am deeply informed by the work of Parker Palmer and critical theory in my search for a theoretical framework. As an educational theory, critical pedagogy expresses the belief that educational systems are based on power structures and that schools tend to serve the interests of those in power, intentionally or unintentionally (Billings, 2008). In our schools, norms for social interaction, expectations and behaviors are perpetrated without rigorous review. Biases are taken for granted. Critical pedagogy expresses a belief that teachers and students must constantly question their world, both inside and outside the classroom. Critical pedagogy is committed to the transformative power of education. It places a strong emphasis on diversity (Billings, 2008; Gay, 1995; Nieto, 2002,). Freire (1970) calls educators to name, to reflect critically, and to act. Wink (2005) marks these three phrases as the best definition of critical pedagogy. Critical pedagogy has its roots in the work of Paulo Freire, a Brazilian educator who worked to develop a method of teaching literacy to indigent farm workers in order to empower them to vote. Freire published his theories of social justice and education in *Pedagogy of the Oppressed* (1970). Critical pedagogy works against the norm that would reproduce current power structures, or devalue inquiry, skepticism and disagreement (Billings, 2008).

Essential to critical pedagogy is the concept of critical consciousness. Critical consciousness is *"an awareness of the invisible oppression in society through education and activism"* (Billings, p.3). Historic examples of invisible oppression are extensive. The issue of slavery in Great Britain and the United States is one example and the issue of suffrage is another. Billings reminds us that it is far easier to see "invisible oppression" through an historic lens than it is to recognize it in the here and now. Today, critical consciousness might encourage individuals to question "English only" policies in the United States or the use of tracking systems in education. Critical consciousness is a necessary element of critical pedagogy. Awareness is essential and awareness comes through the disequilibrium of questioning discourses.

Another essential component of critical pedagogy is hidden curriculum. Giroux (1983) added strength to our understanding of critical pedagogy in his work on hidden curriculum. This concept builds on Freire's belief that much of what is taught is unquestioned. *Hidden curriculum notes that much of what is learned in school is not part of the official curriculum but rather involves subtle socialization in norms and mores of social interaction.* Hidden curriculum supports the needs and mores of the dominant culture. Wink (2005) lends clarity to how it appears in our schools

The hidden curriculum can be seen in schools when little boys are called on more than little girls, when only Eurocentric histories are taught, when teenage girls are socialized to believe that they are not good in math and sciences, when heroes but not heroines are taught, and when counselors track nonwhites to classes that prepare them to serve (p.47).

Hidden curriculum can be intentional or unintentional. Power struggles between teacher and student can move a teacher to engage hidden curriculum as a way to maintain and/or force power. In my opening story of "Who holds the grade book?" the hidden curriculum was unintentional yet very real to some of the students. This type of instruction can be very dangerous in our schools and foster prejudice.

A third component of critical pedagogy is that of dialectic. *Dialectic is the tension between opposing thoughts, ideas, concepts, values and beliefs* (Wink, 2005). The position of dialectic is a normal part of the learning process. While binary systems inform us and often are at the root of technological advances, in education, holding opposing tensions is often at the root of profound understanding. Consider the honest thinking of Winston Churchill who stated: "I am always ready to learn although I do not always like being taught" (Hume, p.24).

Dialectics are important in the learning process. Wink (2005) further explained Dialectic involves seeing and articulating contradictions; it is the process of learning from the oppositional view. Dialectic brings to light a more comprehensive understanding of the multiple facets of the opposite. As we learn while teaching and teach while learning, we are in a dialectical process (p.41).

Often, the dominant paradigm in the classroom is that the students are there to learn from the teacher. The teacher is present to "profess" or dispense knowledge and wisdom. When teachers see that they can learn from the students and students can see the teacher willing to learn from them, then the dialectical process is set in motion. Additionally, once this give-and-take learning process is cultivated between teacher and student, then students are better able to see and engage in learning from each other.

It is impossible to discuss critical pedagogy without discussing literacies. Critical pedagogy recognizes the many forms of literacies that inhabit our world. Refusing to limit the discussion to the reading and writing of language, *literacies implies all of the ways in which individuals and societies make sense of their world* (Wink, 2005). Literacies are defined as reading, writing and reflecting (Wink, 2005). Literacies are the underlying ways of knowing, thinking and making complex meanings. Forms of literacies include academic literacies, functional literacies, workplace literacies, and emergent literacies. This list is not exhaustive. The literacies we use to understand the complexities of life are extensive. There is great power in literacies, power to name the world around us.

Equally powerful is the ability to silence. Silence can be present in a classroom when particular issues are not discussed, when students are discouraged from talking, or when attention is not given to the lives and experiences of students. While silencing may not often be consciously intended, it is often consciously felt by the individual or individuals whose voices have been stilled. Wink (2005) explores it in the following

Often,
Those who have more, silence those who have less;
Those who are from the dominant European American culture silence
Those from the non-European American cultures;
Boys silence girls;
Men silence women.

Often,
Men don't know it;
Boys don't know it;
European Americans don't know it, and
Those with more don't know it (p.58).

Critical pedagogy is dedicated to giving voice to each individual who inhabits a classroom or a community. It is about the thoughtful, analytical understanding of power and how it forms our institutions and us.

Having explored Freire's ideology, it is essential for me to link Freire's text to the work of Parker Palmer. To move from the work of a Brazilian lawyer turned educational activist to an American Quaker from the Midwest may seem something of a stretch but in reality, much of their work is compatible on several levels. Palmer (1998, 2007) expresses his beliefs regarding pedagogy in his classic *The Courage to Teach*. Palmer moves from a focus of educational pedagogy on the learner or the methodology of delivery systems, and focuses squarely on the interior life of the teacher. His haunting question remains "Who is the self who teaches?" This focus moves us away from educational techniques and into the realm of personhood.

An emphasis on the "who" of teaching, necessarily removes us from a discussion of external factors and requires us to look deeply within. Palmer asks the question, "How does the quality of my selfhood form—or deform— the way I relate to my students, my subject, my colleagues, my world?" (p.4). Such an interior focus may seem at odds with critical theory's focus on power structures however, external systems are changed by interior thoughts and commitments. The two are not independent of each other. Palmer argues for a strong spotlight to be placed on the interior life of the teacher in an effort to effect change in the external systems of education.

Identity and integrity are at the core of Palmer's work. These two elements comprise the core of the self that teaches. Identity is defined as

> The evolving nexus where all the forces that constitute my life converge in the mystery of self: my genetic make-up, the nature of the man and woman who gave me life, the culture in which I was raised, people who have sustained me and people who have done me harm, the good and ill I have done to others and to myself, the experience of love and suffering — and much, much more" (p.14).

Integrity is identified as the ability to relate to those forces "in ways that bring me wholeness and life rather than fragmentation and death" (p.14). The manner in which each individual teacher integrates the forces or discourses of life into their person has an enormous impact on the self and the work of teaching that the self has engaged.

This focus on self does not mean that Palmer is opposed to discussing methodology. At the core of Palmer's thoughts on methodology is the principle of paradox. While appreciative of the scientific advances that a binary system of thought has given the world (p.64), Palmer reminds us that paradox is an essential tension in teaching, just as paradox is an essential practice in breathing. Perhaps the paradox that most deeply touches any educator is Palmer's recognition that "the knowledge I have gained from the thirty years of teaching goes hand in hand with my sense of being a rank amateur at the start of each new class" (p.66).

Teaching is immersed in paradox. Teaching requires the intellect and the heart to work in concert. Teaching requires intentionality to merge with flexibility. Teaching honors the individual stories of students and the corporate stories of the disciplines. Good teaching "supports solitude and embraces community" (p.77). These paradoxes are as essential to methodology as state standards are to outcomes. Critical pedagogy and the focus on the interior life of the individual who teaches are the theoretical frameworks from which this experience is discussed. They are the lenses through which I viewed my experience in the classroom.

THE CLASSROOM: AS IT COULD BE

After more than thirty years of teaching I have come to understand that good teaching does not come from learning a certain technique or formula. Teaching cannot be reduced to such prescriptive measures. Instead, good teaching comes from the identity and integrity of the teacher. I firmly believe that learning is a process, not a final performance. It is ongoing and needs to be allowed to grow and evolve for each individual. The learning process involves allowing each student to discover what is important to him or her and it is my responsibility to help provide a safe environment where that learning process can take place. In his work *Gestalt Therapy Verbatim*, author Fredrick Perls (1969) summarize this principle very well when he notes

> Right now I can only hypnotize you, persuade you; make you believe that I am right. You don't know. I'm just preaching something. You wouldn't learn from my words. Learning is a discovery. There is no other means of effective learning. You can tell a child a thousand times, "the stove is hot." It doesn't help. The child has to discover for himself. And I hope I can assist you in learning, in discovering something about yourself. (p. 1)

I think the mistake that many professors make is that they truly believe that as a "professor" it is their job to "profess" to their students how much they know and make sure to remind the students on a regular basis how little the students know. As a result, long lectures ensue with students expected to hang on every dripping syllable and are then punished when they are unable to regurgitate those same syllables verbatim on an exam. This is not dialogue, this is monologue, and nothing very good ever comes out of monologue. Monologue is driven by power. I think teachers forget that they possess the power to create an environment that can either help students want to learn or can keep them from caring about learning at all.

The type of environment Perls refers to must come from a place where "connection" happens – where student and teacher connect not because the teacher is cool or popular, but they connect because there is trust. Parker

Palmer (1998) argued, "Good teachers possess a capacity for connectedness. They are able to weave a complex web of connections among themselves, their subject, and their students so that students can learn to weave a world for themselves" (p.11). Connections can only emerge from dialogue – not monologue.

It is very tempting when teaching a course such as gender and communication to want to scream out in monologue "Look, everything you believe about yourself is wrong!! You've been brainwashed by dominant cultural norms!!" But that is preaching, not teaching. Real teaching involves making the type of connections that allow for discovery. A person is much more likely to embrace an ideology when they believe they have discovered this new found truth on his/her own. Discovery, however, is often only obtained through dialogue. Each student must be able to share their story, their personal narrative in an environment where that narrative may draw ridicule or disagreement. My job as a teacher is to create a classroom environment where these narratives can be told safely. Thus I am confronted with my first challenge – a safe environment where dialogue flourishes.

ERADICATING THE CULTURE OF FEAR

My challenge is compounded when I factor in the reality that a classroom is a breeding ground for fear on every level. Fear breeds prejudice. Both teachers and students are afraid of failing. Teachers fear not being validated as a good teacher with good student course evaluations, not having their love for the subject matched by a room filled with eighteen and nineteen year olds, not engaging in cutting edge research and publishing in the "right" journals, or not being respected by their colleagues and peers. These fears can unknowingly turn the classroom into a battlefield where egos are defended and dialogue is quickly replaced with monologue because monologue allows for greater control [and power].

Teachers often get labeled as arrogant at this point as they defend their positions and ideologies and must always be right because if they cannot defend their position, then their fears are no longer imagined but real. Arrogance is often used as a mask for fear. The more I am afraid the greater my level of resistance. If I do not resist dialogue, then my fears may overwhelm me. I must insist on monologue to mask my fear.

If blinded by their own fears, teachers can quickly forget how afraid their students are. When confronted with the possibility that how they have viewed the world (or maybe have been told how the world is to be viewed) for more than eighteen years, the fear can become crippling. Parker Palmer (1998) writes of this fear when he reminds us "Students, too, are afraid: afraid of failing, of not understanding, of being drawn into issues they would rather avoid, of having their ignorance exposed or their prejudices challenged, of looking foolish in front of their peers" (p. 37).

Courses such as Gender and Communication can feed these types of fears like a wildfire. When told that they are born with their sex but have chosen their gender based upon a number of factors, the threat to their own identity can confront students with a paradigm shift that can be scarier than anything they have ever experienced. Prejudice is fueled by homophobia, insecurities, and ignorance. Even if they are not confronted with a paradigm shift, students can find themselves having to risk self-disclosure and potential ridicule should they dare to engage in dialogue and share their stories. A Gender and Communication course can become a living nightmare of fear for the ill prepared student especially when led by a teacher who is crippled by his or her own fears. In order for true dialogue to emerge both teacher and student must be aware of, and confront these fears.

Additionally, a course such as Gender and Communication can become a breeding ground for issues of diversity. If personal narratives are dialogued, then multiple perspectives on any topic must also be embraced. This gives birth to a room filled with diversity that only exacerbates prejudice and fear. Palmer (1998) identifies this problem by explaining "If we embrace diversity, we find ourselves on the doorstep of our next fear: fear of the conflict that will ensue when divergent truths meet" (p.38). While a small portion of the population have learned how to manage conflict in a positive manner, it is safe to say that a majority of people tend to either avoid conflict for fear of it damaging the relationship, or they confront it head on with a "win-lose" mentality and embrace conflict only because they want to win the conflict.

To tolerate narratives that are the antithesis of a persons' worldview creates a wonderful opportunity to engage diversity. It also engorges the culture of prejudice and fear. It becomes very, very important for me as a teacher of a course such as Gender and Communication to remember that my classroom has the potential to become this breeding ground for prejudice. If not, I can quickly miss-diagnose my student's attitudes and responses. How I diagnose my student's mindset has a tremendous impact on the type of cure I offer for their fears. Thus I am confronted with my second challenge - to confront and diffuse the culture of fear for both my students and myself but without the introduction of force or power.

BUILDING A COMMUNITY OF TRUTH TELLING

In the Socratic tradition, the purpose of dialogue is to foster the discovery of truth telling. If true dialogue is to happen in the classroom, then the true goal of the classroom is to discover the art of truth telling. The goal then is to create an environment where truth telling is practiced. But truth telling has functioned far too long from a flawed model. The dominant model of truth-knowing and truth-telling functions from a "top-down" perspective. Palmer (1998) identifies this problem and argues that there is a difference between the mythical but dominant model of truth telling and a true community of truth tellers. The difference lies in the four major elements of the mythical model as described by Palmer

> There are "objects" of knowledge that resides "out there" somewhere. There are "experts" who are people trained to know these objects. There are "amateurs" who are people without training and full of bias who depend on the experts for pure knowledge of the objects. Finally, there are "baffles" at every point of the transmission that allow knowledge to flow downstream while preventing subjectivity from flowing back up. (p. 100-101)

Information is clearly a monologue and flows down, from the object rather than the object being the center of attention. For example, in a Gender and Communication course, a teacher (expert) enters a classroom prepared to "teach" gender (Object) to students (amateurs). The teacher brings his/her own baffles (bias, life experiences, opinions, power struggles, hidden curriculum, etc.) regarding the topic into the classroom. Students receive the information through their own baffles (or filters of biases, life experiences, opinions, power struggles). Without dialogue, those baffles are never addressed or broken down. The teacher's expert opinion rules the classroom and only monologue transpires. No one learns from each other. This model creates in invisible oppression (critical consciousness), as students feel little freedom to challenge the expert. The hidden curriculum is evident in the teacher or "experts" dissemination of information. Dialectic builds as tension between ideas is never resolved. Literacies are ignored since all students are expected to learn one way (and not everyone learns the same way) and the power differential in this model fosters silence (See Figure 1).

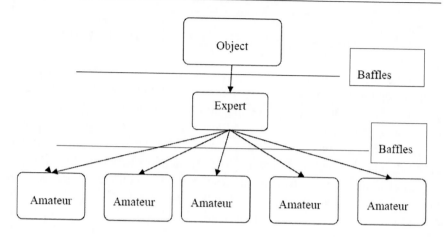

Figure 1. Traditional Truth Model.

Palmer further explains the problems of this model when he argues:

> In the model, truth flows from the top down, from experts who are qualified to know truth to amateurs who are qualified only to receive truth. In this myth, truth is a set of propositions about objects; education is a system for delivering those propositions to students; and an educated person is one who can remember and repeat the experts' propositions. The image is hierarchical, linear, and compulsive-hygienic, as if truth came down an antiseptic conveyer belt to be deposited as pure product at the end. (p.101)

Any student (amateur) who can easily memorize and regurgitate what the "expert" has disseminated on the "object" on an exam or in a paper, can get good grades, excel in the classroom and be rewarded with honors. However, that student may never have "learned" anything.

Obviously, this traditional model does little to foster dialogue as it screams monologue. An alternative model is needed, one which radiates dialogue. Palmer (1998) provides this alternative in the form of a "community of truth" which places the "subject" in the middle surrounded by "knowers" (p.101). Palmer explains, "In the community of truth, there are no pristine objects of knowledge and no ultimate authorities . . . The community of truth is, in fact, many communities . . . At the center of this communal circle, there is always a subject" (p.101). By switching truth from an object (as in the other model) to a subject, we make the subject the center of our attention and the result is that we give it respect and authority that is normally reserved for human beings. This relationship begins, Palmer argues, "When we allow the subject to occupy the center of our attention" (p.103). (See Figure 2)

Palmer elaborates on how the community of truth functions when he explains:

> As we try to understand the subject in the community of truth, we enter into complex patterns of communication – sharing observations and interpretations, correcting and complementing each other, torn by conflict in this moment and joined by consensus in the next. The community of truth, far from being linear and static and hierarchical, is circular, interactive, and dynamic. (p.103)

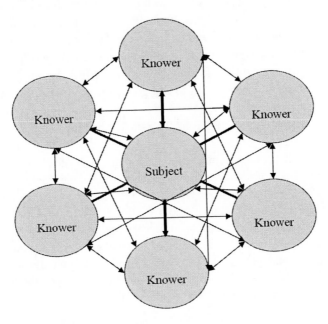

Figure 2. Interactive Truth Model.

In this model the subject and knowers are interwoven. The teacher (now no longer the "expert") enters the classroom ready to allow the subject and knowers drive the course. The model shuns invisible oppression, does not allow for hidden curriculum, tension between ideas is lessened, literacies are embraced, and no one is allowed to silence anyone.

Given this model, I am left with a third and final challenge – how to create and nurture a community of truth telling in my Gender and Communication course.

RIDING THE BUS: A TRANSFORMATIVE TEACHING STRATEGY

My challenge seemed daunting. How do I address dialectic without power, foster diverse literacies, address hidden curriculum while removing the critical consciousness and subsequent prejudice and fear fostered in a course such as Gender and Communication? In order to confront and address these issues in my Gender and Communication course, I knew that I needed to create an environment where dialogue flourished, the culture of fear disappeared, and the community of truth telling emerged. This was not going to be easy. I realized that I was going to have to accomplish these goals by laying some ground rules and establishing a presupposition for all discussions that everyone in the course would need to understand and support. I also had to lay these ground rules through dialogue and not monologue. My solution came in the form of using a metaphor of riding a bus. On the first day of the semester, I informed the class that we would all be going on a bus trip this semester. I announced that we would be taking a ride south down Highway 1 along the coast from Portland to San Francisco. The story is as follows:

"We will all be boarding the bus for the same destination – San Francisco. Some of you will get on the bus and sit in the front row where you can look out the front window of the bus and see everything possible along the way. That is what you know, what you do, and what you are comfortable with. You will take in everything around the bus and see every detail and embrace it all. Some of you will get on the bus on the left side. That is what you know, what you do, and what you are comfortable with. As we travel south, you will look out the window on the left side and see the mountains and the trees and all the beauty the hillsides have to offer.

Some of you are going to get on the bus and sit on the right side. That is what you know, what you do, and what you are comfortable with. As we travel south, you will look out your window on the right side of the bus and see the beach, the ocean, the seagulls and maybe some dolphins or sea lions along the way.

A few of you are going to head right to the back of the bus to the five seats in a row that look like a nice bed. You are going to lie down and sleep the entire trip and not see a thing. That is what you know, what you do, and what you are comfortable with.

When we arrive at San Francisco, we will all have gone on the same journey together and we will all arrive at the same destination together. But some of you will get off the bus and say, "Wow, what a journey, those mountains were incredible!" Some of you will get off the bus and say, "What are you talking about? There were no mountains on that journey, all we saw was this awesome ocean." The left side mountain people will exclaim, "What do you mean no mountains? That's all there was for hours and hours. There wasn't any ocean!" Someone will eventually turn to a front of the bus person and ask, "Did you see the mountains?" And they will respond, "Oh, yes I did, it was wonderful!" Then an ocean person will step in and say, "What about the ocean – didn't you see the ocean?" Then the front of the bus person will reply, "Oh, yes, we saw the ocean too and it was wonderful as well!" While they are all standing there arguing, the back of the bus bench people will exit the bus and say they have no idea what either of these people are talking about.

How can this be? How can a group of people all take the same journey together on the same bus, yet have such completely different perspectives of what happened during that journey? The key is "perspectives." Just because the mountain people did not see the ocean does not mean the ocean is not there. Just because the ocean people did not see the mountains does not mean the mountains were not there. Just because the back of the bus people did not see any of it does not mean none of it was there! It is all real and it is all valid. I hope that during this semester you get to look over at the other side of the bus. If you are a mountain person, I hope that you can at least learn to glance over at the right side and see the ocean. You do not have to like it and you do not even have to enjoy it. I just want you to look over and say, 'Hmmm, I did not know that was there.' The same thing goes for the ocean people. Every now and then, I just want you to glance over at the other side of the bus and see that the mountains are indeed there.

For some of you, my desire is that you discover that the ocean is there for the very first time. And not only do you discover that it is there, I hope that maybe a few of you scoot over and sit in the seat on the right side for a while. Some of you may even say, 'Hey, this is really much better than the mountains. I think I will sit on this side of the bus for the rest of the trip.' I hope the same thing happens for some of you ocean people as well. This will happen in part when those on the ocean side of the bus begin describing what they see to the people on the mountainside of the bus. The people on the mountainside of the bus should do the same for the people on the ocean side. For those of you sitting in the front of the bus, I expect you to help everyone else by describing what you see from your perspective since you see both sides at the same time. Then maybe, just maybe, those of you who are in the back of the bus, if you can at least just listen to the descriptions – you do not even have to look out any windows, just listen to the conversations – I hope you can at least understand that the descriptions you hear are very real to the people describing it for you. Just because it is not on your side of the bus does not mean it is not valid or very, very real for that person who is on that side of the bus. So, are you ready? Let's ride the bus!!"

This inclusion of the "back row sleepers" is a very important piece of the puzzle because it helps to remove power from the situation. (If prejudice is present, it tends to come from the back row sleepers). When given the option to not engage the front, left, or right sides of the bus the student does not feel forced to have to engage in the journey. While no one should get to "ride the bus for free," the use of power and/or force is not teaching or learning. By being enrolled in the course, the students must go on the journey but the goal is to try to remove any power or pressure to "have" to engage in any paradigm shifts.

Once the bus metaphor is established, continually revisited, and bought into by the students, Palmer's community of truth telling emerges and critical pedagogy can thrive. The knowers and the subject work together to drive the learning. Critical pedagogy is allowed to thrive in the classroom. When every student's position on the bus is acknowledged, accepted and embraced, there is little invisible oppression. All knowers have equal ownership in the "ride." Even the "back seaters" know they are welcome and part of the ride. There is little opportunity for hidden curriculum as the knowers all drive the course content. A simple reminder of the metaphor easily and quickly diffuses tension between ideas. Each knower is allowed to explore learning through the method best suited to them, which embraces literacies. The open dialogue prevents anyone from being silenced.

At the beginning of each class, I write a brief lecture outline on the board. At the top of the board, every day, I always write, "Let's Ride the Bus," "The Bus is Ready to Roll!!" or "The Bus is Leaving the Station!!" I remind the student's daily of our ride together. This sets the foundation for classroom discussions. When a topic is addressed that someone says they cannot relate to, I remind them that they are looking out a different part of the bus right now. When two people disagree on a topic, I can remind them that they are merely looking out different sides of the bus. Neither person is right nor wrong – in fact, they are both right in their views. It is not a right verses wrong issue. It is merely a "what side of the bus are you on" issue. Falling back upon this metaphor has allowed me to diffuse many potential conflicts in the classroom. The opportunity to teach tolerance toward diversity is quite obvious.

CONCLUSION

By using something as simple as a metaphor of riding a bus, I am able to address all of my challenges. By embracing multiple perspectives and allowing each person to share their stories, we find ourselves in the middle of dialogue that helps diffuse prejudice. The students begin teaching each other and the course begins teaching itself. As the dialogue flourishes and students begin to feel safe, the culture of fear dissipates. When each story is validated, there is little fear of failure. When no one is allowed to invalidate or belittle a story, fear of rejection and prejudice is diminished. When truth telling is collectively shared through individual stories, a community of truth tellers emerges. Truth telling is no longer an object to be passed on by an expert to some amateurs. Truth telling becomes the central subject around which the entire community gathers and discovers and explores. Hopefully, somewhere along the line, as a result of all of the above variables, the struggle for power dissipates.

Once when a male student expressed his support of rape myths (look what she was wearing, she deserved it!) a female student was able to speak up and tell her story of being raped while wearing a sweat suit. The male saw out of the other side of the bus and even changed seats. He overcame his prejudice, but only because a community of truth telling existed and the culture of fear had been removed. He brought a dialectic based on a paradigm of power but because power was not a dominate paradigm in the classroom, a rape victim felt free to engage in dialogue. Literacy's were shared and understood and voices were expressed.

Once, when a female student shared that she did not mind being whistled at and honked at by passing cars, another female spoke up and shared her story of how that type of activity led to her being sexually assaulted. The first female was able to see how the act of objectification could dis-empower a person and cause another person to want to oppress her with power. This hidden curriculum went beyond anything I could have prepared or planned for that day. Males in the course also heard how most of the women were hurt by this type of intimidation and expressed that they had no idea it was so hurtful.

More prejudice was dissipated. One time, when a male shared that from his side of the bus he enjoyed women used as set decorations in advertisements, a woman shared her journey into eating disorders and her shattered self-esteem because she could not look like the models in the ads.

Not everyone changes seats on the bus. In fact, some students embrace the back row. This raised a daunting question for me: "What do I do when a student does not experience a paradigm shift or does not learn?" In time, I began to see it in a different way. Any perceived lack of change was still a teaching victory for me. The dialectic is possibly so threatening that some students chose not to engage in it. They chose silence to be their voice. This demonstrates to me the lack of power in the course. These students do not feel threatened by the dialectic and are content with silence. They do not feel defensive nor do they feel the need to defend themselves and exercise their prejudice. They feel free to choose to disengage. This can only be possible when fear and power are absent. While I would prefer that the "backseaters" not get a free ride, by not feeling the need to flex their prejudice in class, I feel that a small victory toward a paradigm shift has taken place.

There is an ancient Chinese proverb that proclaims, "When the pupil is ready, the teacher will appear." Forcing a student to learn introduces power in to the classroom. When that happens, learning and teaching stop and the teacher disappears. Riding the bus is an attempt to create the best possible environment for a resistant and prejudice audience.

Change can be very scary and threatening to many people. A course such as Gender and Communication can require a student to have to confront change in his or her ideologies. The threat of that change can create resistance fueled by prejudice in the course. Teachers must be aware of the roots of that resistance and be prepared and equipped to handle it in a healthy and constructive way. When faced with prejudice, cultivating a community of truth telling can diffuse a great deal of the hostility projected into the course and toward the professor. A simple metaphor such as riding a bus can go a long way to diffuse prejudice and cultivate a culture of truth telling in which each person can be humanized and valued.

REFERENCES

Billings, S. (2008). *Critical Pedagogy*. Critical Pedagogy—Research Starter Education.

Freire, P. (1970). *Pedagogy of the oppressed*. New York: Seabury Press.

Gay, G. (1995). Mirror images on common issues: Parallels between multicultural education and critical pedagogy. In C.E. Sleeter & P. McLaren (Eds.), *Multicultural education, critical pedagogy, and the politics of difference* (p.155-190). Albany: State University of New York.

Ginott, H. G. (1972). *Teacher and child: A book for parents and teachers.* New York: MacMillan.

Giroux, H. A. (1983). *Theory and resistance in education: A pedagogy for the opposition. Critical perspectives in social theory.* London & Exeter NH: Heinemann Educational Books.

Hume, J. C. (1995). *The Wit and Wisdom of Winston Churchill.* New York: Harper Perennial.

Nieto, S. (2002). *Language, culture and teaching: Critical perspectives for a new century.* Mahwah, NJ: Lawrence Eribaum.

Palmer, P. (1998/2007). *The courage to teach: Exploring the inner landscapes of a teacher's life.* San Francisco, CA: Wiley.

Perls, F. (1969) *Gestalt Therapy Verbatim.* New York, New York: Bantam Dell Publishing Co.

Wink, J. (2005). *Critical pedagogy: Notes from the real world.* Boston, MA; Allyn and Bacon.

In: Communicating Prejudice   ISBN: 978-1-53610-167-6
Editors: S. Camara and D. Drummond   © 2016 Nova Science Publishers, Inc.

Chapter 8

THE LATINO/A IMMIGRANT MYTH AND THE (IM)POSSIBILITY OF REALIZING COMMUNAL APPRECIATION

Wilfredo Alvarez
Northeastern Illinois University, Chicago, IL, US

ABSTRACT

In this chapter I examine my interpersonal experiences as a Latino immigrant negotiating a predominantly white cultural space. I apply semiotics theory to analyze my time as a graduate student of color at a predominantly white institution (PWI) and city. I discuss how my body and some of its most "repulsive" emanations (i.e., my phenotypic traits and accent) act as signifiers and the discourse of "threat" acts as a signified that together form a sign that many whites "read" as "Latinos/as as a Threat" in everyday interactions. I reframe the communication theory of identity to propose ideas for transformative dialogue, to further understanding of intergroup relations, and to help realize communal appreciation.

As soon as the adversaries are in the ring, the public is overwhelmed with the obviousness of the roles. As in the theatre, each physical type expresses to excess the part which has been assigned to the contestant. Thauvin, a fifty-year-old with an obese and sagging body…displays in his flesh the characters of baseness…The physique of the wrestlers therefore constitutes a basic sign, which like a seed contains the whole fight. (Barthes, 1972, p. 17)

MY BODY'S MARKING AND COMMUNICATING PREJUDICE

Like Thauvin in Barthes' story, in four years in the city of Boulder, Colorado, my physical presence carried the seeds of meaning necessary to make sense of my complex being. The barrage of (non)verbal messages directed at my person revealed a culture in which there was a shared understanding of my being as fundamentally repulsive. Similarly to how the audience in that arena might have reacted to Thauvin's obese body, people's reactions to my presence communicated some degree of "disgust" with me and my various social performances (e.g., language use). The continuous (non)verbal feedback made me feel that my body was marked. The sum of my interactions with whites in Boulder show that I had a "mark" that triggered prejudicial behaviors and these behaviors seemed to be the norm for many of them.

By the time I left this milieu, I was so psychologically beaten that in my psyche there had been few affirming interactions with the majority of whites in Boulder. I write this essay as self-reflexive practice that helps me seek healing and make sense of my unsettling lived experiences. But also, I offer practical ideas to disrupt and rearticulate communication systems that (re)produce cultures of prejudice (Hecht, 1998). My ultimate goal is to promote social justice-oriented critical dialogue that promotes individual and group agency and resiliency. Lastly, my intention is to "plant" discursive "seeds" that equip people to resist and transform oppressive communication systems and generate appreciative communities of people.

In this chapter, I highlight communicative behaviors that exemplify the extent of my experiences with interpersonal prejudice in Boulder. I present four vignettes that illuminate how race-based prejudice is communicatively constituted in mundane interactions. My experiences show both subtle and overt behaviors that demonstrate people's commonplace reactions to my presence in various social settings. I only provide four examples of practices that were common occurrences in Boulder as I experienced them in daily life. To elucidate my experiences with prejudice, I use Roland Barthes' (1972) semiotics theory. Specifically, I deconstruct the factors that lead to the (re)production of white supremacist cultural spaces. I also apply the communication theory of identity (Hecht & Choi, 2012) to offer suggestions for communication practices to achieve social and cultural change. I start with four vignettes illustrating what I characterize as prejudice.

WELCOME TO "LIBERAL" BOULDER

Racial prejudice is deeply ingrained in the fabric of Boulder's sociocultural milieu. The edifices, the bodies that occupy it, whites and nonwhites' routine discourse about race indicating acute anxiety towards it, and Black, Latino/a, Middle Eastern colleagues and undergraduate students' unceasing stories about hurtful encounters with whites, tell a particular kind of story about the extent of Boulder's implicit and explicit biases. I rely on my interpretations of these previous factors and my direct personal experiences to contend that racial prejudice is a constitutive feature of Boulder's culture. I begin with some of my early experiences at the University of Colorado (CU) as a new arrival from New York City.

I was euphoric to be in Colorado to begin my graduate studies in interpersonal and intercultural communication. Soon after my arrival, my excitement turned into perplexity when I began to experience regular distressing interactions with white students, faculty, staff, and city residents. It was during my first year in Boulder when I realized that the culture there was distinctively different than in New York City. But before I discuss aspects of Boulder's "cultural distinctiveness" I provide some background information. One of the reasons why I chose to attend graduate school in Boulder is that it is considered a "liberal" city and it lies in the outskirts of a major U.S. metropolis (i.e., Denver). Compared to the other rural and less diverse locations where I was accepted for graduate school, the Boulder-Denver metro area was the most cosmopolitan choice my partner and I had. Having moved to Boulder with such degree of excitement made my overall experience there even more disappointing and infuriating.

As I reflect on my time in Boulder, I realize that Boulder is "liberal" as much as the "American Dream" was a reality for *all* U.S. citizens in the 20th century. Both themes "Boulder as Liberal" and "The American Dream" are the illusions of a privileged collective. What is an illusion if not the inability to see what lies beyond our immediate lived experience. "Boulder liberals" could only understand the concept of "liberalism" in the context of a racially homogenous society. Boulderites' liberalism was a regional whites only version of it. By default, it excluded my New York influenced ideas about liberalism. Just like the "American Dream" was an idea that mainly made sense to whites in the white supremacist sociocultural imagination of the time. The "Dream" was specifically for anyone designated as "white" during the period of prosperity between the early to middle 20th century. As history shows, all others were, and have been, living in an "American Nightmare" (Ore, 2014). The common denominator is the same in both cases. Evocative of the ignominious "Whites Only" signs of the past, these grand narratives are only inclusive of the white lived experience in the United States.

When nonwhite characters become part of this "whites only" story, the narrative and the symbols that people use to communicate can become unintelligible for whites. In this milieu, routine communication with the new characters becomes a challenge as diverse meanings, for ideas such as "liberalism" and "American Dream," must now be negotiated from various standpoints. For instance, to me, the idea of "liberal" meant something quite different coming from a "liberal" place like New York City. In sum, my move to Boulder, considering my high hopes and excitement, is comparable to the anticlimactic experience of the euphoric romantic partner who has high expectations for a fledgling relationship only to find out that the person is as good for them as Marilyn Monroe was for JFK. Overall, the constraints in which it exists will cause the relationship to end disastrously regardless of how hopeful of its potential and enthusiastic the partners are at the outset.

Two particular events epitomize many whites' toxic and insidious attitudes, assumptions, and perceptions of people of other races and ethnicities in Boulder. The first episode was when I was teaching my first class as a Teaching Assistant and a student had an antagonistic response to something that I said during the lesson. The second episode was during a conversation with a faculty member who was giving a workshop about effective teaching to a new cohort of graduate students.

"WHY DON'T *YOU* LIKE IT HERE?"

It was the beginning of the fall semester my first year as a doctoral student at the University of Colorado. I was in my Perspectives on Human Communication course teaching a lesson about mass communication when the subject of "conservative and liberal news media" surfaced. I stood in front of the classroom discussing the day's lesson with a group of mostly white students when one student interrupts me without raising his hand, and in a defensive and antagonistic voice tone says, "There are people jumping that [southern] border everyday so they seem to like it here, so why don't *you* like it here?" The tension in the classroom was palpable and the other students stared at me with eyes of anticipation wondering what I would do or say next. Surprised by the student's response, and questioning what relationship it had to my lecture, I paused and deflected the student's comment to somehow bring it back to the lesson. Masking my irritation, I asked the student to see me after class; he nodded his head to signify agreement. We talked after class ended and were able to resolve the "misunderstanding" without further complications.

I thought about this student's comment soon after the episode occurred and in the months and years that followed. In retrospect, I feel that his comment was a reaction to something beyond the lesson's content. That student's antagonistic reaction was triggered by my presence in front of the classroom. This white upper-class student was challenged by, and struggling with, the reality of having a Latino immigrant as a communication professor. This student's reaction also seemed to have an undercurrent of frustration and confusion. Interestingly, his emotional tone communicated to me some of the same emotions that I was feeling at the time. In addition, this student's emotional response illustrates how many whites expressed emotionality when in my presence. As I began to notice that such behaviors were becoming a pattern, I deduced that many individuals were as mystified as I was to be in a position where we had to negotiate each other. I believe we simply lacked the discursive resources for such gargantuan task. Our various layers of difference proved to be overpowering and this was demonstrated by the many negative interactions I had with whites. The exchange with my student in the classroom is only a prologue to what turned out to be a prolonged period filled with unsettling experiences with interpersonal prejudice in Boulder. Just a couple of days after the student's antagonistic comment, a professor made a distressing remark related to my ethnicity and ability.

"THAT'S VERY GOOD *FOR A HISPANIC*"

Days later, with my student's comment still fresh on my mind, I found myself sitting in an auditorium at a teaching workshop. A veteran professor, a master teacher and scholar, was facilitating the workshop. It was a dynamic and engaging presentation. I approached the professor after the presentation to introduce myself and to ask some questions about pedagogy. I also wanted to get some advice as I was experiencing much confusion and uncertainty about my new role as a doctoral student—the so-called, "impostor syndrome." A few minutes into our conversation, the professor says to me, "you will be fine, you are in communication and you have done well enough to be here. That's very good for a Hispanic."

Similar to my reaction to my student's comment, I stood there perplexed and unresponsive wondering what to say and in what manner. Part of me felt that there was nothing that I could say or do to remedy the situation—for some strange reason, I felt this state of inertia in responding to people's insulting statements throughout my time in Boulder. Maybe part of me just felt the impotence that many Blacks and Latinos/as have felt when dealing with systemic prejudice (i.e., racism). How does one person fight a system? This feeling can be consuming after dealing with injuring experiences over a long period of time. There is a sense of overwhelmedness that renders the person emotionally incapacitated. Cose (1993) referred to this state as "coping fatigue" in *The Rage of a Privileged Class*. I compare it to the physical fatigue a person must feel when swimming in turbulent ocean waters. I assume that after paddling one's arms and legs for a long time, fatigue begins to set in and it can eventually paralyze the body. In response to the professor's comment, I remember trying to end the conversation so that I could leave and go wallow in my grief. What I found most disturbing about the professor's remark, and what was consistent in encounters with many whites in Boulder, was that this person seemed completely oblivious of the problematic nature of his remark.

This professor's troubling comment exemplifies a collective attitude toward nonwhites at the university and beyond its walls. Interestingly, however, in the four years that I spent there, many people's hurtful comments came across as unabashedly unremorseful. Over time, the consistency and variety of people's responses showed that the problem lied beyond ignorance; this was indeed a culture. In sum, many whites' verbal and nonverbal messages were consistent and intentional in their aims to offend me and others like me. In addition to this professor's subtle yet perturbing assumptions about my ethnicity and ability to perform academically, I provide two more instances that show how prejudice was a constitutive feature of Boulder's (white) residents' orientation toward someone like me (a "biracial" looking Caribbean immigrant).

MY ACCENT'S "UNINTELLIGIBILITY"

Nonverbal messages often communicate more powerfully than verbal messages. Nonverbal channels mediated many of my interactions with people in Boulder. This includes paralinguistic behaviors such as voice tone, volume, pitch, also, eye behavior, facial expressions, as well as body language such as postures, gestures, touch, etc. Two events further highlight my experiences with what I characterize as racial prejudice. Both events took place at gatherings off campus, one to celebrate a friend's birthday and the other at a party at a professor's home. Both exchanges were with people who were my colleague and professor's acquaintances and city residents but had no affiliation to the university.

I was at a friend's birthday party when a white woman in her twenties asked me, "Why is your accent *so thick*?" Both her facial expressions and tone of voice when she asked the question communicated confusion and repulsion. Her frowning, akin to when our palate interacts with an unpleasant food, and how she placed emphasis on the last two words in that question sent a message of rejection. I considered what this person might have meant based on the manner in which she asked the question. Was there a subtext here of any kind? Was she really asking, "Where are you from?" As thoughts raced through my head, I pondered how to respond in a competent manner considering the context. I proceeded to share with her my country of origin (Dominican Republic) and native language (Spanish). She could not have seemed more disinterested in the information that I shared with her. After the fleeting exchange we both realized that we needed to make strategic efforts to ignore each other the rest of the time at the party and we did.

On another occasion, I was at a gathering at a professor's home, when Simon and Garfunkel's song "Mrs. Robinson" came on and I started to sing it out loud when a middle aged white woman looked at me with raised eyebrows and seemingly bewildered mentioned, "Yes, but they don't sing it with *that accent*." I paused and stared at her momentarily, after which I continued to sing the song out loud. Shortly after, I made my way to another room in the house. Like a slow water drip, I noticed these subtle instances of intolerance kept happening in routine interactions. Once again, this person had placed a strong emphasis on the last two words in that statement as if wanting to emphasize my distinctiveness in that context. In each of these instances, the verbal and nonverbal messages operated in concert to express unease with my linguistic performance, particularly how I pronounced words in English. These individuals' reactions are symbolic of various issues operating at the signification level.

My accent, a paralinguistic device, was a seed of meaning through which individuals made sense of and assigned significance to my complex being. These examples show that how I talk has implications for how people respond to me. More specifically, in a place like Boulder, my accent functioned as an invitation to be prejudicial, as dialect is one of the most common ways in which in-group and out-groupness is constituted and negotiated in U.S. society (Lippi-Green, 2003). Over time, my interactions with whites in Boulder created a context of discursive closure (Deetz, 1992). My ability to express myself in complicated ways was constantly restricted by the myopic idea that people had of me. This context of discursive closure was mediated in part by my phonetic language use.

Because of the consistency and vitality with which I endured prejudicial verbal and nonverbal attacks, I began to perceive that the onus was on me to adapt to my surroundings (coping fatigue). People's profoundly prejudiced discourse disciplined and regulated my social performances in powerful ways. I wanted to be my authentic self in interpersonal encounters but could not due to having a constant fear of rejection. In social occasions, I felt like I was "passing" to reinforce others' expectations of me at the expense of my individual integrity (Spradlin, 1998).

The last two individuals' comments represent distancing at the group level, enactments of ethnolinguistic vitality (Giles & Sassoon, 1983). Their remarks embody the presumed and automatically expected normativity, purity, and ideal within communication systems imbued with the ideology of white supremacy. It is in discourse (at micro, meso, and macro levels) that white supremacy is maintained through a dominant iconography that signifies that "white" is a norm that is always "natural" and "neutral" in relation to others (Allen, 2011). Everyday discourse in tandem with macrolevel systems of signification perpetuate a structure that determines where, when, and how Black and Brown bodies become unintelligible (Butler, 1995), uncivilized (Cisneros, 2005), and a threat (L. Chavez, 2008) to the white establishment. I use Barthes' semiotics theory to further explicate how these processes are systematically and systemically constituted through communication.

BOULDER: A PRODUCTIVE "MYTH-MAKING" SITE

Semiotics, as coined by French semiologist Roland Barthes, is the study of sign systems and their meanings. According to Barthes, all signs exist in a system and have a mutually constitutive relationship. Signs are the connections between signifier (the object or material form) and the signified (the symbols that we use to refer to the material form). In this conceptual framework, a myth is the connotative meaning associated with signs. In the remainder of this chapter, I engage semiotics theory's concepts to analyze my experiences with prejudice in Boulder. Furthermore, I apply communication theory of identity to discuss why achieving communal appreciation among diverse cultural groups has been difficult to fulfill and the potential for incorporating this ideal to produce enduring societal and cultural changes.

SIGNS, SYSTEMS, MYTHS, AND THE "LATINO/A IMMIGRANT THREAT"

"Why are *gringos [whites]* so repulsed by us [Latinos/as]?" was a question that one of the Latino janitors that I interviewed for my dissertation project raised (Alvarez, 2011). To me, this question encapsulates thoughts and emotions that many nonwhites think and feel everyday in the United States. What are the main factors giving shape to a culture of prejudice? How can whites' attitudes toward different others be explained? I address these questions by considering salient relationships between the social construction of human differences in the United States, dominant meanings and labels assigned to nonwhite bodies, and how those meanings function as signs that structure sense making (in)directly creating "myths" such as the "Latino/a immigrant Threat."

The signification of the "Latino/a immigrant" is a "myth" that automatically disqualifies people like Jose (pseudonym), the janitor who asked the question, and me (K. Chavez, 2009). Jose's question is a valid one. Why do so many whites have such visceral hostile reactions toward Latino/a, and Black, bodies? I posit that in a white supremacist communication system, Latino/a bodies are always already disqualified (Butler, 1995). This reality is exponentially accentuated in predominantly white cultural spaces like Boulder. The dominant meanings and labels ascribed to Latino/a bodies are so demeaning and totalizing that, for many whites, empathizing, or engaging with them in complicated ways, is virtually impossible. It is in this type of communication system that whites attempt to make sense of people like Jose and me.

In the white European American sociocultural imagination (Flores, 2000), Latino/a immigrants' bodies are often "read" through lenses that are "scuffed" with disparaging connotations. In places like Boulder my body acts as a signifier and symbols that many people typically associate with it, "uncivilized," "repulsive," "a threat" act as the signified and the sign (the combination of the two) reads "Wilfredo is uncivilized, repulsive, a threat." If language is the reservoir of meanings from which individuals construct social reality, then for many Boulder whites, "reality" is that my body carries at least some of those meanings and when people interact with me, those meanings are part of the central reservoir from which they extracted symbols to make sense of me.

As a result of this communication system, prevailing meanings are foregrounded in people's perceptions and communicative deployments. Further reinforced by ubiquitous one-dimensional caricatures of Latinos/as in popular culture (L. Chavez, 2008), the persistence of segregated cultural spaces such as white suburbia and black and brown inner cities (Allen, 2011), and the lack of prolonged interactions with different others (Orbe, 1998), many whites' idea of people like me are myopic at best and fictional at worst. This situation engenders a communication system where my person is totalized, my existence trivialized and thus I am always already disqualified in spaces like Boulder. A constructive outcome from this experience is that as a Latino immigrant, my standpoints offer useful knowledge necessary to illuminate and understand my, and my Black and Latino/a colleagues, experiences with racial prejudice in white America (Hill Collins, 1986).

According to Barthes (1972), there are ideological subtexts in everything that signifies (i.e., symbols). In my Boulder experience, my body acted as a "text" whose "subtext" partially stemmed from historical relationships between Anglo-Saxons and Latinos/as (Mexicans in particular) in the western United States (Rodriguez, 2007) where the two groups fought for resources and land, and more recently as harmful meanings became inscribed in the geography of segregated ethnic communities (Grosfoguel, 2003). The "subtext" inherent in the "Latino/a Threat" narrative creates a discursive framework where whites might perceive someone like me as undesirable, unassimilatable, and thus a perpetual foreigner (L. Chavez, 2008). As a society, people can dissipate harmful narratives such as the "Latino/a Threat" by proactively nurturing their understanding of social differences and their meanings and ultimately put ourselves in a position where we can appreciate different others.

However, the continuous commitment to a system of "whiteness" (Lipsitz, 1998), fueled in part by the institutional maintenance of dominant values (e.g., through mass media messages) (Hall, 1996), crafts a discourse of difference which ideological underpinnings promote images of whites as coherent, civilized, and thus as bodies that people can learn to appreciate. Within this racially insular communication system, whites' relationship with the sign

"Latinos/as as a Threat" is problematic and therefore learning to appreciate it becomes difficult, lessening the possibility of reaching genuine intergroup appreciation. The social constitution and pervasiveness of the "Latino/a as a Threat" sign disseminates a myth that mediates and mystifies whites' understandings of those who embody it. For Barthes, who studied ideology promoting myth-making sites, Boulder would represent the crystallization of such sites as related to the making and maintenance of the "Latino/a Threat" myth. Myth-making sites are dangerous because they function to maintain the dominant social group's narrative of normativity and naturalness at the expense of nondominant groups' lived experiences (in the U.S., cities like Levittown, NY in the mid 20th century, and current-day Boulder, CO and Phoenix, AZ exemplify such myth-making sites).

The white supremacist communication system in Boulder illustrates a linguistic structure that fundamentally labels and defines my Latino body punitively. This linguistic structure possesses a highly sophisticated connotative system (myth) through which people comprehend and relate to my "brown" body (Barthes, 1972). A parallel conceptual example is when I, an able-bodied person, interact with a person with a visible disability. If cognitively I make the person the disability (totalization), I cannot identify with and relate to them in complicated ways. Essentially, if I am part of a system of meaning that totalizes me, then empathizing, relating, or appreciating someone like me, becomes onerous to most people. When it comes to whites' relationships with Latino/a immigrants for instance, appreciation is an ideal with which this country is still struggling. Reconfiguring the current social milieu requires a major shift in the connotative system (our myth-making sites). Such reconfiguration also requires a multifaceted communicative approach that can eventually result in the formation of sustained cultures/sites of communal appreciation.

REALIZING COMMUNAL APPRECIATION

No matter what the durability to date, virtually any pattern of social action is open to infinite revision. Accepting for a moment the argument of the social constructionists that social reality, at any given point, is a product of broad social agreement (shared meanings), and further granting a linkage between the conceptual schemes of a culture and its other patterns of action, we must seriously consider the idea that alterations in conceptual practices, in ways of symbolizing the world, hold tremendous potential for guiding changes in the social order. (Cooperider & Srivastva, 1987, p. 134)

Humans create, conserve, and change societies and cultures through communication (Gergen, 1982). The human sociocultural environment is fundamentally an ever-changing symbolic universe. A shift in orientation towards "the other" is possible insofar as there is a commitment to cooperating in the pursuit of a collective awakening in consciousness. This renewed state of social consciousness will lead to a more nuanced understanding of society as a web of shifting and contentious meanings, ideas, beliefs, and interdependent relationships that if properly harnessed can produce effective systems (Cooperider & Srivastva, 1987). This reality possesses a seed of potential to create cultures of communal appreciation.

In this section, I apply the communication theory of identity (Hecht & Choi, 2012) to stimulate critical dialogue necessary to imagine and realize communal appreciation. I also draw concepts from Cooperider and Whitney's (2005) appreciative inquiry (AI) model to highlight key processes necessary to achieve intergroup appreciation. My hope is that the ideas in this essay serve as an instrument with which people can disrupt communication systems of oppression and discrimination. I also seek to foster communities where diverse people can be empowered by a renewed sense of respect and appreciation for one another. The ideas that follow rest on the premise that all humans have the potential for public leadership, which emanates from the self and out into the person's spheres of influence. Tapping into the human potential for social influence through inquiry (of both self and other) is essential, and a core principle, to transform the status quo related to intergroup relations.

The communication theory of identity (CTI) (Hecht, Jackson, & Ribeau, 2003) is a useful conceptual framework to illustrate the processes through which cultures of communal appreciation can develop. CTI is a theoretical perspective that views communication as a dynamic and fluid process that (re)creates identities with the self and others. CTI advances four layers central to everyday identity enactment and management. The four layers are the personal, enacted, relational, and communal (Hecht & Choi, 2012). Figure 1 captures (below) how these four layers are interconnected and mutually influential.

The personal layer refers to the individual as the main source of identity (analogous to the self-concept). The enactment layer is when we use communicative behaviors to perform our identities with others. The relational layer is when people co-construct shared identities in communication via relational ties. Lastly, the communal layer is where collective identities, as a group/community, are constituted through communication. As Figure 2 below shows, this layered framework is useful because it provides a context to situate the concept of "appreciation" as communicatively (re)produced and as having complex "layers" from the individual to the community level.

In this model of communal appreciation, the concept of appreciation is fundamentally rooted in individuals and permeates into the communities that individuals occupy through communicative enactments, relationship building, and ultimately the formation of cultures of appreciation. Hecht and Choi (2012) posited, "...communication is an element rather than a product of identity" (p. 139). I reformulate this statement to claim that appreciation is a central element of identity. Appreciation is a communicative achievement that has the potential to influence and transform people's spheres of influence. CTI is fitting to develop the idea of appreciation because it provides "...a more comprehensive or synthetic view of identity integrating community, communication, social relationships, and self-concepts, while "locating" identity in all these layers" (Hecht & Choi, 2012, p. 139).

My definition of appreciation places the onus of action on individuals. Individuals must develop nuanced sensitivities toward self and other. According to CTI, the personal layer is akin to the self-concept or the articulation of a unique individual self. The self is communicatively constructed and defined in relation to others in society (Jackson, 1999). For appreciation towards different others to take hold, there must be meaningful prolonged interactions, which plant the seed for an awakening of consciousness. For instance, based on my Boulder experience, it seemed that there was such a "shock to the system" for whites and me that the state of affairs challenged our self-concepts. In the presence of "the other," many of us could not articulate our selves in ways to which we had been accustomed. This created a demanding discursive environment that often lead to conflict.

Interactions with different others can help stimulate internal dialogue that create opportunities to question taken-for-granted assumptions about self, other, and behaviors toward others. Cooperrider, Whitney, and Stavros (2008) call this process "dream[ing]" in their model of appreciative inquiry. The authors assert that "It [dream[ing]] occurs when the best of "what is" has been identified; the mind naturally begins to search further and to envision new possibilities. Valuing the best of "what is" leads to envisioning what might be" (p. 6). In a culture of communal appreciation, individuals must "dream" together what appreciation means to their community's health, display that

Wilfredo Alvarez

enhanced understanding in everyday interactions, and have a collective willingness to engage the "messiness" of intergroup relations (Orbe, 1994).

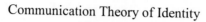

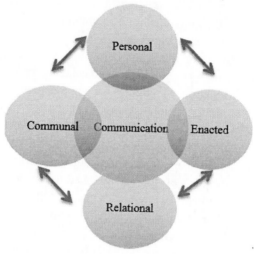

Figure 1. Relationship among four layers of CTI.

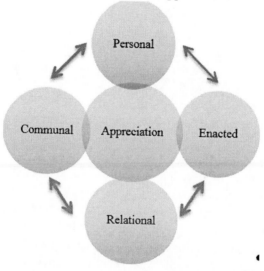

Figure 2. Process of realizing communal appreciation and its four interrelated layers of enactment.

This shifting collective outlook is expressed through internal and external processes of inquiry. For example, for whites who showed a prejudicial attitude toward me in Boulder, the process of change would be set off by internal explorations with questions such as "how do I feel about x group of people and why?" This inquiring practice encourages people to become more curious and probe into the reasons for their own and other in-group members' rigid mindsets. Cooperrider, Whitney, and Stavros (2008) refer to this process as "discovery." They claim that "As part of the discovery process, individuals engage in dialogue and meaning-making. This is simply the open sharing of discoveries and possibilities" (p. 6). This stage is when the seeds of appreciation are planted. Individuals begin to understand that valuing others is necessary for the system's effective functioning (Cooperrider & Srivasta, 1987). Developing an inquiring orientation can be a bold step for individuals and communities alike, which can promote exchanges of thoughts and feelings about culturally different others. Ultimately, there must be a genuine connection between individuals' deeper (personal layer) and surface level communication (enactment layer).

As individuals begin to process the idea that appreciating different others can be a constructive endeavor for all stakeholders, they begin to demonstrate that mental paradigm shift in everyday interactions. For example, the whites with whom I had positive interactions in Boulder were the ones who were genuinely curious about my lived experiences. Those individuals inquired about my background and wanted to know what it was like living in Dominican Republic and New York City for instance. In other words, those individuals intentionally sought some degree of immediacy with me. These communication behaviors are critical allies in triggering attitudinal changes from out-group members.

Additionally, individuals' communicative choices have ripple effects on the formation and maintenance of positive/negative attitudes towards our own and others' cultural groups. I recall moving to a new city after Boulder and being unreasonably unfriendly toward many whites in the new city. The seeds of animosity that many whites in Boulder planted in me were being manifested in various ways months after I had left. In some ways, and without trying to diminish anyone's experience, I was experiencing a type of post-traumatic stress disorder (PTSD.) My experiences during and after Boulder demonstrate that the extent to which cultural group members move beyond "watching" each other as habitual practice and instead, through small actions, begin to "design" a new culture where appreciating others becomes a norm determines our ability to move past destructive intergroup dynamics. Designing this type of norm requires that people "...coconstruct the future by the design of an organizational architecture in which the exceptional becomes every day and ordinary" (Cooperrider, Whitney, & Stavros, 2008, p. 7).

"Designing" (Cooperrider & Whitney, 2005) happens in people's spheres of influence (i.e., the primary social contexts that they occupy in daily life). When I teach intercultural communication, I always invite white students to consider their privilege, based on social status, as having an obligation to challenge dominant perceptions of "the other" and educate people in their spheres of influence. I tell them that they are being exposed to information that requires them to enact more mindful attitudes, beliefs, and behaviors toward nonwhites than previous generations. My hope is that those students return to their spheres of influence and share the information with others. This process can include metacommunicating about appreciation (i.e., talking about appreciation and its benefits). After all, it is possible that several people in the students' spheres of influence have not been exposed to the information to which they are exposed. This scenario highlights the significance of the relational layer in cultivating communal appreciation.

Cultures of appreciation are cultivated when individuals generate "feedback loops" with in-group and out-group members. In this process, individuals respond to feedback as they regularly enact appreciative behaviors. For example, I had a relationship with one of my white neighbors in Boulder that was diametrically opposed to the negative interactions I had with most whites. This person was curious about me, kind, and thoughtful. We exchanged food and she even gave me a plant for my home. Our relationship was what I hoped it would with most whites in Boulder. We formed and developed a healthy relationship where there were constant "feedback loops" about how much we appreciated each other. I believe this relationship helped me to not completely "lose faith" in the potential of ever having nurturing personal relationships with white Americans.

People develop appreciative identities and enlist others' support as they collectively become more appreciative towards others. Thus, appreciative relationships are ones where people give each other room to "mess up" because they perceive that the other person is interested in exploring each other's idiosyncrasies in nonjudgmental ways. The result is social contagion (Christakis & Fowler, 2012). According to Hecht and Choi (2012), the extent to which our identities are central part of a community helps determine the group's well being. Similarly, this idea represents the basis for the possibility of creating enduring cultures of communal appreciation.

As appreciation becomes mutually co-constructed, outcomes in relationships with different others, people begin to lay the foundation for larger appreciative structures. The group is a vital entity as group processes have the potential of becoming large-scale structures (Poole, 2013). For instance, small groups of people contributed to the formation and expansion of the modern Civil Rights Movement of the 1950s and 1960s. Those groups working together toward a shared vision largely influenced the policies and practices that emerged from that social movement. Reaching that level of influence is a crucial goal of the process of creating and cultivating cultures of intergroup appreciation.

As cultural groups form communal identities related to appreciation, individuals will begin to uphold new understandings and values. The proverbial "power in numbers" takes hold. As group identities develop, "group members share common characteristics, histories, and collective memories that transcend individuals and result in commonly held identities" (Hecht & Choi, 2012, p. 142). Group identification is critical because it leads to the emergence of symbols, legends, stories/narratives, and a redesigned culture of intergroup relations. This type of shared effort will catapult cultural groups into a different kind of "destiny" (Cooperrider, Whitney, & Stavros, 2008). This new "destiny" will move cultural groups away from the intercultural status quo in U.S. society. "This [destiny] is important because it is precisely through the juxtaposition of visionary content with grounded examples of the extraordinary that AI [Appreciative Inquiry] opens the status quo to transformations via collection action" (Cooperrider, Whitney, & Stavros, 2008, p. 7).

A group-level shift in awareness can be achieved with the support of social institutions (e.g., education systems). Engaging conversation topics around questions such as "why are the concepts of diversity and inclusion important?" and "why is intergroup appreciation necessary in a culturally diverse complex global society?" as early as middle school can advance this dialogue and raise the nation's public consciousness. Education settings provide forums where people are exposed to different others and engage in critical dialogue about difficult topics in a supportive communication climate (Allen, 2011).

Educational institutions are core socialization spaces where cultures of appreciation can be nurtured. Related to education, for cultures of communal appreciation to take shape, three central interrelated factors must be present: 1) a commitment to providing everyone with access to a constructive primary, secondary, and postsecondary education, 2) this approach will foment people's understanding of the human condition, 3) the first two factors will lead to more mindful and intentional individual and group action. As communities' discourses of diversity change, so will the insidious cultural codes that perpetuate enduring prejudicial attitudes toward culturally different others.

The four layers outlined in this chapter—personal, enactment, relational, and communal— are closely interconnected. As individuals develop a sense of the importance of the concept of appreciation and begin to express it, this opens the door to engage with different others. As relational partners begin to have conversations about intergroup appreciation, this expands the number of people who will consider genuinely appreciating others to be a significant notion in their lives. For these reasons, these four layers must be understood as inextricably linked and interdependent.

Oppressive communication systems (Kramarae, 2005) must change if the U.S. is to rise above Social Darwinist structures (Ore, 2014). The implications of such paradigm shifts are significant for intergroup relations and the social system's effective functioning. The United States cannot consider itself a "civilized society" when marginalized groups are still considered sub-human and treated like second-class citizens. For this forward movement to happen, the interracial status quo must be challenged, disrupted, and permanently transformed. A commitment to communicating compassion and empathy and finding moments to engage openness can transcend conventional sociocultural roles and engender systemic transformation (Alvarez, 2013).

In closing, expanding our vocabularies about culturally different others can contribute to social transformation and the formation of communities of appreciation. This transformation process entails making individual adjustments, which require a commitment to constant self-reflection, consciousness raising, and the courage to engage difficult conversations inside and outside of our spheres of influence. This commitment to being present and engaging different others in our everyday interactions will foster influential relationships leading to the formation of cultures of communal appreciation. The result is mutually respectful and empowered diverse communities of people.

REFERENCES

Allen, B. J. (2011). *Difference matters: Communicating social identity* (2nd ed.). Long Grove, IL: Waveland Press.

Alvarez, W. (2011). *Communication experiences of Latina and Latino custodial workers in a university setting.* Unpublished doctoral dissertation. University of Colorado Boulder.

Alvarez, W. (2013). Finding "home" in/through Latinidad Ethnography: Experiencing community in the field with "my people." *Liminalities: A Journal of Performance Studies, 9*(2), 49 – 58.

Barthes, R. (1972). *Mythologies.* New York, NY: Hill and Wang.

Butler, J. (1995). Contingent foundations for a careful reading. In S. Benhabib, J. Butler, D. Cornell, & N. Fraser (Eds.), *Feminist contentions: A philosophical exchange* (pp. 35 – 57, 127 – 143). New York, NY: Routledge.

Chávez, L. R. (2008). *The Latino threat narrative: Constructing immigrants, citizens, and the nation.* Stanford, CA: Stanford University Press.

Chávez, K. R. (2009). Embodied translation: Dominant discourse and communication with migrant bodies-as-a-text. *Howard Journal of Communications, 20*, 18 – 36. doi:10.1080/10646170802664912.

Cisneros, J. D. (2008). Contaminated communities: The metaphor of "immigrant as a pollutant" in media representations of immigration. *Rhetoric & Public Affairs, 11*, 569 – 602. doi:10.1353/rap.0.0068.

Christakis, N. A., & Fowler, J. H. (2013). Social contagion theory: Examining dynamic social networks and human behavior. *Statistics in Medicine, 32*, 556 – 577. doi: 10.1002/sim.5408.

Collins, P. H. (1986). Learning from the outsider within: The sociological significance of black feminist thought. *Social Problems, 33*, S14 – S23. doi:10.1525/sp.1986.6.03a00020.

Cooperrider, D. L., & Srivastva, S. (1987). Appreciative inquiry in organizational life. *Research in Organizational Change and Development, 1*, 129 – 169.

Cooperrider, D. L., & Whitney, D. D. (2005). *Appreciative inquiry: A positive revolution in change.* Oakland, CA: Berrett-Koehler Publishers.

Cooperrider, D. L., Whitney, D. D., & Stavros, J. M. (2008). *The appreciative inquiry handbook: For leaders of change.* Oakland, CA: Berrett-Koehler Publishers.

Cose, E. J. (1993). *The rage of a privileged class: Why are middle-class Black angry? Why should America care?* New York, NY: HarperCollins.

Deetz, S. A. (1992). *Democracy in an age of corporate colonization: Developments in communication and the politics of everyday life.* Albany, NY: State University of New York Press.

Flores, J. (2000). *From Bomba to Hip Hop: Puerto Rican culture and Latino identity*. New York, NY: Columbia University Press.

Gergen, K. (1982). *Toward transformation in social knowledge*. New York, NY: Springer-Verlag.

Giles, H., & Sassoon, C. (1983). The effects of speaker's accent, social class background, and message style on British listeners' social judgments. *Language & Communication, 3*, 305 – 313. doi:10.1016/0271-5309(83)90006-X.

Grosfoguel, R. (2003). *Colonial subjects: Puerto Ricans in a global perspective*. Berkeley, CA: University of California Press.

Hall, S. M. (1996). Cultural identity and cinematic representation in black cultural studies. In A. Baker Houston, Jr., Manthia Diawara and Ruth H.Lindeborg (Eds.), *Black British Cultural Studies: A Reader (Black Literature and Culture)* (pp. 210 – 22). Chicago, IL: University of Chicago Press.

Hecht, M. L. (Ed.). (1998). *Communicating prejudice*. Thousand Oaks, CA: Sage.

Hecht, M. L., Jackson, R. L., & Ribeau, S. A. (2003). *African American communication: Exploring identity and cultural*. Mahwah, NJ: L. Erlbaum Associates.

Hecht, M. L., & Choi, H. (2012). The communication theory of identity as a framework for message design. In Hyunyi Cho (Ed.), *Health communication message design* (pp. 137 – 152). Thousand Oaks, CA: Sage.

Jackson, R. L. (1999). *The negotiation of cultural identity: Perceptions of European Americans and African Americans*. Westport, CT: Praeger.

Kramarae, C. (2005). Muted group theory and communication: Asking dangerous questions. *Women & Language, 28*, 55 – 61.

Lippi-Green, R. (2003). *English with an accent: Language, ideology, and discrimination in the United States*. New York, NY: Routledge.

Lipsitz, G. (1998). *The possessive investment in whiteness: How white people profit from identity politics*. Philadelphia, PA: Temple University Press.

Orbe, M. P. (1994). "Remember, it's always whites' ball:" Descriptions of African American male communication. *Communication Quarterly, 42*, 287 – 300. doi:10.1080/01463379409369935.

Orbe, M. P. (1998). An outsider within perspective to organizational communication: Explicating the communication practices of co-cultural group members. *Management Communication Quarterly, 12*, 230 – 279. doi:10.1177/0893318998122003

Ore, T. E. (Ed.) (2014). *The social construction of difference and inequality: Race, class, gender, and sexuality* (6th ed.). New York, NY: McGraw-Hill.

Poole, M. S. (2013). Structuration research on group communication. *Management Communication Quarterly, 27*, 607 – 614. doi:10.1177/0893318913506265.

Rodriguez, G. (2007). *Mongrels, bastards, orphans, and vagabonds: Mexican immigration and the future of race in America*. New York, NY: Pantheon Books.

Spradlin, A. (1998). The price of "passing:" A lesbian perspective on authenticity in organizations. *Management Communication Quarterly, 11*(4), 598 – 605.

In: Communicating Prejudice
Editors: S. Camara and D. Drummond
ISBN: 978-1-53610-167-6
© 2016 Nova Science Publishers, Inc.

Chapter 9

FROM MAJORITY TO MINORITY: A PERSONAL NARRATIVE

Deanna F. Womack

Kennesaw State University, Kennesaw, GA, US

ABSTRACT

I use my life experiences as stories to help students in my intercultural classes better empathize with different experiences. I tell stories of living and beginning high school during the civil rights struggles in Birmingham, Alabama. My own later experiences as minority group member living in Taiwan allow me to identify with several difficulties typical of minority experience. The experiences of my teenage daughters, who were born in China, allow me to provide examples of intercultural identity development. By publicly telling my own story, by supporting students brave enough to tell theirs, and by choosing educational materials with which both minority and majority students can identify, I believe I have been successful in helping some of my students become more sensitive to prejudice, even their own.

INTRODUCTION

When I began teaching intercultural communication several years ago, I decided to use my experiences as a majority, a minority, and a parent of international adoptees to prompt my students to take others' perspectives as we discuss course material. My personal experiences have influenced the way I teach intercultural communication, and I hope have provided a richer academic environment for students.

My experiences as a teenager were those of a privileged majority member in the Deep South. When I started high school in 1963, my father, S. Grady Fullerton, was Director of Finance for the city of Birmingham. He reported to the four county commissioners, one of whom was the infamous Eugene "Bull" Connor, who sent police with cattle prods and firefighters with hoses turned on full blast to break up nonviolent protests that he and most people I knew termed "riots" during the civil rights demonstrations of the early 1960s. For two years in my twenties, I lived in Taichung, Taiwan, Republic of China and experienced life from the perspective of a visible minority. Beginning in my forties, I became a member of a mixed race majority-minority family when my husband and I adopted twins born in China. Now, as a teacher of intercultural communication in a School of Communication and Media that is 71% white, 14% black, 6% Hispanic, and 9% other, I draw on these varied experiences to enrich my course and to help my students, both minority and majority, identify with my experiences that are similar to and different from their own. I hope they are better able to understand and empathize with others' experiences through the stories I tell and the feelings I share.

My Majority Experiences

I started high school in Birmingham, Alabama, in 1963, the first year the Birmingham Public Schools were integrated. I was fourteen when I began ninth grade at Ramsay High School. In 1962, all of the approximately 800 students in ninth through twelfth grades were Caucasian. In 1963, four African American students were enrolled, one student in each grade. Adding only four Black students, who formed about .005% of the student body, still led to community uproar. After several days' delay to calm the situation and plan for crowd control, school began. For the first two weeks, when I entered the building, I saw and heard loud States' Rights Party demonstrators at one end of the block-long street and pro-integration demonstrators at the other. In between were national and local news crews and the police, who formed a line through which students passed.

As a teenager, I received mixed messages about integration. The evening before my first day of high school, my mother warned me that some students might walk out at lunch the next day, but I was not to join them. She said this, not because she supported integration, which my parents tended to see as a movement fomented by "outside agitators," but because polite Southern girls (of both races) did not "make trouble" or "cause a scene."

I remember no incidents during the school day; I don't believe the walkout actually occurred. I never even saw any of the African American students, though I heard rumors that one day the senior put his head down on his desk and cried. Two years later, after my family moved to Houston, Texas, I entered eleventh grade at Robert E. Lee High School. The school was integrated with enough African American students that I was aware of them, but I do not remember any difficulties related to integration in the Southwest.

The next year, my family returned to Birmingham for a visit and attended the annual church picnic. I was very uncomfortable when an elderly lady who happened to be sitting at the wooden picnic table with my friends and me animatedly expressed her views about integration. She said, "Why, you'd think they were people just like we are!" I thought – but did not say – "but they are people."

Why I thought differently from my parents and my community, I cannot say. Perhaps it was because the adults in my community had been influenced by unchallenged community attitudes that desegregation was "right," "the way things ought to be." By the time I grew up, attitudes were slowly beginning to change. My parents' textbooks taught that African Americans were inferior. My textbooks focused on Caucasian accomplishments, but at least they did not explicitly present African Americans as an inferior race. I also think exploitation theory or perhaps scapegoating theory (Schaefer, 2009) may help explain the difference. Caucasians may have wanted to restrain African Americans so that they could have higher status and power, and thus feel superior. Or lower-class Caucasians may have scapegoated African Americans, as taking away jobs that should have gone to them. While those attitudes persisted when I was growing up, they were less often publicly expressed, and I was not conscious of sharing them.

In teaching a course in intercultural communication, I use these experiences when I show most of the "Ain't Scared of Your Jails (1960-1961)" section of the video *Eyes on the Prize* (Blackside, 2006) in class. Most of the Black Southern students in class have seen the video more than once. Many of the White Southern students have never seen it nor been made so vividly aware of the violence that the peaceful protestors, often led by college students, faced. In class I talk about my high school experiences and answer questions about living through those times. Since I am White, I believe my

White students are less defensive when they view the film in class than students are when my Black colleague teaches the course. As a member of the Majority, I have freedom to criticize the Majority in ways that she believes she does not.

MY MINORITY EXPERIENCES

How did I change from being surrounded by attitudes of racial discrimination to openly trying to combat them when I teach intercultural communication at my university? I believe my two years' experiences of being a member of a minority race when I lived in Taiwan hold the key to indicating how attitudes can be transformed and have also informed the teaching techniques and materials I use in my intercultural communication class.

I learned what it was like for others to perceive and judge me primarily by the color of my skin or some other stereotypical characteristic and how annoying that was. Although my experiences were primarily positive, I grew tired of being a walking representative of a country or religion different from that of the majority. Sometimes I was cheated, as when a shopkeeper charged me three times what she should have for a fish. I had not seen her put her thumb on the scale when she weighed it, but the Chinese owner of the grocery store at Tunghai University, where I was teaching, reweighed it, explained to me what likely had happened, and told me I must be more careful watching the store clerks.

When I rode public buses to and from school, I was usually the only Westerner in a sea of Chinese at least a foot shorter than I. I felt the junior high school boys riding with me were talking about me, though I eventually learned enough Chinese to discover that they were discussing more interesting topics. My self-consciousness had led me to feel singled-out, and sometimes I was. Once when I got lost in downtown Taichung, a little girl saw me and went running to her mother, exclaiming, "American! American!" in Chinese. In 1975-1977 Westerners were much less common except in the capital of Taipei, and we were in Taichung, about mid-island, so farmers coming to town on Sunday, their one off day, tended to stand close and stare at my face. One school holiday two little girls, who likely had never seen a Westerner or at least been so close to one, were sitting behind me on a bus. I felt a tug on my hair and thought they must have been overcome by curiosity. I learned that being different opens one up to being treated as a representative of a race or culture.

Consequently, frequently being judged by my race, nationality, or religion rather than as an individual quickly became old. Even though there were more than twenty Western faculty members teaching at Tunghai University, some students treated me only as a representative of my country or my religion and wanted detailed explanations of US foreign policy or my religious beliefs. I thought then how my Jewish high school friend who had given us a small oil lamp, as a wedding gift must have felt when I assumed the lamp had some religious significance. I was interpreting many of his actions not as the result of individual decisions but as though he had only one dimension, his religious identity.

As a woman, I have often found myself in situations in which I am a minority, and I weave those experiences as well as my international experiences into class discussions. I mention how uncomfortable I was during a job interview when I realized that I was the only female in the room. Although the department had many women faculty members, all seven members of the department search committee were male. I tell the story of having trouble convincing a furniture salesman that the wrong size mirror had been delivered. After four telephone calls, I had my husband initiate a conference call. For the first time, the salesman asked that I measure the existing mirror. When I told him the measurements, he exclaimed that the mirror was clearly meant for another piece of furniture! Other than sexism, I have no explanation for why he didn't believe me or ask me to tell him the measurements during the first three calls. He did eventually send the correct mirror.

Because of the power of my own personal experiences that allowed me to relate to "different" others, I work to create experiences that foster student understanding of others' perspectives without making them resentful. I was horrified the first time I taught intercultural communication when one of my best male students said, after reading an important chapter, "OK, I get it. I'm a Caucasian male, and it's all my fault." As lifelong Southerners, my parents may have had similar feelings, that people who didn't understand them were blaming them for an inherited system. My experience has been that making people feel defensive leads to resentment, not understanding.

Thus, in my intercultural communication classes, I encourage students to speak about discrimination experiences such as "dwb," "driving while Black," and being stopped by police for no reason. I show the film "A Tale of 'O': On Being Different in an Organization" (Kanter & Stein, 1980) because it does not focus on specific groups, but on the experience everyone has had of being different from a majority. At some time everyone has felt like an outsider (an

"O") in a group of insiders ("Xs"). Because the film presents specific "outsider" experiences that help "outsiders" understand their feelings and experiences without making "insiders" feel guilty, I find students are open to it. I have had White students say they could relate to that video better than more group-specific videos used in diversity training.

TEACHING ABOUT ETHNIC AND CULTURAL IDENTITY DEVELOPMENT

Finally, I use my personal experiences as an adoptive parent and a member of a mixed race family to help students understand the challenges in minority identity development. My experiences as a minority group member have also helped me understand the struggles my daughters have to reconcile their multiple cultural identities. Like children born of parents who immigrated to America, they are not completely American, nor completely members of their birth parents' culture. I discuss these struggles in the identity formation unit in my intercultural communication class and use my daughters' experiences as examples.

I tell the class that placing my teenagers at a particular point along the five-stage racial-ethnic identity model is difficult (Cross, 1991, adapted by Ting-Toomey & Chung, 2012). These models "tend to emphasize the oppressive-adaptive nature of intergroup relations in a pluralistic society" (Ting-Toomey & Chung, 2012, p. 83). They also emphasize a pre-encounter phase, in which ethnic persons' identities are influenced by the dominant culture's values and norms; at this stage, individuals are unaware of being "ethnic" or different. During the encounter phase, individuals become aware of their ethnicity because of a negative event such as encountering racism. This is the encounter my daughters claim they have not yet experienced. However, as teenagers, they are already negotiating multiple identities.

The conceptualization that best describes my daughters' experience seems to be Berry, Kim, and Boski's (1987) model, which captures identity challenges related to both cultural and ethnic differences. I also discuss the identity experiences of one of my daughter's Vietnamese-American friends who calls himself a "banana": Asian (yellow) on the outside but American (white) on the inside. He reads, writes, and speaks fluent Vietnamese at home. He was born in a local hospital in Georgia, but did not become fluent in English until he started kindergarten. Even so, he considers himself American and operates comfortably and effectively in both cultures. I also state that I hope my daughters develop a bi-cultural identity, in which they strongly identify both with the dominant culture in which they were raised and the culture of their birth. Research indicates that the majority of American adoptive parents with Chinese daughters hope to communicate to their daughters that they are Chinese-American (Gao & Womack, 2013). Research with Korean adoptees now in their twenties and thirties indicates that, though they identified with the majority US culture growing up, as adults they have begun prefer the company of Koreans and now emphasize the Korean part of their identities (Tuan & Shiao, 2012).

I use the examples of identity struggles and bi-cultural identities to prompt students in the class to tell their own experiences. Majority students can better identify with the identity struggles discussed in the textbook when they realize what some of their classmates may be experiencing. In various semesters, a Norwegian immigrant, a Korean-American student, a gay student, and an African-American student have been brave enough to discuss their experiences, both positive and negative, with the class. I believe some students in these classes were able to learn better from these testimonies than from reading about the reasons for racial discrimination (Schaefer, 2009) or the difficulties of negotiating multiple cultural and ethnic identities (Berry, 1994, 2004).

CONCLUSION

I use my life experiences as stories to help students in my intercultural classes better empathize with different experiences. I tell stories of living and beginning high school during the civil rights struggles in Birmingham, Alabama. My own later experiences as minority group member are the best explanation for why I have rejected as best I can the racism with which I was raised. They allow me to identify with several difficulties typical of minority experience: being singled out as different and being stereotyped based on skin color, sex, or religion (even though the cultural stereotypes I experienced were overwhelmingly positive). When I encountered members of the majority society, the encounters began with ambiguity and prompted me to be wary lest I be mistreated. It took me much longer to trust members of the majority culture. Even when initial encounters with particular individuals were positive, I was on guard because I expected that I would eventually be stereotyped and no longer treated as a unique individual.

I try to use these experiences to prompt my students to take others' perspectives. Both my individual experiences and my experiences as the parent of international adoptees have influenced the way I teach intercultural communication and, I hope, have provided a richer experience for students. By publicly telling my own story, by supporting students brave enough to tell theirs, and by choosing educational materials with which both minority and majority students can identify, I believe I have been successful in helping some of my students become more sensitive to prejudice, even their own.

REFERENCES

Berry, J. (1994). Acculturation and psychological adaptation. In: A. Boury, F. van de Vijver, P. Boski, and P. Schmitz (Eds.), *Journeys into cross-cultural psychology* (pp. 129-141). Lisse, The Netherlands: Swets and Zeitlinger.

Berry, J. (2004). Fundamental psychological processes in intercultural relations. In: D. Landis, J. Bennett, and M. Bennett (Eds.), *Handbook of intercultural training* (3rd ed., pp. 166-184). Thousand Oaks, CA: Sage.

Berry, J., Kim, U., and Boski, P. (1987). Psychological acculturation of immigrants. In: Y. Y. Kim and W. Gudykunst (Eds.), *Cross-cultural adaptation: Current approaches* (pp. 62-89). Newbury Park, CA: Sage.

Blackside. (2006). *Eyes on the prize: America's civil rights movement 1954-1965.* (Season 1) Dvd. PBS: American Experience.

Crohn, J. (1995). *Mixed marriages: How to create successful interracial, interethnic, and interfaith marriages.* New York: Ballantine/Fawcett.

Cross, W., Jr. (1991). *Shades of black: Diversity in African-American identity.* Philadelphia: Temple University Press.

Gao, H.M., and Womack, D.F. (2013). How Caucasian parents communicate identity to adopted Chinese daughters. In: Gonzalez, A., and Harris, T. M. (Eds.). *Mediating cultures: Parent communication in intercultural contexts* (pp. 45-58). NY: Lexington Books.

Intercountry adoption statistics. (2014, January 1). Retrieved October 1, 2014, from www.http://travel.state.gov/content/adoptionsabroad/en/about-us/statistics.html).

Kanter, R. M., and Stein, B. (1980). *A tale of "O": On being different in an organization.* New York: Harper and Row (Video available on Youtube: www.youtube.com/watch?v=p56b6nzslaU).

Schaefer, R. (2009). *Racial and ethnic groups* (12th ed.). New York: Prentice Hall.

Ting-Toomey, S., and Chung, L. C. (2012). *Understanding intercultural communication* (2nd ed.) New York: Oxford University Press.

Tuan, M., and Shiao, J. L. (2012). *Choosing ethnicity, negotiating race: Korean adoptees in America*. New York: The Russell Sage Foundation.

In: Communicating Prejudice   ISBN: 978-1-53610-167-6
Editors: S. Camara and D. Drummond   © 2016 Nova Science Publishers, Inc.

Chapter 10

THE NATURE OF PREJUDICE: ORIGINS, CONSEQUENCES, AND THE CASE OF TRAYVON MARTIN

Bobbi Van Gilder

Northeastern University, Boston, MA, US

ABSTRACT

This chapter summarizes prejudice literature, explains the ways in which socialization processes influence prejudicial thinking and social cognition, and then uses this information to analyze and explain the case of the Trayvon Martin shooting. Prejudice is a natural human phenomenon resulting from social categorization systems that are developed early on in an individual's life span and are then reinforced through social interaction. As a result of the socialization process, stereotypes become a well-learned set of associations and are *automatically* activated in the presence of a member of the target group (Devine, 1989). Consequently, stereotypes and prejudices influence individuals' perceptions of events, as well as their emotional and physical responses to stimuli. These in-group out-group distinctions can result in harmful consequences, which are made evident by shooting of Trayvon Martin. This chapter highlights the implications of negative intergroup prejudice and offers thoughts for social change.

Keywords: prejudice, stereotyping, social cognition, socialization, Trayvon Martin

INTRODUCTION

Forming groups is a natural animal (or human) behavior. In fact, throughout history, human beings have formed groups because of the survival benefits provided by group life (e.g., fighting off predators, raising offspring, protection, etc.) (Nelson, 2002). However, with group formation, there is a natural, often inevitable, production of intergroup prejudices. In forming close ties with members of one's own group (i.e., in-group), human beings have a natural tendency to be suspicious and rejecting of members of other groups (i.e., out-groups). As such, evolutionary psychologists have suggested that in-group preferences and hostility toward out-groups are adaptive and therefore innate (Nelson, 2002), so human beings can do little to avoid prejudice and stereotyping. Of course, prejudice is not *always* a bad thing.

As Paul Bloom (2014) has attested, prejudice is not only natural, but can often be rational, and even moral. In his presentation at the 2014 annual TED conference, Bloom (2004) notes that, "for the most part, we make good guesses both in the social domain and the non-social domain, and if we weren't able to do so, if we weren't able to make guesses about new instances that we encounter, we wouldn't survive" (n. pag.). He goes on to argue that even educated individuals who might believe that they do not participate in the prejudicial treatment of out-group members accept that there should be "some pull towards the in-group in the domain of friends and family, of people you're close to, and so even [they] make a distinction between us versus them" (Bloom, 2014, n. pag.). In cases such as these, the preferential treatment of our in-group members is often something individuals are proud of, rather than ashamed of. And, while these group distinctions that humans make are natural, and moral by our cultural standards, there are times when such distinctions can become problematic, and even harmful. Put simply, there are times when in-group out-group distinctions are irrational, wrong, and may lead to immoral consequences. Racial stereotypes for instance, have become a prominent source of immoral consequences. And, important to this essay, "these stereotypes and biases have real-world consequences, both subtle and very important" (Bloom, 2014, n. pag.).

By studying prejudice then, individuals may be better able to understand how to make sense of prejudices when the use of prejudice goes wrong.

Further, by understanding the social processes of prejudice and the ways in which biases influence thoughts and behavior, individuals may work to develop their communication skills to more effectively engage in intergroup communication. As such, this essay highlights the importance of practicing mindfulness in intergroup encounters. By practicing mindfulness, and by communicating respect and appreciation for difference, negative prejudicial behaviors and the harmful consequences of such actions may be reduced.

Although prejudice is inescapable, the study of prejudice enables us to understand the negative influence that prejudicial thinking can have on the thoughts, feelings and behaviors of human beings in their everyday lives. As noted by Nelson (2002),

> Virtually all of history's wars, battles and other acts of group violence have been driven by some form of prejudice, stereotyping or discrimination. For example, in the Spanish Inquisition, the American Civil War, the American slave trade, the Holocaust, and the genocide in Rwanda and Yugoslavia, the prejudice and intergroup hostility that groups had toward each other led to unparalleled bloodshed. (p. 2)

The study of prejudice is essential to helping us understand how negative attitudes and prejudices form the basis for subsequent negative intergroup behavior (Nelson, 2002). Furthermore, although prejudice could never be fully eliminated, human beings can practice mindfulness by attempting to embrace their prejudices and their emotional responses to racial stimuli with awareness (Cargile, 2011). The purpose of this chapter then, is to examine the ways in which prejudice is produced and maintained through communication, or social interaction. This essay will provide an overview of prejudice literature and will explore a case example that illustrates the cognitive processes that influence thoughts and behaviors. Finally, this essay will conclude with some best practices for reducing discriminatory behavior through conscious awareness, or mindfulness.

KEY CONCEPTS

Allport (1979) defines prejudice as "antipathy based on faulty or inflexible generalizations. It may be felt or expressed. It may be directed toward a group as a whole, or toward an individual because he is a member of that group" (p. 9). Discrimination refers to the acting out of prejudice. Discrimination has serious and immediate consequences, and comes about when we deny individuals or groups of people equal treatment (Allport, 1979). Finally, a stereotype, "whether favorable or unfavorable... is an exaggerated belief associated with a category. Its function is to justify (or rationalize) our conduct in relation to that category" (Allport, 1979, p. 191). In sum, stereotyping is a mental shortcut, a process of categorization, and is at the root of prejudice.

Prejudice stems from a process of social categorization, which all humans engage in. In fact, academics have worked for centuries to delineate and classify human beings into categories, using classifications to better understand the natural world. In 1735, Linnaeus developed a classification of all living phenomena, which provided a framework, or overarching logic, for others as they attempted to understand the human population (Connolly, 1998). Most notably, Cuvier, in 1805, argued that there were three major races (i.e., White, Black, and Yellow) within the human population and that these races could be ordered hierarchically on the basis of their intellectual and physical abilities (Connolly, 1998). This type of categorical racial thinking had significant consequences. For instance, this categorization system was used to justify the enslavement and inhumane treatment of Africans in the United States, and was later modified to justify colonialism (Connolly, 1998). Although these classification systems of biological distinctions between races have been repeatedly falsified in scientific research, this discursive logic continues to influence attitudes and behaviors. In fact, similar attempts at classification are unconsciously employed in our everyday interactions.

As Nelson (2002) explains, when humans encounter others, they tend to automatically assess and perceive that person on the basis of his or her features. Almost immediately, when individuals encounter a stranger, they tend to categorize people along a few broad categories (e.g., race, sex, age, etc.). These broad categories are often referred to as basic, or primitive categories. Primitive categories have been found to have a strong impact on how the perceiver interprets most, if not all, other information about that stranger (Nelson, 2002). This practice occurs so quickly and so frequently that categorization becomes a non-conscious process. Further, categorization is not only directed toward the out-group, but people also use *self*-categorization in the development of their social identities.

Social identity theory introduced the concept 'social identity' and the ways in which group memberships explain intergroup behavior. *Social identity* is a person's sense of who they are based on their group membership(s). In other words, individuals typically view themselves as members of certain social categories such that one's group membership(s) becomes a key component of his or her individual identity (Turner, 1987). As such, the groups (e.g., social class, family, ethnic group, football team, etc.) to which individuals belong are a significant source of pride and self-esteem for group members.

Group membership gives individuals a sense of belonging to the social world, which is developed through a process of social categorization (Turner, 1982). Social categorizations are intermittent divisions of the social world into distinct classes or categories (Turner, 1982). And, through this process of categorization, individuals tend to exaggerate intergroup differences while minimizing intragroup differences. As explained by Turner (1982), "the accentuation of intraclass similarities and interclass differences is further enhanced by the value significance of the classification" (p. 28). Consequently, this process of categorization leads to the homogenization and depersonalization of out-group members.

Along with the homogenization of out-group members, in-groups also tend to be biased in favor of their own groups. This is referred to as in-group bias, or in-group favoritism (Nelson, 2002). Individuals typically attempt to boost the status(es) of their own in-group(s). In fact, the central premise of social identity theory is that members of an in-group will seek to find negative aspects of an out-group in an effort to enhance their own self-image. The desire to develop and maintain a favorable self-image motivates people to "enhance the status of the groups to which they belong (in-group bias) and to diminish the status of other groups (out-group derogation)" (Tyler, Kramer, & John, 1999, p. 2). When the group identities are more meaningful (e.g., groups based on race or gender), out-group derogation often takes the form of sexist or racial discrimination (Nelson, 2002). Social identity theory thus predicts certain intergroup behaviors on the basis of several characteristics: perceived group status differences, the perceived legitimacy and stability of those status differences, and the perceived ability to move from one group to another. Such behaviors might include stereotyping, prejudice and discrimination.

HOW CULTURE BREEDS PREJUDICE

While social categorization is a natural human phenomenon, the question remains as to how these categorization systems are developed. In answering this question, researchers should examine culture as a breeding place for the development of categorization systems and prejudice. Jacobson (1996) defines culture as, first and foremost, "a shared way of making sense of experience"

(p. 16). Culture is thus a shared meaning system through which individuals learn to define and interpret experiences. Social learning theory argues that learning is a cognitive process that takes place within a social context and occurs through observation or direct instruction (Bandura, 1971). So, as social learning theorists argue, individuals can learn culture through observation, participation, and explicit communication (Schild, 1962).

Importantly, "culture profoundly influences the contents of thought through shared knowledge structures" (Nisbett & Norenzayan, 2002, p. 567). *Schema*, for example, "refers to knowledge structures that govern thought by selective attention, retention, and use of information about a particular aspect of the world" (Nisbett & Norenzayan, 2002, p. 567). Related to this concept is *cultural schema*, which are patterns of schemas that make up the meaning systems for cultural groups. Cultural schemas influence peoples' behaviors, preferences, and social judgments (Sanchez-Burks, Nisbett, & Ybarra, 2000). *Cultural models* refer to those cultural schemas that are intersubjectively shared in a group. Cultural models govern the ways by which people interpret their experiences and also guide peoples' actions in a variety of life domains (Nisbett & Norenzayan, 2002). A *script* then, is an especially significant type of cultural model, as scripts stipulate "the people who appropriately take part in [an] event, the social roles they play, the objects they use, the sequence of actions they engage in" (Nisbett & Norenzayan, 2002, p. 568). This notion of schema thus explains how the content of the human mind can differ so significantly across cultures.

As constructivist theory explains, "symbolic actions in the world are formed by ways of knowing" (Littlejohn & Foss, 2011, p. 158). One of the core assumptions of constructivism is that "persons make sense of the world through systems of personal constructs" (Nicotera, 1995, p. 52). *Constructs* are interpretive schemes that identify something as within one category or another. These interpretive schemes develop as individuals mature, moving from relative simplicity to relative complexity. Developmental changes in children's social perceptions are understood to reflect progressive transformations in the system of cognitive structures, or constructs (Delia & Clark, 1977). This theory emphasizes the role of interpretive processes in human interaction. According to the theory, individuals interpret and act according to their mind's conceptual categories, which, as explained previously, are a product of culture. As such, individuals subconsciously communicate through stereotypes.

NEUROSCIENCE OF SOCIAL COGNITION

As evidenced in the preceding paragraphs, the development of stereotypes results from a process of cultural learning, a process that occurs early on in an individual's life span. Importantly, the stereotypes developed through the cultural learning process influence the cognitive responses of humans when they encounter individuals that fit within one of their conceptual categories. As such, to further understand the intricacies of prejudicial thinking and its influence on human behavior, we must examine the neuroscience of social cognition.

As explained by Adolphs (2009), both automatic and controlled responses contribute to social cognition. Controlled processes are slow, reflective and arise much later in cognitive development (Adolphs, 2009). Further, controlled processes often involve "language-based declarative reasoning and reflective thinking" (Adolphs, 2009, p. 697). Alternatively, automatic processes tend to be faster and more spontaneous (Adolphs, 2009). Automatic processes often involve emotions and tend to influence social judgments and behaviors without reflection (Adolphs, 2009). Hence, much of our social cognition is rapid and fraught with biases and stereotypes; it is automatic. As a result of the socialization process, stereotypes become a well-learned set of associations. And, because they have been frequently activated in the past, they become automatically activated in the presence of a member of a target group (Devine, 1989). Devine's (1989) model holds that "this unintentional activation of the stereotype is equally strong and equally inescapable for high- and low-prejudice persons" (p. 6).

Selective Attention and Inattentional Blindness

According to Allport (1979), "nothing strikes our eyes or ears that directly conveys meaning" (p. 165). Anything obtained through the senses is perceived. Social cognition thus refers to the way individuals selectively perceive people and their behaviors (Licu, 2012). As noted by Licu (2012),

> With the process of visual perception we can say that reality is constructed and reconstructed in all three stages of social perception: in the phase of selecting the information (we see what we want to see), in the phase of interpreting the information (which depends less on the behaviour observed than on the reading key applied), as well as in that of

storing the information (which is not stored equally, but with varying degrees of accuracy and accessibility). (p. 89)

As such, visual perception often deceives us and misunderstandings can be the result of a false perception of reality. Allport (1979) also explains this phenomenon, noting that humans select evidence by focusing attention on certain signs, accentuating these signs, and deliberately overlooking other signs. Put simply, human beings select cues that they believe to exist, accentuate them in their minds, and then interpret the whole of the situation to conform to their prejudices (Allport, 1979).

Thinking can be viewed as an endeavor to anticipate reality. Thinking is an active function of remembering, perceiving, judging and planning (Allport, 1979). Inattentional blindness then, refers to "the failure to see an unexpected object that one may be looking at directly when one's attention is elsewhere" (Koivisto & Revonsuo, 2007, p. 845). As Koivisto and Revonsuo (2007) explain, conscious visual perception is closely related to attention, as individuals with normal vision are often "blind" to the unexpected if they are, at the same time, performing an attention-demanding task. Despite the salience of the unexpected stimuli, the stimuli typically go undetected. Our focus is immediately drawn to features of a stimuli that conform to our expectations (our stereotypes), so we often fail to detect disconfirming stimuli. This can become especially problematic in stressful situations when one is forced to respond to a stimulus quickly. For instance, the presence of a black face might cause one to focus on the ethnic features of the figure without noticing other salient aspects of the situation, thus triggering an automatic fear response, which could prompt a harmful reaction.

The Amygdala and Emotional Fear Response

The amygdala is located in in the limbic areas of the brain, which is where many of our habitual and automatic behaviors are processed (Cargile, 2011). As researchers have recently discovered, "the amygdala can provide rapid and automatic processing that could bias social cognition" (Adolphs, 2009). Specifically, the amygdala produces automatic emotional responses (e.g., fear or anxiety) when being exposed to a stimulus. These automatic emotional reactions do not require conscious recognition of the feared stimulus (Davis, 1992). Hence, the fear response in learned. The stimulus that produces the emotional response may have initially been emotionally neutral, but the consistent pairing of the neutral stimulus with an aversive stimulus produces an acquired automatic emotional response, or a conditioned fear response (Davis, 1992).

Fear is defined by Öhman (2005) as "an activated, aversive emotional state that serves to motivate the organism to cope with threatening events" (p. 954). Further, individuals attempt to cope with this fear, and coping attempts tend to focus on more metabolically demanding defensive behaviors (e.g., immobility or freezing, escape, or attack). And, important to this essay, the activation of the amygdala correlates with racial stereotypes. In fact, Cunningham et al. (2004) examined brain activations of white participants responding to racial stimuli (black and white faces) and found larger amygdala activation (a stronger emotional psychophysical response) to black than to white faces. Even though the white participants in this study reported to hold no racial prejudices, they showed automatic emotional response to black individuals (Öhman, 2005). This was associated with an implicit racial bias. While "individuals [are not] consciously aware of neural activity deep within their brain (i.e., amygdala activation) and may not notice the tensing of their own muscles... the reaction nevertheless exists" (Cargile, 2011, p. 13).

While animals learn that a stimulus predicts an aversive event by experiencing the aversive event, humans have the ability to learn indirectly (Phelps, 2006). With the symbolic means of communication, or language, humans are able to acquire the emotional properties of a stimulus without aversive experiences (Phelps, 2006). For instance, "one could learn to fear and avoid a neighborhood dog by being bitten, an example of learning through direct aversive experience. However, one could also learn to fear and avoid a neighborhood dog by listening to a neighbor discuss how the dog is mean and dangerous" (Phelps, 2006, p. 31). So, when the dog is encountered, a fear response will be activated even though there is only symbolic knowledge of the dog's emotional properties. This explains how the fear response becomes automatically activated in the presence of a black person, given the consistent pairing of black men to criminality, violence, and other emotionally charged stereotypical representations from the media. Further, the social stigma associated with the black identity is continuously reproduced through social interaction, thus instructing a fear response. This can be illustrated by the case of the Trayvon Martin shooting.

CASE EXAMPLE: TRAYVON MARTIN

The stereotype of Black Americans as violent criminals perpetuates dominant cultural discourses of race and ethnicity (Eberhardt, Purdie, Goff, & Davies, 2004). The robustness and the frequency of this stereotype association produces harmful outcomes such as,

> People's memory for who was holding a deadly razor in a subway scene (Allport & Postman, 1947), people's evaluation of ambiguously aggressive behavior (Devine, 1989; Duncan, 1976; Sagar & Schofield, 1980), people's decision to categorize non-weapons as weapons (Payne, 2001), the speed at which people decide to shoot someone holding a weapon (Correll et al., 2002), and the probability that they will shoot at all (Correll et al., 2002; Greenwald et al., 2003) (as cited by Eberhardt et al., 2004, p. 876).

This association between Blacks and crime is consistent, frequent and strong, but it also appears to be automatic. The mere presence of blacks, or even merely thinking about blacks, can lead people to miscategorize, misinterpret, and/or misevaluate behaviors or objects, and may even lead to people shooting too quickly (Eberhardt et al., 2004).

The association between blacks and crime directs people's eyes, their focus and their interpretations of the stimuli (black person) with which they are confronted. These associations "cause people to see (and not to see) in similar ways, despite individual differences in explicit racial attitudes" (Eberhardt et al., 2004, p. 877). Our visual perception and attention is thus influenced by the presence of black faces.

Heuristics refers to the human tendency to use decision-making shortcuts by reducing complex decisions to simpler assessments. Conscious thought and action are influenced most often by fast, intuitive, and typically non-conscious mental processes (Richardson & Goff, 2012). These mental shortcuts, most of the time, allow for individuals to understand their social worlds quickly and somewhat accurately. However, such shortcuts can also lead to systematic errors in judgment (Richardson & Goff, 2012). The shooting of Trayvon Martin, for instance, is a concrete example of this type of judgment error. While most people think that they have conscious agency and control over their thoughts, feelings, and judgments, the automatic unconscious processes "are often the primary source of our conscious impressions, beliefs, feelings, intuitions, and choices" (Richardson & Goff, 2012, p. 299).

Trayvon Martin was a 17-year-old African-American high school student who lived in Miami Gardens, Florida. On February 26, 2012, Trayvon Martin was walking from a house, where he and his father were staying, to a local 7-Eleven (Blow, 2012). On his way back to the house he caught the attention of George Zimmerman, a neighborhood watch captain at the Retreat at Twin Lakes gated community in Sanford, Florida (CNN.com, 2013). At 7:09 pm, when George Zimmerman saw Trayvon, a black teenager, walking the streets of his community, he called 911 to report "a suspicious person" in the neighborhood (CNN.com, 2013; Beety, 2012-2013). Referring to Trayvon Martin, who was wearing a hooded sweatshirt, Zimmerman reported that the boy looked "real suspicious" (Blow, 2012). The 911 operator told Zimmerman that officers were being dispatched and instructed Zimmerman not to get out of his SUV or approach the person. Despite the instructions of the dispatcher, Zimmerman followed Trayvon Martin. Several moments later, Zimmerman shot Martin, and claimed that the shooting was in self-defense. Yet, Martin was unarmed (CNN.com, 2013). He had only a bag of skittles, a can of iced tea, and his cell phone (Blow, 2012). Zimmerman had a 9-millimeter handgun. So why did Zimmerman find Trayvon suspicious?

In the case of Trayvon Martin, the victim's appearance and race made him susceptible to stereotyping. Trayvon was black, and Zimmerman was not. As explained by Beety (2012-2013), Zimmerman could only identify Martin as an African-American male in his late teens. And, the hoodie worn by Martin "blinded Zimmerman by enhancing his personal blind spot of conscious and subconscious bias, and by acting as a physical block to Zimmerman's view of Martin" (Beety, 2012-2013, p. 335). The Trayvon Martin case reminds us that, even today, Black men are subject to the "Black-as-criminal" stereotype that links blacks with violence and criminality (Lee, 2013).

As stated previously, many of our habitual and automatic behaviors are processed in the limbic areas of the brain (Cargile, 2011). The conditioned fear response is processed in the amygdala (Davis, 1992). Thus, when a conditioned stimuli was presented (e.g., African-American male), the amygdala produced a fear response (Cunningham, et al., 2004). This automatic fear response resulted in the shooting death of an unarmed teenager. As previous research has demonstrated time and time again, "individuals are quicker to identify weapons and slower to recognize harmless objects, like tools, in the hands of Black persons than in the hands of White persons" (Lee, 2013, p. 127). This commonly reported "shooter-bias," was evident in Zimmerman's decision to shoot the unarmed teenager in "self-defense."

Zimmerman was found not guilty on the basis that this shooting was in self-defense. However, while the doctrine of self-defense in criminal judgments may seem reasonable to many, Richardson and Goff (2012) note that such doctrines fail to account for the fact that those who are stereotyped as criminal are at greater risk of falling victim to mistaken judgment, which, in this case, produced a deadly consequence.

THOUGHTS FOR SOCIAL CHANGE

While some prejudices can produce detrimental consequences, there are ways to combat the influence of prejudice on negative intergroup behaviors. Three practices will be described in the following paragraphs: (1) engaging in intergroup communication, (2) practicing mindfulness, and (3) empathetic listening. The first practice for the development of more effective intergroup communication is for individuals to engage in more frequent, and more intimate, communication with out-group members. Similar to the ideas set forth in Kim's (2001) cross-cultural adaptation theory, the activity of communicating across group boundaries can potentially result in a transformative learning process. Transformative learning is a gradual process that is largely unconscious, resulting from participation in social communication activities with out-group members (Kim, 2001). When stereotypes are salient, particularly negative stereotypes regarding racial identities, the interactant may experience stress or fear, an automatic response to the racial stimulus. However, through repeated exposure, the interactant may be able to overcome the challenges he or she encounters and can learn from these experiences. From these experiences, individuals have the potential to develop a more inclusive and integrative perspective (Mezirow, 1991; Taylor, 1994). Of course, as Cargile and Giles (1996) argue, various aspects of an interaction can worsen an already developed cognitive predisposition to rely on stereotypes when communicating with out-group members, and responses from out-group members may diminish the chance for favorable interactions all together. As such, this approach is dependent upon the interactants and their willingness to learn from one another and engage with one another with an open mind.

While interacting with members of an out-group is important, the practice of mindfulness is crucial to the development of intergroup communication effectiveness. Mindfulness was described by Langer (1989) as a way to encourage individuals to conscientiously tune in to their mental scripts and preconceived notions, which are habituated into their everyday communication. As explained by Cargile (2011), "mindfulness attempts to extend conscious sensing beyond the surface of our reactions to their deep, tangled, and conditioned roots" (p. 17). For instance, if a feeling of discomfort arises when an individual encounters an outsider, the individual should attempt to recognize the feeling he or she is experiencing, and then consider *why* this feeling is being experienced. Mindfulness is thus "a readiness to shift one's frames of reference, the motivation to use new categories to understand cultural or ethnic differences, and the preparedness to experiment with creative avenues of decision making and problem solving" (Ting-Toomey, 2012, p. 46).

Finally, individuals should attempt to engage in empathetic communication. In fact, as Wang et al. (2003) explains, "developing and drawing on ethnocultural empathy (i.e., empathy directed toward people from racial and ethnic cultural groups who are different from one's own ethnocultural group) has been suggested by scholars as a promising way to promote the mutual understanding between various racial and ethnic groups, on both cognitive and affective levels" (p. 221). By listening intently and by attempting to empathize with the experience of the "other," an interactant may be better able to appreciate the experiences of the out-group member. This practice of perspective taking may enable for new understandings and promote mutual respect between groups.

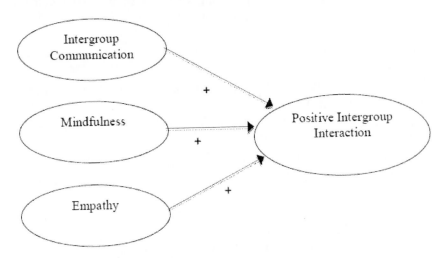

Figure 1. Improving intergroup relations.

CONCLUSION

In sum, prejudice is an inescapable consequence of our cultural upbringing and our social interactions. The stereotypes that are created and maintained through our social development processes become so deeply engrained in our subconscious, that they are automatically activated in the presence of targeted groups, or group members. Prejudices are further maintained and perpetuated in the dominant cultural discourses of American society. As noted by Connolly (1998), discourses represent "the social construction of language and knowledge, organizing the ways in which we think about the world and what we come to regard as appropriate, valid and true" (p. 11). Further, discourses provide the logic for how we "attempt to understand each other in the social world" (Connolly, 1998, p. 12). This is especially evident in discourses of race, religion, sexual orientation and gender. These discursive patterns have real and material consequences (i.e., the shooting of Trayvon Martin). However, three approaches described in this chapter (i.e., intergroup interaction, mindfulness, and empathy) may work to develop and enhance effective intergroup communication skills.

REFERENCES

Adolphs, R. (2009). The social brain: neural basis of social knowledge. *Annual review of psychology*, 60, 693-716. doi: 10.1146/annurev.psych.60.1107 07.163514.

Allport, G. W. (1979). *The nature of prejudice*. Cambridge, MA: Perseus Books.

Allport, G. W., and Postman, L. J. (1947). *The psychology of rumor*. New York: Russell and Russell.

Bandura, A. (1971). *Social learning theory*. New York: General Learning Press.

Beety, V. E. (2012-2013). What the brain saw: The case of Trayvon Martin and the need for eyewitness identification reform. *Denver University Law Review*, 90, 331-346.

Bloom, P. (2014, January). *Can prejudice ever be a good thing?* [Video Recording]. Presented to TED Conference in Ney York, NY. Retrieved from: http://www.ted.com/talks/paul_bloom_can_prejudice_ever_be_a_ good_thing.

Blow, C. M. (2012). The curious case of Trayvon Marin. *The New York Times*.

Cargile, A. C. (2011). Being mindful of the habitus of culture. *China Media Research*, 7(3), 11-20.

Cargile, A. C. and Giles, H. (1996) Intercultural communication training: Review, critique and a new theoretical framework. In: B. R. Burleson (Ed.) *Communication Yearbook*, 19, 385-423.

Connolly P. (1998). *Racism, gender identities and young children: Social relations in a multi-ethnic, inner-city primary school.* Routledge: London.

Correll, J., Park, B., Judd, C. M., and Wittenbrink, B. W. (2002). The police officer's dilemma: Using ethnicity to disambiguate potentially threatening individuals. *Journal of Personality and Social Psychology*, 83, 1314-1329. doi: 10.1037/0022-3514.83.6.1314.

Cunningham, W.A., Johnson, M.K., Raye, C.L., Gatenby, C. J., Gore, J.C., and Banaji, M.R. (2004). Separable neural components in the processing of black and white faces. *Psychological Science*, 15(12), 806-813. doi: 10.1111/j.0956-7976.2004.00760.x.

Davis, M. (1992). The role of the amygdala in fear and anxiety. *Annual Review of Neuroscience*, 15 (1), 353-375.

Delia, J. G., and Clark, R. A. (1977). Cognitive complexity, social perception, and the development of listener-adapted communication in six-, eight-, ten-, and twelve-year-old boys. *Communications Monographs*, 44(4), 326-345.

Devine, P. G. (1989). Stereotypes and prejudice: Their automatic and controlled components. *Journal of Personality and Social Psychology*, 56, 5-18.

Eberhardt, J. L., Goff, P. A., Purdie, V. J., and Davies, P. G. (2004). Seeing black: race, crime, and visual processing. *Journal of personality and social psychology*, 87(6), 876-893.

Greenwald, A. G., Oakes, M. A., and Hoffman, H. (2003). Targets of discrimination: Effects of race on responses to weapons holders. *Journal of Experimental Social Psychology*, 39, 399-405.

Jacobson, W. (1996). Learning, culture, and learning cultures. *Adult Education Quarterly*, 47, 15-29.

Kim, Y. Y. (2001). *Becoming intercultural: An integrative theory of communication and cross-cultural adaptation.* Thousand Oaks, CA: Sage Publications, Inc.

Koivisto, M., and Revonsuo, A. (2007). How meaning shapes seeing. *Psychological Science*, 18(10), 845-849.

Langer, E. (1989). *Mindfulness*. Reading, MA: Addison-Wesley.

Lee, C. (2013). Making race salient: Trayvon Martin and implicit bias in a not yet post-racial society. *North Carolina Law Review*, 91, 101-157.

Licu, M. (2012). Cross-cultural psychology and its possible applications in the school environment. *Euromentor Journal-Studies about education*, 2, 84-95.

Littlejohn, S.W., and Foss, K.A. (2011). *Theories of human communication* (10th ed.). Long Grove, IL: Waveland Press Inc.

Mezirow, J. (1991). *Transformative dimensions of adult learning*. San Francisco, CA: Jossey-Bass.

Nelson, T.D. (2002). *The psychology of prejudice*. Boston, MA: Allyn and Bacon.

Nicotera, A.M. (1995). The constructivist theory of Delia, Clark, and associates. In: D. Cushman and B. Kovacic (eds.) *Watershed research traditions in human communication theory* (pp. 45-66). Albany, NY: State University of New York Press.

Nisbett, R. E., and Norenzayan, A. (2002). Culture and cognition. In: D. L. Medin (Ed.) *Stevens' handbook of experimental psychology* (pp. 561-597) New York: John Wiley and Sons, Inc.

Öhman, A. (2005). The role of the amygdala in human fear: Automatic detection of threat. *Psychoneuroendocrinology*, 30, 953-958.

Phelps, E.A. (2006). Emotion and cognition: Insights from studies of the human amygdala. *Annual Review of Psychology*, 57, 27-53.

Richardson, L. S., and Goff, P. A. (2012). Self-defense and the suspicion heuristic. *Iowa Law Review*, 98, 293-336.

Sanchez-Burks, J., Nisbett, R. E., and Ybarra, O. (2000). Cultural styles, relationship schemas, and prejudice against out-groups. *Journal of Personality and Social Psychology*, 79(2), 174-189. doi:10.1037/0022-3514.79.2.174.

Schild, E. O. (1962). The Foreign Student, as Stranger, Learning the Norms of the Host-Culture. *Journal of Social Issues*, 18(1), 41-54.

Taylor, E. W. (1994). Intercultural competency: A transformative learning process. *Adult Education Quarterly*, 44, 154-174.

Ting-Toomey, S. (2012). *Communicating across cultures*. Ney York, NY: Guilford Press.

"Trayvon Martin shooting fast facts." (August, 2013). CNN US Retrieved on December 1, 2013 from http://www.cnn.com/2013/06/05/us/trayvon-martin-shooting-fast-facts/.

Turner, J.C. (1982) Toward a cognitive redefinition of the social group. In: Tajfel (ed.) *Social identity and intergroup relations* (pp. 15-40). Cambridge university press.

Turner, J.C. (1987). *Rediscovering the social group: A self categorization theory*. Oxford: Blackwell.

Tyler, T.R., Kramer, R.M., and John, O.P. (1999). Introduction: What does studying the psychology of the social self have to offer psychologists? In: T.R. Tyler, R.M. Kramer, and O.P. John (Eds.) *The Psychology of the Social Self* (pp. 1-10). New Jersey: Lawrence Erlbaum Associates, Inc.

Wang, Y., Davidson, M., Yakushko, O. F., Savoy, H., Tan, J. A., and Bleier, J. K. (2003). The Scale of Ethnocultural Empathy: Development, validation, and reliability. *Journal of Counseling Psychology*, 50(2), 221-234. doi:10.1037/0022-0167.50.2.221.

In: Communicating Prejudice ISBN: 978-1-53610-167-6
Editors: S. Camara and D. Drummond © 2016 Nova Science Publishers, Inc.

Chapter 11

THAT WILL NEVER BE ME: A NARRATIVE INQUIRY ON EMPOWERMENT AND VIOLENCE AGAINST WOMEN FROM THE CLOTHESLINE PROJECT

Karen Sorensen-Lang, PhD
Azusa Pacific University, Azusa, CA, US

ABSTRACT

This narrative inquiry examines how a national organization, The Clothesline Project, engages students on an undergraduate college campus around issues of sexual assault and domestic violence. Through the researcher's personal narratives, in-depth interviews with women's center staff, and text analysis on t-shirts where students write the stories of their own experiences with domestic violence and assault, the study draws out observations on current articulations of empowerment and women's issues. It also analyzes perspectives on positive rhetoric around feminist advocacy work and shares findings regarding the metaphor of voice and "healing-freeing" writing.

INTRODUCTION

Universities and organizations, both domestically and globally, stage Clothesline Project events—visual art and performance rhetoric displays where the stories of domestic violence are shared on t-shirts with stories written on them by victims. More than 100 groups are self-registered with the national Clothesline Project, and thousands of victims every year create shirts at their events in order to speak about violence against women. The metaphor of a clothesline is employed to represent a place where, for many generations and in many cultures, women gathered to share their stories with each other at the clothesline, one of the few safe places women had to talk freely. Now, at Clothesline events, people who have been victims of domestic violence and sexual assault write their message or ideas about their experiences on a t-shirt and hang their story on a public clothesline. At the start of the week displaying the clothesline, organizers hang shirts made during previous years and leave open space on the line for people to write new shirts and hang them for public reading. The four goals of the national organization are: "1. To bear witness to the survivors as well as the victims of the war against women. 2. To help with the healing process for people who have lost a loved one or are survivors of this violence. 3. To educate, document, and raise society's awareness of the extent of the problem of violence against women. 4. To provide a nationwide network of support, encouragement and information…" (Clothesline website accessed July 8, 2013).

The college Women's Center that participated in my study has staged the event for ten years. I interviewed an intern, a half-time staff member, and the director. Their goals for bringing Clothesline Project to their campus, as reported during the interviews, are to express that women's issues are not lost in the midst of what's going on in the world or in the busy lives college students lead, and especially to offer an arena for healing and processing experiences of violence against women. They emphasized the "healing-freeing factor" that writing and sharing personal stories with others can provide. Also, key goals for the organizers are to respect the stories of victims and to join with women across the nation about raising awareness for domestic violence and sexual assault. One Women's Center staff member shared that even though people may know violence is prevalent, they need to know that it is personal, too. An individual woman's words on a shirt humanizes the statistics and closes the distance from the issue of domestic violence for those who may not have experienced domestic violence or assault. My study's participants say

Clothesline Project allows women to say, "It happens; it happened to me. Please hear me."

The research questions that guided this inquiry were:

1. How are advocacy workers making use of writing to help women address domestic violence and sexual assault traumas?
2. What are the feminist principles and orientations that guide the staffs at the non-profits?

For the writer or the reader at the clothesline, both come in contact with the stories of domestic violence and enter what many describe as a sacred space where the written texts on the shirts do the talking for victims. The Women's Center intern who hosted the week-long Clothesline event at my site says it is programming that encourages emotional growth in the students who take part. It raises awareness to promote safety and reduces naivety about how prevalent violence against women is across all social contexts.

NARRATIVE INQUIRY METHODOLOGY

My data gathering is governed by narrative inquiry that focuses on how people make meaning of life and events through story. A simple description of this methodology from Schaafsma, Pagnucci, Wallace, and Stock says it is "research in the form of story," or "exploring the world by telling a story about it" (282). The data is story gathering, and the report of findings is told in story, often including elements of character, scene, and dialogue. Shaafsma and Vinz pose the question, "In what sense can we think of narrative as 'provocateur,' this is provoking new thoughts, questions, and possible explanations for the issues and situations we are trying to understand?" (9). The responses to my research questions were gathered through narrative research via in-depth interviews and text analysis of the clothesline t-shirts as I discovered "the ways individuals and groups shape their identities through stories" (Spector-Mersel 215).

Connelly and Clandinin make the important point that "humans are storytelling organisms, who, individually and socially, lead storied lives" (2), and humans make sense of life through stories. How we make meaning and come to know things often happen through narrative understanding. When researchers study narrative, they study the way in which humans experience life, according to the authors. For my study, I explore what experiences were important to the advocates and when and where they started to experience their own power. At the start of my research project, I recognized that I am not trying to prove what factors limit women at large, or make an empirical case for what helps women increase the sense of agency in their lives. I interviewed at one site and had three interviewees, each with follow-up interviews; this is not a far-reaching pool of participants, but a specified group of interviewees doing work with hundreds of women each year on an undergraduate college campus.

Other studies have looked at the issue of women's identity development, empowerment and voice with sample sizes that parallel my own (Blakslee and Martin; Van Vlaenderen and Cakwe; Allen). Sample sizes in these studies included six women in "Influences on Identity: A Grounded Theory Approach to Descendants of Freedmen," ten women in "Women's Identity in a Country in Rapid Social Change: The Case of Educated Black South African Women," and ten interviews in "Violence and Voice: Using a Feminist Constructivist Grounded Theory to Explore Women's Resistance to Abuse." These sample sizes are not meant to be representative of a population, but instead, they provide data toward the goal of developing theory and insights about women.

I see my research as the authors of "Composing Storied Ground: Four Generations of Narrative Inquiry" describe their narrative research: "We weren't trying to *prove* anything. We were *exploring!*" (Shaafsma, Pagnucci, Wallace, and Stock 290). The authors reject the values of hard science such as validity and proof in the study of human beings, and they work toward focusing on differences in the data. Sometimes narrative researchers record certain stories and sense they are significant without really knowing why at first. Pagnucci explains the writing of his narrative dissertation this way: "I started to write, telling a story I'd experienced, leaving the question of why I was telling that story up to the story itself. I trusted that somewhere in the course of writing that narrative I'd figure out why I needed to write that story" (Shaafsma, Pagnucci, Wallace, and Stock 295). Narrative inquiry does not follow traditional conventions of research. It provides space in the research process to grapple with what sometimes cannot be consciously known at the start, and to follow instincts about what resonates with the researcher. "Stories connect what we know to what we're trying to understand. They make things personal, give things meaning. They make things matter" (Pagnucci 9).

My Day at the Clothesline

When I went to write on my shirt at the Clothesline Project also staged at my campus, I thought I was ready. I had visualized this moment for five years—going into the space, writing my story, and discovering what this might do for me. I picked a bright purple, large marker. As I wrote, my heart picked up its pace. My knuckles tingled and my printing got more labored with each letter.

"I said, it will never be me too." And it was. "Black and Blue." I write the words and draw in the five splotches mimicking the grip of a hand on my arm.

I couldn't get myself to display my shirt as long as students were in the amphitheater ambling through the clothesline reading shirts others had hung. I stood with a rumpled t-shirt and two wooden clothespins in my hand, waiting to go to work. I sat back down at an empty table and wrote my last name in the crewneck on the inside seam. I thought about writing my grandmother's name there also.

My grandmother used to sew her own clothes. She, like me, was too tall for conventional sizes in the stores. She made patterns for her suits and dresses with the inches of fabric needed to accommodate her long torso. Sitting in the amphitheater that day, I wore a Clothesline promotional t-shirt I ordered a size too big just to make sure it would be long enough to cover to my waistline.

I write her name above mine. Daisy. A woman whose stories of being abused heightened my awareness against such treatment. I knew that, as a teenager, she had locked herself in an outhouse at her in-laws' farm when her husband was at war and his brothers were trying to rape her. I knew she had been knocked over a couch backward by a boyfriend later in life. She had been beaten while pregnant. When I heard mention of these stories, the tape always played in my mind: "That should never be me. That will never be me."

But it was, for a flash. He taught at my university. He grabbed my left arm when I defied what he wanted. We had called off our wedding and now, he wanted the ring back and he wanted to date. And I didn't. He taught feminist literature. I tried to leave and step around him in the doorway. Then I couldn't. He slammed me against the wall. I could have called for friends nearby, just around the house in the front yard—the embarrassment held me back. I folded.

I scrambled in the backdoor of my house once he left and I stood with my hand still on the deadbolt and thought of Daisy. I was she in that moment.

Each year following when I walked by the Clothesline Project at my university, I thought about stepping in and making a shirt with black and blue marker on the sleeve where I once wore bruises for more than a month. Five years later I contributed to the shirts on the line because I finally wanted to engage with my story and I wanted more control over it. I had things I wanted to say about it. That even smart professors like him don't practice what they teach. Even smart professors like me can be battered. Even my grandmother, who stopped going to school in the fifth grade, who worked at a BB gun factory as a test shooter with the meanest aim and perfectly fitting pants she sewed herself, could be battered. Even Daisy, even me.

That semester I shared the story in my classroom for the first time. We were discussing violence and power in a Gender Communication course. We talked about how we language violence and how we talk about survivors and how survivors talk about violence. One student, Mandy, shared her story of abuse in a methodic but invested tone for a few minutes. I sucked a quick breath in and decided that for the first time, it seemed like a space and time to join a student like Mandy in sharing what had happened to me. I briefly talked about it with a steady voice as my heart jumped in my chest again. And, I made sense of it a little more that day with my students. I had already written it down on a t-shirt and I hung it up on a clothesline. I had included my last name where the tag should have been and I did it in a world where I am known by that name, as Professor Sorensen-Lang. I think it took the sting out of the memory. Writing about it made it useful to me. The abuse and the hit to my identity could then make its way into my classroom and into some learning. The story entered my most important place and I liked that it did.

It all sounds a little intellectual describing that teaching experience now, but the classroom is my most consequential place to be. Relaying it to an audience, I experienced the assault again, and I felt all the nerves about being judged, I thought about my professionalism, and I talked back to that with a feminist challenge about not dividing the personal and the public. What made telling my story feel right was that I owed it to Mandy to stand with her. At my point of healing and processing, I would have felt dishonest not saying, "I get it. Me too."

Part of the Women's Center Director's Story

I find my way to the Women's Center on her campus and locate Monica's office. She is newly appointed as the full-time director to the Women's Center, a job she did half-time before the university funded a full-time position. I am Monica's first appointment after her having been out of the Women's Center for a week at a conference. When we step into her office, I notice two small, potted plants on her desk. Next to them, her staff has placed a sign in bubbly, markered letters that says, "Happy Bosses Day!" She stares for a moment at her gifts and comments to me how thoughtful this is. "I mean, truly, truly thoughtful," Monica exclaims. She begins to tell me the devastating news that her house burned down over the summer, just a few weeks before our scheduled interview. Her staff at the Women's Center knows one of the many things she has lost includes a vibrant collection of houseplants. The plants on her desk are a small bit of greenery compared to the domestic grove she had cultivated for 30 years in her home. But she receives them enthusiastically as yet another new start in her life.

Why Monica Works on Behalf of Women

She was the fourth of five kids in her family and said she always needed to find herself or she'd get lost in the crowd. In her traditional culture, the father was in charge and the mother would say so too, if asked. "But she was always running the show from behind the scenes," Monica said. When people would tell this future women's advocate she couldn't do something because she was a girl, she would say, "Just watch me." Her rise to administration in higher education came about in large part because of the male mentors who pulled her into meetings with the higher-ups and invited her to give input in decision-making. But her most significant mentor was the first female Latina administrator at her school who told her, "People might treat you differently because of your gender or your ethnicity, but don't play the victim role. Because you're not." She encouraged her to never think of herself as the token female on a committee or the token person of color. Instead, she thinks of herself as a person with diverse experiences and values to bring to circles of influence, even if the committee gets extra points for diversity if she's there. Monica chose to trust that people were including her because of what she uniquely had to offer. She clings to assuming the best of others even though she has had interactions that devalued her. One colleague said he would never get a promotion if he were up against her because she is a woman and she is a minority. "I was just like, really? You would actually say this? It has nothing to do with the fact that I might be more qualified than you are? But his fighting words were that I was a woman and I was a person of color. He was a white male. I was so appalled by it."

I asked Monica, "What's your story of coming to voice? How did you arrive where you are now as an advocate for women?" Monica didn't want to share the details of her story, but simply said after ten years of marriage and being a stay-at-home mom, she found herself divorced and needing to support her children. "All the things that men held dear, you know, 'the buck stops here' or 'I get to decide everything,' it all fell to me, whether I asked for it or not," she explains. "I wouldn't say I had to develop a different skill set, but I had to understand that I was capable of this skill set." She wanted to be in a line of work where she could help women understand that they could make it too.

Monica says the word empowerment is overused, but that's what she wants for women—to empower them through education and support. She wants women to determine what success means for them and she wants them to know they have their own stories and their own paths. "Women have so many things and so many issues that we don't even talk about," Monica says. "So many women are walking around campus doing extracurricular and doing everything so well, but they're carrying a load around. What if they didn't have to carry that load with them? What if we could actually meet some of that need here?"

Monica had the right people investing in her path, and she broke new ground by achieving dean status at her college. She regards giving back and community as cornerstones of her work. "I believe we all stand on somebody else's shoulders. If someone else can stand on my shoulders, then I did my part. To know that there is someone else who stood before me and paved the way, it gives me the responsibility to do my part to make sure that women's voices are heard." She lives with the belief that she is shaping others' opinions of hiring women in their male-dominant workplace. If she creates a positive experience working with a woman, she opens the door for more women to move up. Even as she functions as the prototype of the female administrator on her campus, her message to educators about women is, "Don't stereotype them. And don't make assumptions about their stories because they come from different experiences. In order to validate their voices, you've got to listen."

Rachel's Story as a Women's Center Advocate

As the graduate intern for the Women's Center, Rachel says it's scary that she went through four years of undergrad and never discussed women's issues or feminism in her classes. When she became a resident advisor looking out for 40 freshman women, she said she realized what women's issues are and what needed to happen to address them. When a speaker came to campus to speak about sexual assault awareness, some big conversations in Student Life programming took place, but soon after, the topic was dropped. Rachel started to ask her faculty mentor questions about why there were no resources on campus for victims of sexual assault and why was there no visible advocacy or information for women about sexual assault awareness. She decided to start a group with her friend that would continue the conversation. "I was so willing to help with the group, but I was not going to talk about me," Rachel said. She had been assaulted as a 16 year old, but didn't talk to anyone about it until her junior year of college. When her faculty advisor questioned her about why the sexual assault awareness work on campus was so important to Rachel, she started to talk about the experience. "I'm really grateful to the faculty members who really pushed me and said, let's get personal," she said.

Rachel says what motivates her to be an advocate for women and work at the center is mostly frustration. She qualifies that it's not anger toward men, but a frustration about silence and not having a voice for years about her own abuse. She also values working with other women to improve women's lives. When one of her friends attempted suicide their senior year, she was the second person in to visit her. She simply said, "This isn't you. What's up?" Rachel believes it was the pressure around body image and all that's required of women to be valuable that pushed her friend toward suicide. As the intern for the Clothesline Project, Rachel hosted women around the clothesline as they wrote their stories and shared their thoughts about violence against women. Her favorite shirt was one jam packed with text. "What I think I loved was that it took me five minutes to read it. And I had to sit there, and I had to just be with it." On the sleeve the author had written, "This is just a snippet."

THEMES FROM THE CLOTHESLINE

The stories from this Women's Resource Center are organized below by themes that emerged from interviews and are grouped into four categories for discussion: women's issues, the metaphor of voice, ideas about writing for empowerment, and feminist principles. Additional results from the Clothesline Project t-shirt texts, as well as promotional and explanatory documents used on site during the event are included at the end of this section. These results reflect the experiences and opinions of staff members at a Southern California, four-year-college's Women's Center.

Women's Issues

When the director of the center did a survey of the female student body in order to access programming needs, she was surprised by the results. The results did not report the usual topics Women's Centers like hers tend to address: sexism in culture and media, sexual assault and rape, body image struggles, or awareness raising about traditional women's issues like representation and access. Monica was surprised the survey findings reported that female students wanted resources to help them navigate romantic relationships, female friendships, and demanding schedules/stress management. Interestingly, these results may substantiate the suggestion that the four staffers shared in separate interviews in response to the question about what limiting factors they see at work in the context of the women's lives where they work. They all said women they work with are not aware enough of women's issues and aspects of themselves that relate to gendered concerns. Part of their work at the Women's Center is to value women's experiences and concerns, but also to name gendered struggles that exist both personally and systemically.

One intern said, "Women would rather just not think about it."

"It?" I asked.
"Think about inequalities, think about violence against women, and the areas of the world that are still a man's world."

The director said women's issues just aren't named and analyzed enough among the students she works with. "There's a misconception that women have made a lot of gains, so we turn our attention to something else," Monica said. She says pervasive patriarchy is a major limiting factor for women, but even more so if they do not know what it is or see its role in culture.

T-shirt texts from the clothesline:

"I'm tired of being objectified. I feel expendable. I feel used. Why would you do that to your granddaughter? Why do you still think of me this way? I distrust older men."

"My best guy friend gave me a "gift" I'll never forget. Happy birthday to me."

"Don't go back to that person who thought he was a 'man.' There is other love out there."

"Men define sex in today's culture, but women uphold that. I'm sick of being treated like a sexual object. I'm NOT! No woman is!"

The staff also reported concerns about the disconnect between positive beliefs about women and actions or living out these beliefs. "If I could change something about legitimizing women's issues, it would be to not just know we are capable of doing anything we want, but to see more women actually doing it," one intern said. Monica used the metaphor "voice" when she said that for her, voice isn't just what you say, but a sense of personal efficacy that backs up what you are saying. She observes the growth in students she works with and believes that for a female student to most authentically have a voice in her own life, her actions change to begin to reflect her beliefs and personal values. "They start to respect themselves and stop doing things that are hurting themselves," she said. "They do things like choose the major they are passionate about and not just do what others want or think they should do." She did not think that the root problem is confidence issues for women, since they often report they are empowered and they feel empowered—this is a group of women who grew up wearing "girl power" shirts—but Monica does not see this translating enough to action for individuals. "They know women can, but they don't see that they personally can," Monica said.

The other limiting factors reported during interviews looked at the issues of "space," meaning both gathering places and conversations with people, as in moments of time, to engage in women's issues. "There's a perception that women can talk and talk, but we hear from them that they don't have places or people to talk with," Monica said. Monica has noted that in recent years, female students express one-on-one to her the need to talk about topics that have been traditionally viewed as male issues, such as addiction to porn or the pressure to achieve. The social events, small group talks, mentoring situations and awareness raising projects like Clothesline are all part of what the Women's Center does to value women and value the things women care about. They emphasize holistic development of the self and not compartmentalizing the female as separate or unimportant aspects of the self, whether it is as students live out their identities as academics or athletes, or as they pursue their hobbies and career plans. Monica said, "The ones who get stuck on one part of their identity, they seem to struggle because they're never satisfied with the perspective of who they are." She hopes that when students come in contact with Women's Center staff and events, they see some of how to acknowledge the complexity of the self.

The Metaphor of Voice

T-shirt texts from the clothesline:

"I am not the moment you took from me. Nor will I ever be. My voice will not be silent no longer."

"If you feel trapped or isolated, talk to someone. My best therapy was sharing what happened to me!"

"It doesn't matter if it doesn't seem like a big deal. It is...don't be afraid to talk about it."

"For 13 years I kept it a secret as if I had done something wrong. Don't tell me I am beautiful and expect me to forget. I have three years of guilt and I need time to forgive."

Metaphoric and strikingly eerie, the shirts on the clothesline give voice to 95 women out of the larger group of the incoming freshman class on the campus who, according to statistics, will be sexually assaulted during their college experience. "The more moving stories we have being told, the more people will be moved by them to action," one Women's Center intern said. The connection between voice and audience is indivisible within this advocacy work. With a general goal to improve women's lives, the Women's Center staff says, "prompting the audience to act" is a major benefit of voicing personal stories. The staff points out that personal stories, more so than stats or research, are simply more inspiring and, most importantly, memorable. Also, their main effort while staging the event goes into advertising the Clothesline Project in order to get an audience of readers to the clothesline. Without an audience, there's not the validation that the project is hoping to provide to women. "When we are available to listen to them, we validate them and let them know they are not ignored," Monica said. Rachel said about writing, that the sense of connection and communicating shared experiences are the motivations behind what writing means to her and why writing is a powerful part of this event. When an audience connects with what a person writes and validates where that person finds meaning, she says it is gratifying. The overlap between what she sees the goals of writing are and the goals of her women's advocacy are here: it is all for connection with others and finding meaning in experiences. Monica said the opposite of having a voice is feeling as though your story does not have a place in society or in whatever community you may be a part of, in her case, a school campus. To feel voiced is to know you can share your story and share the views that you have, including those that have formed because of your past and because of who you are as a woman. "We need to tell our stories," Monica said.

Along with the issue of audience and voice is the issue of space and voice. A dominant thread of discussion among Women's Center staff was women "having a way to talk about experience" and how this becomes a major factor in how to understand voice in advocacy and writing. Monica said, "Everyone doesn't need permission to speak or sit in a situation, but they need space to do it." The interviewees repeatedly said women need space to speak and to voice ideas and space for a woman to say or not to say what is on her mind. Students may be writing and expressing ideas day in and day out on campus, but the students the Women's Center works with ask again and again for programming and opportunities to talk about the topics that are important to them. "Until you can talk about it, abuse or something that's important to you, I don't think you can really start to define your voice," Rachel said.

Ideas about Writing

"The power of what's written on shirts, for so many it is forgiveness and for so many others it is anger. And, both are so powerful and they're powerful to one another," Rachel said.

As the Women's Center intern in charge of staging the event, Rachel said it is the power of writing that makes the event effective—it makes experiences more real where needed and it provides a way of expressing what is going on inside the woman. "When you write, it becomes a reality and no longer just in your head. Through this type of writing, we're acknowledging what's there," one Women's Center staff member said. "It gives women who write the shirts some power over the abuse. She can say, 'I'm in control enough that I could write this." Rachel said, "It takes courage to write things down." In this context, writing often documents a survival story or healing process. It provides victims of violence opportunities to write a different story amidst their ongoing stories of surviving and hopefully healing.

The Women's Center director said for her, this particular use of writing makes experiences more real, but the beauty of it is that it also sets some parameters on the emotions and thoughts that come with remembering. "It doesn't go on forever. It's discrete. You can write it down and say, 'here's the beginning and here's the end.' " In this way, writing about experiences with violence puts stakes down in the journey. The personal stories may describe how the woman is writing and talking about it for the first time or write something that expresses, "I have overcome," or "I'm not defined by this." And, the staff believes that part of acknowledging the importance of the stories, or "stakes in the journey," put down on the shirts is that every year, the shirts are carefully folded and stored to be displayed again the next year. The staff wants to metaphorically speak continuity of support and the validation of personal stories for any woman who writes on a shirt. The writing is never tossed aside, but instead, it has readers year after year.

T-shirt texts from the clothesline:

"He found and raped me when I was 14. God found me and healed me. For 3 years I walked passed the Clothesline terrified to even hint at my story, ashamed of the molestation and of the rape. But now I'm here and I refuse to let the abuse define me. Healing is possible."

The Clothesline Project interviews noticeably brought in ideas about audience and its role for writers. Although this was not a primary line of questioning, participants emphasized how an audience to read the shirts represents community, and that is a core need for humans. We need connection and we need to be acknowledged, they said. The staff works hard to promote the event and to bring an audience in to read the t-shirts. "Sharing writing educates others. The author gets to say, 'I'm not the only one,' and the reader gets to say, 'This stuff does happen to people I know,' " one staff member said. "I think the power of seeing the other stories goes a long way for other victims to say, I can tell my story too." The idea that people care about the content on the shirt emerged as important to the staff. When one graduate intern discussed her views about writing and how key an audience is, she noted that, in her academic writing, she wants professors to really engage with her ideas instead of providing simple formatting feedback. "I want you to care about the content," she said of her readers. She said writing should provide a sense of connection and validate what the author finds meaningful. This kind of statement is one that threads together composition values and feminist advocacy. The writing that goes on at the clothesline gives an audience a chance to connect with the authors' journeys in their stories of violence. In their effort to create a sacred space for the telling of stories and voicing of experience, the staff provides an example of how key acknowledgement is to humans. In this case, it is for the author/victim and her story/text as she acknowledges her story to herself in her willingness to write it and allow it to be read by others in her willingness to share it. The Women's Center honors the courage it takes to write and the courage it takes to share personal, powerful stories with others.

Feminist Principles

I ask Monica what feminist values she thinks her Women's Center embodies or upholds. She asks me to define feminism. I smile and say that's kind of part of what I'm studying. Are women's advocates using that label anymore? "It depends on who is here. If we feel like we're in a safe place and we're talking to faculty who work with feminist theory or women-focused classes, then we have a different way of embracing that language and talking about it, exploring it," she explains. "But if we have other people who have not read as much or heard as much, who have a view that if you say 'feminist,' then they can't hear the rest of your conversation." In looking at the themes from interviews to draw out feminist traits, it is clear that representation is a key feminist value at work in the Women's Center. They want to see women in positions of influence and they want to encourage young women with the belief that they can go anywhere and do anything. The staff also defines their feminism in context as not "bashing men." They speak often of "balance" about how they talk about women's issues and patriarchy concerns. "We don't want to tear men down by building women up. We're looking for balance," one intern said of her staff. The director often defends the need for a Women's Center by saying, "Men's issues are women's issue and women's issues are men's issues." She wants to teach both men and women how to respect each other and to build understanding between genders and about gender issues. The staff's goal is to create programming where people do not "attack men," but instead share their experiences in order to have people come to a better understanding for both men and women. "I've seen angry girls. That doesn't help either because they try to push down men," the director said.

Considering the ideas shared during interviews with Women's Center staff, it becomes evident that staff members are hyper-attentive to defying stereotypes about feminism. When feminism came up during interviews, most often the responses and discussion about feminism were their saying what they are *not* as feminists instead of what they *are*. Specifically, they are not angry and they are not pushing men down. One staffer did offer the office motto as her understanding of feminism: to affirm, celebrate, and restore women. The group gave little space to being angry in advocacy, and they framed key definitions and goals in positive terms. Any anger or clash was described as counter-productive in an effort to not embody negative stereotypes of feminism.

T-shirt texts from the clothesline:

> "Feminism taught me that I DON'T HAVE TO PUT UP WITH YOUR SHIT."

> "I am tired of being valued as a woman only by what is between my legs! What happened to equality between genders? Virgin or not, there is so much more to me than the physical."

> "Rape has become normal. It is a symptom of a society that values violence as entertainment, porn, beauty as the measure of a woman, men as leaders and women as support, distinct gender roles. Why is half the population living in fear of the other half?"

The Women's Center's feminism could best be described as solidarity among women. They often say things like, "women need each other," or "we encourage women to value other women." One intern said that, generally, feminist literature focuses on the self or just on the poorest of women, but that she hoped the feminism they were doing at the center would decrease competition between all women and increase their appreciation for each other and for female friendships. One afternoon "talk time" event the center offered focused on the question, "Why do women like to tear up other women?" One senior event ended the school year with a panel emphasizing the importance of female friendships and networking in life beyond college. The staff's structure emphasizes mentoring in its hierarchy, from the director to graduate interns and then toward undergraduate interns and students. The idea of "pouring into" other women was a staff cultural norm, and seeking out other women for advice and support is commonly encouraged. Female togetherness is key to their embodiment of feminism as they go about feminist advocacy, even if they do not identify as "feminist" in their literature or their languaging of their work.

THEMES FROM CLOTHESLINE T-SHIRT TEXTS

Reading over the compiled text of the t-shirts, it is evident that what Monica said about women is true—we should not make assumptions about their stories because they come from different experiences. Even with the common factor of abuse or assault compelling them to write on a shirt, their messages reveal varied perspectives about society and women's sexuality, the journeys toward healing (is it even possible?), and views of the self as victim. Still, there were noticeable recurring ideas and language that emerged on the shirts. Not surprising for those familiar with sexual assault statistics, many of the women wrote about best friends and family members as their abusers. They wrote about broken trust and role confusion regarding the men in their lives. The most prominent word across the clothesline was the word "broken." "He robbed me of so much. What did I do wrong? When can I smile again? Why am I alone? Why do I live in this prison while he is free? I am so broken and so weak…" And, "You broke me. I hate this. Please I'm begging you. It's always there. I want to know what real love is, but I'm so broken." One writer displayed the message of being "broken" while also being OK when she wrote, "BR ok EN." Another woman wrote one or two words on each line, "What   was/Broken/Weak/Hurt/Forgotten/Is/Now/Whole   Strong   Healed LOVED." Much of what was written spoke of the journey of healing, as this shirt does. Another wrote, "Maybe this will be the year that I forgive," and the author drew a broken heart on the chest. One shirt had a simple, honest, and sad thought: "12 years and it's just getting easier." One asked if it was even possible to heal or "get over" the abuse or assaults, while another, cited earlier, made a victorious proclamation: "I refuse to let this abuse define me. Healing is possible." Another wrote of her journey: "Last year I hung a shirt of unforgiving resentment and pain. This year, I'll hang one of redemption, forgiveness and above all, hope."

Two points for consideration regarding women's issues emerge when the texts of the t-shirts are analyzed as a group: 1) the idea that suffering brings women strength and 2) the belief that a woman's sexuality is equated with her entire self, instead of a part. It seems as though a number of the authors make sense of their abuse or assault experiences in part by seeing it as experiences or hurt that made them stronger. After relaying a long story of being abused by her father, being back and forth between foster care and her home, and being beaten by past boyfriends, one writer closes her text by writing, "Pray not for easy lives, pray to be stronger women." Another shirt says she and her mother have taken all that happened to them to turn it into love for others and to let it make them stronger. One shirt says, "I am empowered by my scars," while another gives a lot of purposefulness to the abuse: "Everything is going to be alright. What's happening in my life right now will tie into the big picture. The moments I don't understand and the moments I hurt are shaping me more and more." And lastly on this point, "Thank you God for the pain and for the process. Without it, I wouldn't be who I am today…"

Women's advocates might reframe this narrative that "suffering brings strengths" or it is "just part of life" to instead say, you should never have experienced this abuse to begin with. One woman did write to her abuser and frame her experience as though to say, this abuse should have never happened in the first place: "You told me I was Worthless/Stupid and/Unloved./Too bad you never told me I deserve much better." If women are socialized, or themselves choose, to give abuse or assault credit or simply a place in the grand narratives of what it means to be female, this type of license to abuse or purposefulness in abuse may only serve to normalize oppressive acts against women.

A disturbing trend in the writing was women who appear to equate their entire identity or worth with their sexuality, expressing the idea that they had "lost everything" when they lost their virginity or might now be viewed as "used goods" after being assaulted. One woman writes, "He was my first boyfriend, he told me he loved me! Why would he take advantage of me!!! He took everything I had in one night." The recurring use of the word broken, as discussed earlier, again and again pointed to a total ruin because of unwanted sexual encounters and assault. This assumption that a woman's worth is wrapped up in her sexuality is also revealed in the strong assertions against this thinking when texts say, "I won't be defined by this" or "I'm more than what's between my legs." Whether the authors are addressing their own internalized views on women or are speaking against typical views on women, their statements reveal assumptions that much of women's worth lies in their sexuality, purity, and not being "used up" sexually. "I was raped when I was 14. I'm not sure why things like this happen or why people do things like this to others! Over the years I have been learning that it's not my fault and I'm not 'used goods' in my fiancé's eyes." One feminist voice in the t-shirt texts writes, "I am not broken, guilty, dirty, or unwanted because of some sick man. I am beautiful and whole, and so is every other woman."

The gendered experiences and gender tensions that many women journey through their college years and life with are told in snippets on these clothesline t-shirts. They speak clearly of the epidemic of violence against women and sexual assault realities women fear or face, and give and receive support about on campus and beyond. This public display of women's stories embodies some of the goals of the Women's Center's programming—to raise awareness about very real, though often denied, women's issues and to do so through writing and sharing with an audience. In passive programming like this where women are given space to express themselves but are not directly engaged (unless they choose to connect with the advertised resources at the event such as the counseling center), it is hard to know if the authors experience some of the healing-freeing phenomena the Women's Center is hoping the Clothesline Project will provide. Two of the t-shirts on the line did encourage other women to share their stories: "If you feel trapped or isolated, talk to someone…YOU are never alone! Sharing my story lead me on my path of Healing!" And, "Silence is not the answer!" In this context, the use of the term "voice" can be understood as speaking for the first time about the abuse and not being defined by it. A data source such as the Clothesline Project can be a chilling and sad place from which to draw insights about women and the stories they carry with them into the classroom and into their writing. These t-shirts bear witness to the pervasiveness of violence and sexual abuse women deal with and the ways in which women are or are not valued beyond their sexuality (or how women internalize or address this belief), and then how they journey to overcome and make sense of this too-common oppression women face.

REFERENCES

Blakeslee, Sara E. and Marika L. Martin. "Influences on Identity: A Grounded Theory Approach to Descendants of Freedmen." *Journal of Feminist Family Therapy.* 21 (2009): 271-283. Online.

Clandinin, D J, and F M. Connelly. *Narrative Inquiry: Experience and Story in Qualitative Research.* San Francisco: Jossey-Bass, 2000. Print.

Shaafsma, David, Gian S. Pagunucci, Robert M. Wallace, and Patricia Lambert Stock. "Compositing Storied Ground: Four Generations of Narrative Inquiry." *English Education.* 39 (2007). 282-305. Print.

Shaafsma, David and Ruth Vinz. *Narrative Inquiry: Approaches to Language and Literacy Research.* New York: Teachers College Press, 2011. Print.

Spector-Mersel, Gabriela. "Narrative Research: Time for a Paradigm." *Narrative Inquiry.* 20:1 (2010): 204-224. Print.

Van Vlaenderen, Hilde and Mandisa Cakwe. "Women's Identity in a Country in Rapid Social Change: The Case of Educated Black South African Women." *Psychology and Developing Societies.* 15.1 (2003): 69-87. Online.

In: Communicating Prejudice
Editors: S. Camara and D. Drummond

ISBN: 978-1-53610-167-6
© 2016 Nova Science Publishers, Inc.

Chapter 12

AUTOETHNOGRAPHIC ACCOUNTS OF PREJUDICIAL PRONOUNCEMENTS: ADVANCING PRINCIPLES OF APPRECIATIVE INQUIRY

Sakile K. Camara
California State University, Northridge, CA, US

ABSTRACT

This essay is an autoethnographic account of my time matriculating through the Ph.D. program at a large predominantly white institution PWI) in the Midwest. Using narrative inquiry, I focus on prejudicial pronouncements experienced between 1994-1999 as a context for self-reflection. Despite these challenges, the five principles of appreciative inquiry are used as a theoretical framework for transformation: Constructionist, simultaneity, poetic, anticipatory, and positive. I attempt to understand my limitations, in part marred by my thinking, as I analyze these situations through phenomenological thought.

The idea that Black women have difficulty in higher educational systems, especially at predominantly white institutions (PWIs) is not new. For the past 30 years, literature has established that black women have been in the business of validating their intellect and competence as they struggle through Ph.D. programs and the professorate (see Patricia Hills-Collins, 1986; bell hooks,

1989; & Lois Benjamin, 1997). Some of these experiences are what Howard-Baptiste call "Mammy Moments" (2014). So, my experience is nothing more than a continuation of the many stories from and about other Black women who have entered Ph.D. programs across the country at primarily White institutions (PWIs; see Jones, Wilder, Osborne-Lampkin, 2013) that are often left unheard and unspoken as educational strategies for adult learners, mentoring or teaching strategies. Nonetheless, this autoethnographic narrative brings a certain level of risk and exposure, but also an understanding of appreciative inquiry that engages individuals in self-determined change as a catalyst for new possibilities beyond the lived experience of racial incongruence.

This chapter serves as a qualitative roadmap to encourage others who resonate with my story. I also identify prejudicial pronouncements from, with, between and among my learning community that ultimately extended into my career as a professor. Most pronouncements are evocations. Prejudicial pronouncements are meaningful in two respects: They solicit emotional meanings/reactions of invalidation and they embody social biases. Emotional meanings can vary depending on the purveyor of the pronouncement and the context in which it was provided. Emotional meanings fueled by prejudicial pronouncements are not static and its meaning can change with any individual. Social biases are represented by and include the concepts of prejudice, stereotyping and discrimination. These forms of bias are applied to the other person without regard for truth (Fiske, 2010). Therefore, prejudicial pronouncements are utterances in which the cultural existence (i.e., race, sex, class, sexuality and ability) of person is perceived as being deliberately used as a marker to discredit or invalidate that person's level of competence, credibility and intelligence.

Furthermore, prejudicial pronouncements can exhibit authority over another person because power is relinquished to the person who made the pronouncement. Therefore, the type of existence called into being through past prejudicial pronouncements are psychologically structured, but lie dormant until those deep emotional meanings/reactions are triggered by some act of invalidation. These emotional meanings are generally unexplainable until conscious reflection reveal its point of origination. Therefore, appealing to the pronouncement as the authority distorts how one's current reality is perceived; whether real or imagined. Expressing a link between perception and intention, prejudicial pronouncements are socially constructed as a deliberate act of social bias with the sole intention to doing psychological harm.

The purpose of this chapter and this book is to answer the call articulated in the conclusion of Michael Hecht's *Communicating Prejudice* book published in 1986. Hecht called for an intellectual movement beyond understanding prejudice and its personal and social effects on individuals to a more proactive approach that explores appreciation as a serious subject of investigation. David Cooperrider and Whitney's (1999) five principles of appreciative inquiry (AI) are used as a framework by which the author comes to appreciate challenging experiences through specific change agents.

AUTOETHNOGRAPY: MY METHOD OF INQUIRY

In this chapter, I use autoethnography as my method of inquiry, while also using phenomenology (see Sykes, 2014) to examine not only my lived experience of receiving memorable prejudicial messages but having the responsibility of letting them go. Boyd (2008), suggest that autoethnography is a conduit for transformational learning. Through this essay, I wanted to portray the interactions as vividly as I could, while providing an entrance into my thoughts. Jones (2005), argues that autoethnographers must set the scene, tell their story, weave in theory, explanations, life, and art, while at the same time letting go. Autoethnography requires that the personal aspects of the individual become inverted much like insider perspective (Hayano, 1979). In other words, it is a reflexive process that lets the reader in.

However, autoethnography is recognized as having varied methods. The structure will take the form of note-taking, discussion, emotional recall, reflection and the identification of themes from narratives (Ellis & Bochner, 2000). Data for this analysis are my personal stories vividly remembered from my Ph.D. program. Many of the stories have been told repeatedly with colleagues who were part of my cohort. So I remember the stories as if it were yesterday. In writing these experiences down for the very first time, I had to ensure that each experience was my own and that I wasn't mixing it up and writing across stories. So I spoke with individuals who were in the program with me to ensure the accuracy of the story. In keeping with AI, I also write about my transformation through the Ph.D. program and after.

PREJUDICIAL PRONOUNCEMENT 1: AFFIRMATIVE ACTION ENTRIES

In 1994, I pursued a doctorate at a large Midwestern university. Our cohort was considered the most diverse in the history of the department (i.e., three African American females, two white males, two white females, one female from Sri Lanka, one Indian male, one Asian male and female, one Mexican female, and one Middle Eastern male). When I entered the program, there was only one African American male, and one female from India, so people of color were drastically underrepresented. I was fortunate, however, to be part of this cohort. The graduate experience was both affirming and disconfirming. On one hand, this was the place where I learned how to interrogate the categories of race, class, sexuality and ability, but on the other, the environment was racially disruptive and tense with discourses of affirmative action entries and racial repudiation on the new cohort.

As a black woman growing up in the deep South, I was accustomed to "the look" of non-acceptance. I could tell within days of being on campus that the mostly white faculty were not exactly pleased with the "browning" of the department. According to rumors, there were concerns about the challenges the faculty would face with an assumed "less-than-stellar" class of graduate students. To demonstrate the shock experienced, two African American women in the cohort (aka Paula and Jada) decided to go around and introduce themselves to department faculty to establish a good rapport. They asked me to go but I passed on the offer. When they returned to the Teaching Associates office, they sat in silence exchanging glances. I asked what was wrong. Apparently, as a sign of gratitude, one of the faculty members in the department slammed her office door in their faces stating, "If it looks like I am busy, it is because I am." This behavior caused me great dissonance for two reasons. First, it corroborated what I had already assumed about the faculty; they didn't want us there. Second, I knew that the most critical part of the doctoral process was the faculty-student relationship (Gardner, 2007). This particular display translated to me, whether real or imagined, that my chances of working with someone in this department just got smaller or was going to be that much harder. To my amazement, they got up and tried it again.

By the third week of classes, there was clearly an issue with two of the white male students in the cohort with the students of color that mirrored the faculty rumors. Because we were encouraged to engage in open dialogue with each other, it wasn't uncommon to see graduate students debating various issues in pockets of the department. The claims about people of color in our cohort had trickled down to the cohort. A bold statement was made by one of the white male students, later nicknamed by me and Paula "the golden boy" that a, "better qualified white male student had been turned down so that one of us could get in." We were all assumed to be affirmative action entries and the debate robustly continued.

Because affirmative action discourses are challenging to respond to, students relied on facts from articles, legal narratives, feminist and judicial discourses. Citing them with great confidence, proponents of affirmative actions yelled, "The people who have benefitted from affirmative action the most are white women, not people of color." Others proclaimed that based on statistics of SAT and GRE performance scores, you shouldn't assume that white men would be the recipients of these scholarships because Asians tend to outperform everybody on these exams. I was a supporter of Affirmative Action and believed that it was important since discrimination permeated hiring and university admissions processes. I chimed in on the conversation with, "What difference does it make whether affirmative action gets you in the door? It won't keep you there." Patty was the one white feminist in the cohort who recognized that the golden boy's comment was inclusive of her race, but exclusive of her gender. The last remark came from Paula who said, "I will put my GPA up against anybody's." She verbalized her GPA with confidence. Based on the response of members of the cohort, it was quite evident that Paula had the highest GPA of us all.

After that, the topic of affirmative action was never brought up again by anyone in the cohort, at least not in public. I can't say for sure whether it was knowing Paula's GPA, or the strong arguments made during our discussion that muted any further public conversations about affirmative action. We could only wait and see who would be left to come back the following year. During the heated debate, I was able to forge a relationship with Patty that lasted until graduation and after. Patty introduced me to Mother-Doctor, a black feminist in the field at our first department colloquium. She didn't know it at the time, but she threw me a lifeline of support, because for the next year and a half, I would be resisting a race agenda for my research and publicly sparring with my advisor about race related issues.

PREJUDICIAL PRONOUNCEMENT 2:
THE RACE RESEARCHER EXPECTATION

By the end of the quarter, our cohort had met most of the department faculty through a written scaffold assignment called the "Invisible College." The whole idea behind the assignment was to inspire you to get to know a faculty member's research to prepare you for your dissertation journey and future career in the professorate. When the faculty member I had aspirations of working with attended class, her body of research was challenged for its lack of diversity. As a result, our future interactions led to expectations of me conducting specific ethnic research.

During my advisor's presentation, Paula asked, "Why should a group as diverse as this class be interested in your research since you've only studied white middleclass individuals?" The question was a reasonable one, and the truth was that the lack of diversity within her specific line of research was the same lack of diversity operating in the area of interpersonal communication as a whole. My advisor was pretty rattled because she inquired of me during the break whether I understood why she had not studied other groups. I assured her that I did. After she left the room, the class teased me for wanting to work with her. I defended her as any budding graduate student would. I knew that I had cultural access and a profound interest in relationship maintenance across various communities of people.

However, it became quite apparent to me over the following year, that the only body of research that she wanted me to focus on was interracial relationships (i.e., black and white couples specifically). The more I wanted to mainstream my research and to study interpersonal communication generally, the more she placed me in an ethnic box. As a result of my resistance to interracial romantic relationships, I was eventually encouraged to work with another junior faculty member under the guise of co-advisement. I watched the "golden boy," the same person who teased me about being her advisee, develop a relationship with my advisor, publish articles and graduate. I was troubled, but not surprised. According to Kim and Karau (2009), one of the most consistent predictors of scholarship productivity is faculty-student research interactions, and I didn't have this opportunity.

Our private disagreements about race became publicly displayed in the classroom (see hooks, 1989). On the first day of attending class (mixed grad and undergraduate students), my advisor asked, "How many of you have taken Kai (my middle name) for a class?" After the poll, she stated, "I am going to dispel every myth she's ever taught you." A week later, she suggested that lack of consciousness about sexist behavior did not make one a sexist. Using her father as an example in a scenario, she polled the class as to whether his behavior in the workplace made him a sexist. The undergrads in the class in unison replied, "No." For me, this had implications for race and other categories. So, I disrupted the conversation and said, "Yes, he is still a sexist. Just because he is unaware does not mean he is less sexist." My advisor snapped back and said, "So I guess, according to Kai, if I go somewhere in Africa that I have never been before and say something that is offensive, I guess I am a racist?" I replied, "No, you are unconsciously, incompetent!" Paula, who was sitting in front of me, turned around and firmly suggested in a stern voice, "Stop it right now!" I took her advice and remained silent for the duration of the class.

After class ended, I spoke with Paula about the occurrence. We had a pretty long talk about what was going on and so I decided to drop the course. Another senior graduate student, Darby, suggested this to me, "Sometimes, you have to go outside the field to understand what's going on inside the field." And so I explored other courses in the field of education, English, gender studies, pan-African studies, sociology and agricultural education. A whole new world opened up to me as I began to discover different parts of my identity and the identities of others. These courses gave me a foundation outside of communication studies that helped me understand the intersection of race, gender, and other categories.

PREJUDICIAL PRONOUNCEMENT 3: "YOU'RE A WOMAN AND YOU'RE BLACK"

As I mentioned earlier, the advisor-advisee relationship is a crucial one, and it is the relationship reported by black women in graduate programs to be the most problematic and unsatisfactory (Beeler, 1991; Trotman-Reid, 1990). This was certainly no different for me. The decision to change course and find a new advisor came shortly after I was stopped in the hallway by my co-advisor and another graduate student (white female). The two seemed to be having a discussion about employment opportunities after graduation. I thought it was odd that they would query me considering I was very new in the program. As I write about this experience, I hear this comment echoing among us, "You won't have any problems getting a job because you're a woman and you're black." I couldn't help but internally reflect and appraise the comment by asking myself, "Is there nothing more to me than my sex and my ethnicity?" There seemed to be no suggestion that I was or would be academically qualified. My blackness and the fact that I was a woman was enough to get me a job. There was a serious concern for me that the two categories of gender and race, which had historically been a cumulative negative effect for black women, had now become conceptualized as a cumulative advantage and was prohibiting white females from getting jobs. As a consequence of contributing to this discourse, I thought it necessary to seek out a new advisor, but my options were few. So the same faculty member who shut the door in Paula and Jada's face was reopened for me, but not without consequences.

PREJUDICIAL PRONOUNCEMENT 4:
PEDAGOGICAL BUFFOONERY

By my third year as a Ph.D. student, I was doing pretty well as a teacher. However, black professors generally have more complex experiences in the classroom than their white counterparts (Tillman, 2012) and the black TAs in the department were no exception. I observed on three occasions white male students challenging black female TA's. During the 90s, many black scholars were writing about their classroom challenges (Hendrix, 1995; Smith & Witt, 1993). I received little to no feedback and few complaints in the classroom compared to the other TA's in my first two years of teaching. I attribute that to my prior teaching experience and advice from my former debate coach at a small school in the Southwest. Before I left for my first teaching job at the small university in the Midwest, Dr. Randy, said to me, "Don't you take any S*!% off of those students!" He gave me a big hug and walked away. As brief as the meeting was, it was the best advice he could have given me. The advice came in handy with difficult students and white males who mostly challenged my credibility.

Consequently, the problem I faced wasn't a student-teacher one, but the characterization of my teaching style in peer reviews. As a TA, when given the opportunity to teach a unit on nonverbal communication, I was perplexed that the senior TA lecturer focused her evaluation on my style of presenting rather than the content of my lecture and my ability to manage the classroom. I wanted to know how I handle their questions or whether I engaged with them in a positive way that sustained learning. Yet, all she seemed to notice was that I was "animated." "Animated!" I thought. "What in the hell does that mean?" For many, the phrase may seem harmless, but for others, animated is a word that hinges on racialized politics of black and brown Americans that rehashes a long history of being perceived as exhibiting behavioral buffoonery and jovial acts of humor in professional contexts. I could surmise that the senior TA didn't have the necessary experience to evaluate my teaching beyond her limited focus, however, the term "animated" has appeared in peer evaluation reports with white colleagues since graduate school.

According to McGee (2016), black professors are not only expected to entertain but are often described in ways that characterize them as buffoons that reaffirm racial stereotypes, which has implications for career advancement. Failure to acknowledge the content presented during a lecture is demeaning. The American culture has a long history of understanding word choice, language, what happens when a single word is employed in a sentence, and the meaning potential it carries. Even today, when the most well-intentioned person uses the word "animated" to describe my teaching, I am compelled to speak up. Thus, the controlling images and language to describe pedagogy in an evaluation of any faculty must be laid to rest.

PREJUDICIAL PRONOUNCEMENT 5: "YOU'LL BE A GREAT TEACHER, BUT NEVER A GREAT SCHOLAR"

By the time I was in my 5th year of graduate school, I had passed my general exams and was finally moving toward the writing of my dissertation. My new advisor, Dr. Bendle, met separately with each of her advisees to talk about their respective projects at her favorite Thai restaurant. I was grateful for the extra time she offered me and the meals she provided. At some point during the matriculation process, I gave up resisting being defined an ethnic scholar or conducting "ethnic research." I was winning the battle, but losing the war. Thus, I agreed to use her methodology to focus on racism-*ing*.

To get some grounding in this particular methodology, my advisor piloted a course that focused on racism-*ing*. The experience was bitter and sweet. By the fourth week of class, Dr. Bendle shared her concerns about the emotional reaction of the white students in the classroom to the topic. She noticed the guilt they were experiencing, and felt a need to change the direction of the conversation to offset the emotional turbulence. I fully understood her desire to change the focus of the course, but I believed the feeling of guilt was a necessary step in the process, and I shared that with her. Before we ended our discussion, I wanted to know if she had noticed that the black students had stopped coming to class completely. There was an awkward silence between us. If she wasn't aware before, she was now. Dr. Bendle sent an email to the students to rally them back to class. Many of the students returned, and we were able to finish the quarter on a high note. Others decided not to return and unfortunately suffered the consequences.

Dr. Bendle had a great working relationship with her undergraduate students. Some of her graduate students loved her as well, but there was a tad bit of verbal abuse that some of us endured. She could lift you up in a statement of affirmation and break you down with statements of disconfirmation. This happened periodically. For example, she often told me I was a good teacher. I often wondered how she knew this since she never evaluated my classes or witnessed my teaching. One day when I was sitting in her office, she told me she regularly surveyed her undergraduate classes about good teachers in the program. She said, "Your name comes up often." I was pleased to hear the news. However, there was always bad news to follow like, "You are always in crisis. You need to get your life together," or "You wouldn't make it there," "You need to be a Putnam student to get that kind of job." More often than not, I would just ignore it because I had already parted ways with two previous advisors, and I needed to finish the degree. The next prejudicial pronouncement is what set me on a path to find my final advisor and leave this elite learning community for good without ever looking back.

The big day of prejudicial doom occurred during dinner. As I ordered my favorite Thai dish, Dr. Bendle announced that she wanted to write a book on racism-*ing* and she wanted me to co-author. I was excited and thought the project was awesome, but there was one catch; the book would come before my dissertation would be written. My heart plummeted. I could not financially bear the burden of writing a book while putting the completion of the Ph.D. on hold. During dinner, she shared her projections about what we might find based on some preliminary research we had collected. I knew that I could not reduce those experiences as the same. We bantered a bit about those projections and my desire to finish the program first. Her final retort to my resistance to the timeline and her interpretation of racism experiences was, "You will be a great teacher, but never a great scholar!" As I tried to resist what I heard, the other prejudicial pronouncements that flooded my graduate school experience filled my thoughts like a thick cloud of fog restricting one's visibility. As I sat in disbelief, I felt the tears welling up in my eyes. At that very moment, those words seemed to speak life into me. I excused myself to go to the ladies' room. I put water on my face to remove the tear stains. I didn't want to go back to that table. I could not face her with any level of dignity. After a few minutes, I managed to return to the table with my head up, but my spirit broken. I tried to speak, but I had nothing to give. My utterances were obstructed. The more she talked, the more abusive she became. I couldn't withhold the tears, so I excused myself twice more to go to the restroom. On my final return, I told her I wasn't feeling well and that I needed to go. She bid me farewell.

After I called Paula to debrief the experience, I had a good night's cry. The next day, I started creating my exit plan. After a few phone calls, I got a suggestion to check with the African American faculty member from the department that was merging with ours. I called Dr. Cramer on Monday morning and made an appointment to speak with her. I met Dr. Cramer early on a Wednesday morning. After hearing my story, she sympathized with me and agreed to take me on as an advisee, but there was a catch. I had to notify Dr. Bendle of the change. I cringed in my seat. I had no courage to face Dr. Bendle, but Dr. Cramer was very clear that I needed to communicate that change before she would sign any paperwork to be my advisor. So, I emailed Dr. Bendle and bcc'd Dr. Cramer. She responded with a three-page single spaced email expressing her displeasure with my decision and a few unfavorable comments.

I didn't see Dr. Bendle anymore until the day I rushed into the department office to make copies. I couldn't turn around quickly enough to exit the office without being noticed, so there we stood facing each other. The moment was awkward, and my stomach was in knots. In an effort to reduce my discomfort, I reluctantly greeted her with "Hello Dr. Bendle." The greeting was met with silence, and of course I felt foolish for speaking, but then she spoke, "You know you are wrong. I did so much to help you. You wouldn't have passed your generals if it weren't for me. I did so much for you." She had tears in her eyes. And she was right. She did do a lot for me, and I was truly grateful, but she also did great harm. So, I remained silent and gave a faint smile. The fog returned rendering me silent and unable to speak. Before she exited the office, she said, "You can stand there with that smirk on your face if you want, but you know you are wrong." I made my copies and vowed never to enter the office again. Before I could exit the building, I was approached by Mindy, one of Dr. Bendle's advisees. Mindy was an Asian woman whom I had seen several times at our group meetings at Dr. Bendle's home. With her eyes wide open as if she was in shock, she said, "You left Dr. Bendle. Oh no. You were one of the strong ones. We all thought if you left, it must have been really bad. You were so strong." I smiled and I kindly responded, "I just couldn't take it anymore."

Two years later, I graduated and continued to work at a small private college in the area until I got my first tenure-track position in Houston, Texas. My PhD program immediately became a distant memory. My only correspondence was with my former advisor. She and I worked on two publications together after graduation. However, the words "You'll never be a great scholar," subconsciously haunted me for more than ten years after receiving the doctorate degree. Perhaps it's because the cycle of destruction is much quicker than the cycle of creation. Despite successfully defending the dissertation, graduating, being offered a tenure track position and producing publications, I occasionally experienced invalidation and unwarranted challenges to my credibility that invoked a series of self-deprecating comments about my scholastic ability. The awareness of my emotional meanings had not dawned on me until I was lamenting with Paula about a peer reviewer's comments to one of my articles. As I began to vigorously question my academic ability, Paula says, "Kai, stop it! Girl, she really did a number on you." I immediately knew who the "she" referenced and I began to sob as the memory of that day came rushing back to me. I hadn't thought about Dr. Bendle in years, yet her words, uttered more than ten years ago, resonated with every experience that invalidated my scholarship.

Paula was correct in her assessment. After all she was the first person I talked to after my last meeting with Dr. Bendle. I knew that if I was going to change my outcome, I had to determine how I was going to move forward. As I reflect on these prejudicial pronouncements, an explanation is provided for how these experiences were enhanced and informed by appreciative inquiry, which allowed me to navigate the Ph.D. program, and manage similar interactions and reactions long after graduate school.

THE FIVE PRINCIPLES OF APPRECIATIVE INQUIRY

Despite these prejudicial experiences, I was able to reclaim my voice through imagining something different as mandated by appreciative inquiry approaches. Cooperrider, Barrett, and Srivastva (1995), suggest that through engaging in shared conversations and agreements, change to living social systems happen. The value of the model resides in its capacity to be transferred to a variety of contexts and everyday interactions that promote peace and healing (Cooperrider& Whitney, 2001). Often called the 4-D model, the AI approach uses a cycle of four processes and five principles (see Table 1). I will focus on the five principles: Constructionist, Simultaneity, Poetic, Anticipatory, and Positive.

The first principle is the *constructionist principle,* and it proposes that we create our realities and what we believe to be true with the words that we speak. In other words, truth determines what we do, how we do things and act and this emerges within our relationships with others. So we co-construct our realities with others, which means we have a deep connection with others. While in the Ph.D. program, I realized that I created beliefs through my language and internal thoughts. While prejudicial pronouncements were real and they did happen, the pronouncements manifested and resided in me and became my reality. As a result, I reacted to the words spoken to me. I could never change the impact of the words until I changed the voice inside of my head. The utterance of invalidation was a strong one. Although it didn't stop me from going after my dreams, it created a cycle of belief that robbed me of thinking I was worthy. My personal faith story was that of unworthiness.

Table 1. Summary of the five principles of Appreciative Inquiry

Principle	Summary
Constructionist Principle	Words create reality. Thus, it is socially constructed through language and conversation.
Simultaneity Principle	Inquiry creates change and our method of intervention. When we ask questions, we create opportunities for change.
Poetic Principle	We have a choice in what we learn from experiences, which are endless sources of learning. When we choose to learn, it makes a difference.
Anticipatory Principle	Imagining the future inspires action. Human systems move in the direction of what they can imagine.
Positive Principle	Requires positive affect. Positive questions lead to positive change. Large scale change requires positive questions to amplify the core.

The constructionist principle of appreciative inquiry proposes that through the language and discourse of day-to-day interactions, people co-construct the organizations they inhabit. The principle suggests that we should engage in asking positive questions so as to stimulate new ideas, stories, and images that generate new possibilities for action with others who can help you construct a better world to navigate in and through our organizational structures. I now understand that words construct environmental realities, thus the world of academia I have lived in. When I experience a prejudicial pronouncement, I recognize that my interpretation may not be the originator's intent. I co-construct a new meaning through critiquing its original intent and refocusing my energy to resolve its impact. I ask my colleagues questions that help them understand or discover a feeling about something they had not considered so that meaning is created, shared and understood.

The second principle is the *principle of simultaneity*, which proposes that as we inquire of human systems, we begin to change them. This is often a collaborative process in which we seek out individuals who can set the pace or guide us in the right direction to help us work within and through environments with which we exist. Good questions are asked of the right people who can point us in the right direction. They help us understand our thinking and action. For instance, in my first semester of the Ph.D. program, the department hosted an African American scholar for a colloquium. I was pulled from the hallway by a cohort member to attend. I had no awareness of the scholar then that I now fondly call Mother-Doctor. I introduced myself and whispered, "I'm sorry I won't be able to stay. I have a paper due, and I am drowning in this program." She looked at me, saw the tears in my eyes and kindly handed me her business card. She said, "If you ever need anything, just email me anytime." I took her up on her offer and emailed her periodically to check-in. From 1999-2010, Mother-Doctor met with me for breakfast at our national association conferences just to see how things were going. I made sure to ask every question I needed answers to as I navigated my way through the Ph.D. program and later in tenure-track positions.

Whitney and Trosten-Bloom (2010), suggest that when you ask about peak moments, it sets the stage for life changing experiences. Just having the guidance of Mother-Doctor and hearing her story, great things began to happen for me. My curiosity about how to function in the academy as an African American woman, how to negotiate salary, how to handle difficult situations with other faculty members and how to navigate family life and the workplace began to open up new ways of seeing. I was living in a world that my questions created for me, and I could see the possibility for transformation. Mother-Doctor helped me to understand that scholarship was not just about publishing, but that it was much, much more.

The third principle is **the *poetic principle*,** which recommends that we choose what we want to be by rewriting the stories from the past. No one else could rewrite my past but me. After being told that I would never be a great scholar, I had to redefine what a scholar meant for me. I had no interest in the publish or perish pressure, so I took the advice of one of my professors in the Ph.D. program, who said, "Start at a university where you can grow and develop." In my Ph.D. program, we were under great pressure to apply to Research I (RI) ranked institutions that required heavy publication output. I watched as a few made it, while many did not. Since year three in the Ph.D. program, I knew I wanted to teach at a teaching-centered institution; not so much because of fear of being able to perform at an RI. My passion was teaching and I enjoyed doing research. I didn't want to be in a position of not enjoying research. I also developed two key strategies for producing scholarship that would allow me to conduct research on my own terms: Collaborating with other scholars and mentoring students in the research process.

My first collaborative research project was with Mark P. Orbe. I met Mark in the summer of 1995 at the Black Caucus Summer conference in Kentucky. This was my first conference attendance and the first research paper I had ever presented in public. Mark was the respondent for the panel. Due to time constraints, we had to leave the conference room to hear his responses to our papers. So we moved to the hallway. Sitting on a bed of steps, Mark's opening statement to me was, "Wow! You have something to say and only you can say it..." I felt so affirmed in my research as he went on to tell me about the pros and cons of the paper. From that point on, Mark was my biggest supporter. He dedicated a significant amount of his time mentoring those of us who were not at Historically Black Colleges and Universities (HBCUs). He was incredibly generous and selfless with his time. He modeled research collaboration, and now I institute his process with my graduate students.

The poetic principle allowed me to discover a strategy for producing scholarship and mentoring students into the publication process. Changing the echo in my head from "You'll never be a great scholar" to "You have something to say, and only you can say it," provided me with thick skin during the most formal part of the publication process (peer review). Some reviewer comments could be quite scornful and borderline abusive. For many faculties, those responses hemorrhaged their desire to submit scholarship. Despite receiving rejection letters, or a revise/resubmit status, I used the feedback as an opportunity to advance the work and resubmit to other journals. I never gave up on projects, and I chose to learn something regardless of the outcome or tone of the feedback.

The fourth principle is the *anticipatory principle*. This principle posits that what we can imagine inspires a difference in the future. I began imagining what I could do beyond the academy with the skill set acquired in my field. This principle incorporates the use of two elements in the 4D model: Dream "envisioning what might be" and Discovery "appreciating what gives life" (Cooperrider, Whitney & Stavros, 2008, p. 5). According to Whitney and Trosten-Bloom (2010), when you have an image, you execute or act on it. Thus, appreciative inquiry uses one's history in artful creations out of positive imagery to refashion anticipatory realities. In 1996, while still a graduate student, a very close friend of mine inspired me to start my own business,. I consulted with non-profit agencies during the summers and assessed their after-school programs. I returned to my passion for assessment after I gained tenure and promotion. Using my research background, I was able to write effective designs for digital solutions that aid the academic community in measuring and assessing student learning outcomes better. To date, I have designed six different solutions for the academic community to assess student learning outcomes, monitor faculty-student research mentoring, engage in strategic planning, manage department logistics, collaborate in program review and share successes through e-portfolios.

However, delving into the IT field, more often than not, I have been generously queried about my competence: "What IT experience do you have?" or "What department are you from again?" I fondly reply, "I have dreams," and "I am from XX Department." Let me clarify the dream response. My first product, AMEE (Assessment Made Easy Everyday), was fully developed during the summer of 2010. Step-by-step images of the programs operation appeared to me while I was sleeping. When I awoke from the dream I would go to my computer and type the operations I saw in my dream into my scope document. The dreaming continued for several nights and weeks.

While in my Ph.D. program, I expressed to a colleague that I could remember my dreams and that I have been able to do this since I was a child. He was amazed when I started sharing some of my dreams with him. He was the first to share with me that many dream experts believe that most individuals do not generally recall their dreams (Robbins &Tanck, 1988). He suggested I record my dreams in a journal. I took his advice, but as soon as I started journaling, the vividness of my dreams diminished. When I stopped journaling, the vividness returned. So, I stopped writing about my dreams. However, while recording my dreams of the AMEE solution, none of the details diminished. Was this a paradox or divine intervention? The anticipatory principle of AI helps us understand that if we believe that we can do something, then we conceive it. In other words, once you believe that your possibilities are greater than your dreams, you can manifest that in your waking life. This reminds me of a quote often associated with David Thoreau, "Our truest life is when we are in dream awake."

The final principle is the *positive principle*. This principle proposes that momentum and sustainable change requires developing strong relationships with the individuals in your environment and particularly with those you are in conflict with the most. For excitement, inspiration, and creativity to increase or new ideas to flourish, there has to be a collective movement toward change. Appreciative inquiry theorizes that you can create change by doing more of whatever works rather than paying attention to the problems. At one of the institutions where I worked, there was a faculty member that I referred to as 'the tomato thrower.' The tomato thrower had one job and that was to denounce every proposed issue on the table no matter what. Tomato throwers make affirming and appreciating difficult because whatever is being processed by the group becomes arduous and creativity is stifled.

However, more recently, I have used appreciative inquiry to create change by just acknowledging the tomato throwers process. Acknowledgement identifies and leverages what was once a conflictual process that now encourages and considers that which inhibits progress as part of the positive core. Tomato throwers are necessary within organizational environments because they allow us to carry negative voices over, which broadens our thinking about an issue. This principle assumes that the more positive we are at asking questions to guide the change, the more long-lasting and effective the change will be. In other words, you have to develop a positive process for managing conflict, because conflict will always be there. Conflict doesn't go away, it just looms. Thus, how we navigate through the challenge changes our core way of doing things.

CONCLUSION

While the first work associated with communicating prejudice was published seventeen years ago, the work on prejudice and discrimination is a little longer and very rich across multiple disciplines. Scholars from across all disciplines have spent a significant amount of time trying to understand prejudice as a defective outlook that threatens contact between and among groups of people rather than from a position of appreciation or the benefits gained from the experience. This book, *Communicating Prejudice: An*

Appreciative Inquiry Approach, explores two phenomena; prejudice and appreciative inquiry. The theoretical and practical relevance of prejudice and appreciative inquiry (full and partial) is articulated by blending direct unsettling lived experiences with a deep exploration of how prejudicial experiences can be appreciated, respected and used as a form of empowerment. The chapters in this book have provided a framework that helps clarify the involvement of the two phenomena. Using several methodological approaches, contributors to this text have boldly written about personal experiences with prejudice, reflections on practical emancipatory frameworks that create new directions for future generations, and tools for dialogue. These meta-narratives, ethnographies and studies display the potential for creating opportunities for inclusivity, transformation, growth and social justice.

REFERENCES

Beeler, K. D. (1991). Graduate student adjustment to academic life: A four-stage framework. *NASPA Journal, 28*(2), 163-171.

Benjamin, L. (1997). *Black women in the academy. Promises and perils.* Gainesville: University of Florida Press.

Boyd, D. (2008). Autoethnography as a tool for transformative learning about white privilege. *Journal of Transformative Education, 6,* 212-225.

Collins, P. H. (1986). Learning from the outsider within: The sociological significance of Black feminist thought. *Social Problems, 33*(6), S14-S31.

Cooperrider, D. L, Whitney, D. & Stavros, J. M. (2008). Appreciative inquiry in organizational handbook: For leaders of change. 2nd ed. Brunswick, OH: Crown Custom Publishing, Inc.

Cooperrider, D. L., Barrett, F., Srivastva, S. (1995). Social construction and appreciative inquiry: A journey in organizational theory. In Hosking, D., Dachler, P. &Gergen, K. (Eds.) *Management and organization: Relational alternatives to individualism* (pp. 157–200).

Cooperrider, D.L. & Whitney, D. (2001) A positive revolution in change. In Cooperrider, D. L. Sorenson, P., Whitney, D. & Yeager, T. (eds.) *Appreciative inquiry: An emerging direction for organization development* (pp. 9–29). Champaign, IL: Stipes.

Cooperrider, D.L, & Whitney, D. (1999). A positive revolution in change: Appreciative inquiry. Taos, NM: Corporation for Positive Change.

Ellis, C., &Bochner, A. (2000). Autoethnography, personal narrative, reflexivity: Research as subject. In N. K. Denzin & Y. S. Lincoln (Eds.), Handbook of qualitative research (2nd ed., pp. 733–769). Thousand Oaks, CA: Sage.

Fiske, S.T. (2010). *Social beings: Core motives in Social Psychology* (2nd ed.). Hoboken, NJ: Wiley.

Gardner, S. K. (2007). "I heard it through the grapevine": Doctoral student socialization in chemistry and history. *Higher Education, 54*, 723-740.

Harlow, R. (2003). "Race doesn't matter, but. . .": The effect of race on professors' experiences and emotion management in the undergraduate college classroom. Hayano,D.(1979). Auto-ethnography: Paradigms, problems, and prospects. *Human Organization, 38*, 99–104.

Hendrix, K. (1995). *Professor perceptions of the influence of race on classroom dynamics and credibility.* Presented at the annual meeting of the Western States Communication Association. February, 10-14, Portland, OR.

Hooks, b. (1989). *Talking back: Thinking feminist, thinking black.* Boston: South End Press.

Howarde-Baptiste, S. D. (2014). Artic space, lonely place: "Mammy moments" in higher education. *The Urban Review, 46*(4), 764-782.

Jones, B. T., Wilder, J., & Osborne-Lampkin, L. (2013). Employing a black feminist approach to doctoral advising: Preparing black women for the professorate. *The Journal of Negro Education, 83*(3), 326-338.

Kim, K., &Karau, S. J. (2009). Working environment and the research productivity of doctoral students in management. *Journal of Education for Business, 85*, 101-106.

Linton, J. D., Tierney, R., & Walsh, S. T. (2011). Publish or perish: How are research and reputation related? *Serials Review, 37*(4), 244-257.

McGee, E. (2016). Entertainers or education researchers? The challenges associated with presenting while black. Race, Ethnicity and Education, 19(1), 96-120.

Nettles, M. (1990). Success in doctoral programs: Experiences of minority and white students. *American Journal of Education, 98*, 494-522.

Robbins, P. R., Tanck, R. H (1988). Interest in dreams and dream recall. *Perceptual and Motor Skills, 66*, 291-294.

Smith, E., & Witt, S. (1993). A comparative study of occupational stress among African American and white university faculty: A research note. *Research in Higher Education, 34*, 229-241.

Sykes, B. (2014). Transformative authoethnography: An examination of cultural identity and its implications for learners. *Journal of Transformative Education, 6,* 212-225.

Tillman, L. (2012). Inventing ourselves: An informed essay for black female scholars in educational leadership. *International Journal of Qualitative Studies in Education in Education, 25*(1), 119-126.

Trotman-Reid, P. (1990). African-American women in academia: Paradoxes and barriers. In S. Lie & O'Leary (Eds.). *Storming the tower.* New York: Nichols/GP Publishing.

Whitney, D. &Trosten-Bloom, A. (2010). The power of appreciative inquiry: A practical guide to positive change. 2nd ed. San Francisco, CA: Berrett-Koehler Publishers, Inc.

LIST OF CONTRIBUTORS

Wilfredo Alvarez (Ph.D., University of Colorado Boulder) is an Assistant Professor in the Department of Communication, Media, and Theatre at Northeastern Illinois University in Chicago, IL. Dr. Alvarez teaches courses in communication and difference, intercultural, interpersonal, organizational, conflict, and leadership communication. Dr. Alvarez's research focuses on relationships between communication processes, power dynamics, and social identity categories (i.e., race, social class, immigration, gender, sexuality, and ability status). Dr. Alvarez's research has appeared in *Management Communication Quarterly, Liminalities: A Journal of Performance Studies,* and *Inter/Cultural Communication: Representation and Construction of Culture in Everyday Interaction* (A. Kurylo, Editor).

Sakile K. Camara is Professor of Communication Studies at California State University, Northridge. Her research addresses how acts of power communicatively transpire, are managed, performed and strategically responded to in a variety of contexts across culture and media forms. Camara has published several articles in top Communication Journals and has presented on these topics at national, international and regional conferences. Her recent work in designing assessment software has led to additional research interest that focuses on using communication concepts in the design of technology.

Ellen Correa earned a B.A. in Human Communication from California State University Monterrey Bay and an M.A. in Intercultural Relations from Antioch University MacGregor. Formerly the manager of a local government antipoverty program in California, she left her job to enroll in a doctoral program at the University of Massachusetts Amherst. In May 2016 she was awarded a PhD in Communication and Certificate in Latin American,

Caribbean, and Latina/o Studies. Employing a methodology she calls dialogic performance (auto) ethnography, her dissertation explores the ethical and relational implications of cultural assimilation in her family of Puerto Rican descent.

Darlene K. Drummond (Ph.D., Ohio State University) is an Assistant Professor of Speech in the Institute for Writing & Rhetoric at Dartmouth College. In the context of intercultural communication, she address the maintenance of ethnic and racial identities within intra-and-interracial encounters. Social support, medical adherence, doctor-patient interactions, and health advocacy are concepts explored in the context of health communication. Publications appear in communication and medical journals, and she has presented over 25 papers at regional, national, and international conferences. In addition, she has received awards from the World Communication Association, National Communication Association, and the Southern States Communication Association.

Bobbi Van Gilder (Ph. D., University of Oklahoma) is a Postdoctoral Teaching Associate in the Department of Communication Studies at Northeastern University. Her research interests include intercultural communication, gender and sexuality studies, and interpersonal communication, with particular emphases on identity, difference, and intergroup attitudes. Specific areas of interest include: (a) the cultural and communicative construction of gender and sexuality, (b) social identity and intergroup relations (e.g., ethnic identification, stigmatization, social prejudice, and discrimination), and (c) identity negotiation and identity management.

Tina M. Harris (PhD, University of Kentucky, 1995) is a Professor in the Department of Communication Studies at the University of Georgia. Her primary interest as a communication scholar is in the area of interracial communication. She is co-author of the textbook Interracial Communication: Theory into Practice (2015, Sage Publication) with Mar P. Orbe. Oher interest include communication and pedagogy, diversity and media representation, race and ethnic disparities and religious frameworks in health communication. She has published many articles and book chapters on race and communication, has served as reviewer for many top tier communication journals. She was awarded the UGA Josiah T. Meigs Teaching professorship (highest teaching honor) and the University System of Georgia Board of Regents Award for Scholarship of Teaching and Learning for her research on pedagogy and race.

Michael Hecht (PhD, University of Illinois) is a Distinguished Professor Emeritus of communication Arts and Sciences at Penn State University and president of REAL Prevention, LLC. Dr. Hecht specializes in health, intercultural, and interpersonal communication. His research examines effective inter-ethnic communication and identity, including his work on prejudice as well as his Communication Theory of Identity. This work has been expanded to the study of adolescent identity and the social processes of drug offers as well as narrative and culturally grounding approaches to health message design. This work is the basis for the evidence-based keepin' it REAL, a narrative, multicultural school-based substance use prevention curriculum for elementary and middle school students that he co-created with Dr. Miller-Day. Since its adoption by D.A.R.E. America, keepin' it REAL is the most widely disseminated substance use prevention program in the world, reaching 1 million U.S. youth as well as those in 52 countries around the world. He also was involved in adaptations of the curriculum for use in rural US communities as well as for Nicaraguan youth. Other projects focus on using interactive video games for sex education, narrative HPV vaccination promotion, and media literacy. In addition to D.A.R.E., collaborators include Planned Parenthood and the 4H Clubs of America. This work has been funded by the National Institutes of Health, Robert Wood Johnson Foundation, U.S. Department of State, and the Nemours Foundation among others. Hecht has served on NIH's Community-Level Health Promotion Review Group, including being selected as its chair, as well as on numerous editorial boards in communication and other fields.

Liliana (Lily) Herakova is a faculty member and a Graduate Students Teaching Supervisor at the Department of Communication and Journalism, University of Maine, Orono. She holds a PhD in Communication from the University of Massachusetts Amherst. Lil has worked with various social activist projects and co-founded the Pioneer Valley Bread House, a place for intercultural and intergenerational dialogue around the embodied practice of baking bread with others. Her scholarship and pedagogy explore the interpersonal communicative production of power, knowledge, and identity. Lily's work has been published in *Communication Studies, The Howard Journal of Communication,* and *the Journal of Applied Communication Research*, among others.

Kevin T. Jones is a Professor of Communication Studies at George Fox University in Newberg, Oregon. Kevin holds a Ph.D. in Rhetoric and Public Address from Louisiana State University and has over 30 years' experience teaching at the college level. Kevin has published numerous essays and articles on teaching strategies and techniques based on his years of experience in the classroom.

Susan L. Kline is an Associate Professor in the School of Communication at The Ohio State University. She researches interrelationships between social cognitive processes, interpersonal communication processes and message design practices.

Karen Sorenson-Lang is a rhetorician who studies women's rhetorics and gender communication. She is an assistant professor at Azusa Pacific University in Southern California. Her research interests include service-learning, feminist rhetoric, and composition theory.

Mark P. Orbe (Ph.D., Ohio University) is Professor of Communication & Diversity at Western Michigan University where he holds a joint appointment in the Department of Gender & Women's Studies. His research interests revolve around the inextricable relationship between culture, power, and communication –areas in which he has presented over 100 papers at regional, national and international conferences and published 12 books and over 100 journal articles and book chapters.

Victoria H. Orbe (M.S.W., University of Michigan) is currently Clinician in the Home-based Service Division of Starr Commonwealth in Battle Creek, MI. Within this work, she draws on her academic and research-based accomplishments to serve children, youth, and families. Her research, counseling and community organizing interests continue to focus on intersections of race, gender, and sexuality.

Renu Pariyadath is an Assistant Professor in the Department of Fine Arts and Communication Studies at the University of South Carolina Upstate. She studies solidarity practices in the context of nonprofit and social movement organizing, environmental justice, and global social change.

Robert J. Razzante (M.Ed., Ohio University) is a doctoral student in the Hugh Downs School of Communication at Arizona State University. His research interest centers on intercultural communication through a critical lens with a greater focus on facilitating dialogue about power, privilege and oppression among dominant cultural groups in both formal and informal educational settings.

Emily Reichert (MA, Purdue University) is a Ph.D. student in the Department of Sociology at University of Massachusetts Boston specializing in stigma, health disparities, and disenfranchisement. Emily has contributed to projects funded by NIH as a research assistant for health interventions dealing with adolescent drug use, indoor tanning, as well as projects investigating unconscious bias in graduate admissions decisions.

Karla D. Scott is an Associate Professor of Communication and Director of the African American Studies Program at Saint Louis University. She earned her Ph.D. from the University of Illinois Urbana Champaign where she studied Black women's language use and identity negotiation. Her favorite courses to teach include Intergroup Dialogue, Communicating across Racial Divisions, Black Women in Society, and Language and Cultural Diversity. She is an experienced dialogue facilitator and is a member of the first cohort of the Stirfry Seminars Mindful Facilitation Certificate Program.

Deanna F. Womack (Ph.D., University of Kansas) is Professor of Communication at Kennesaw State University. She has also taught Communication at Emerson College, Northern Illinois University, Rhode Island College, Stonehill College, Harvard Business School, and Tunghai University, Taichung, Taiwan. She served as Department Chair at Stonehill College and Kennesaw State University. She has recently published research on communicating identity to international adoptees and best practices in communication for older adults in residential living settings. She is third author of *Building Communication Theory*. She is also the mother of twins born in 1996 in China and adopted in 1998.

Dianah Wynter is a Professor of Media Theory & Criticism in the Department of Cinema & Television Arts at California State University Northridge. Wynter teaches Media & Society, Film as Literature (Intertextuality and Postmodernism), and Classic Filmmakers. She holds MFA degrees from Yale University and the American Film Institute. She first presented her research on consumer data, ratings and children's programming at the University Film & Video Association Conference in 2013. She us an Emmy nominated television director and recipient of a National Endowment for the Arts Fellowship.

INDEX

R

S